The Learning Society Revisited

Titles of Related Interest

FAGERLIND & SAHA
Education & National Development

HUSÉN & KOGAN
Educational Research & Policy. How Do They Relate?

HUSÉN & POSTLETHWAITE
The International Encyclopedia of Education

McNAY & OZGA
Policy Making in Education

POSTLETHWAITE
International Educational Research: Papers in Honor of Torsten Husén

SIMMONS
The Education Dilemma

A Related Journal

International Journal of Educational Research

Editors:

H. J. Walberg, T. Neville Postlethwaite & B. P. M. Creemers

The International Journal of Educational Research provides a forum for the communication and encouragement of excellence in educational research. The establishment of this forum enables both educators and researchers to benefit from the most significant educational investigations being conducted throughout the world.

The Learning Society Revisited

ESSAYS BY

TORSTEN HUSÉN

PERGAMON PRESS

OXFORD · NEW YORK · TORONTO · SYDNEY · FRANKFURT

U.K.	Pergamon Press Ltd., Headington Hill Hall, Oxford OX3 0BW, England
U.S.A.	Pergamon Press Inc., Maxwell House, Fairview Park, Elmsford, New York 10523, U.S.A.
CANADA	Pergamon Press Canada Ltd., Suite 104, 150 Consumers Road, Willowdale, Ontario M2J 1P9, Canada
AUSTRALIA	Pergamon Press (Aust.) Pty. Ltd., P.O. Box 544, Potts Point, N.S.W. 2011, Australia
FEDERAL REPUBLIC OF GERMANY	Pergamon Press GmbH, Hammerweg 6, D-6242 Kronberg, Federal Republic of Germany
JAPAN	Pergamon Press Ltd., 8th Floor, Matsuoka Central Building, 1-7-1 Nishishinjuku, Shinjuku-ku, Tokyo 160, Japan
BRAZIL	Pergamon Editora Ltda., Rua Eça de Queiros, 346, CEP 04011, São Paulo, Brazil
PEOPLE'S REPUBLIC OF CHINA	Pergamon Press, Qianmen Hotel, Beijing, People's Republic of China

First edition 1986

Library of Congress Cataloging in Publication Data
Husén, Torsten.
The learning society revisited.

1. Education and state.   2. Educational equalization.
3. Education–Social aspects.   4. Comparative education.
I. Title.
LC75.H87   1986   370.19   85–29683

British Library Cataloguing in Publication Data
Husén, Torsten.
The learning society revisited; essays.
1. Educational sociology
I. Title
370.19   LC191

ISBN 0-08-032660-9 (Hardcover)
ISBN 0-08-034037-7 (Flexicover)

Printed in Great Britain by A. Wheaton & Co. Ltd., Exeter

Preface

THE essays collected in this book reflect experiences of scholarly work in education during a research career over some forty-five years. From the late 1940s to the early 1970s I was closely involved in research related to the Swedish school reforms. In the early 1960s I began to turn to educational problems on the international scene, first by becoming Chairman of the International Association of Educational Achievement (IEA) and some years later of the Governing Board of the International Institute of Educational Planning in Paris. Other international involvements were with OECD, the International Council for Educational Development (ICED) and the Max Planck Institute for Educational Research in Berlin.

I did not embark on educational studies and research in the capacity of an educator. As I have spelled out in my autobiography, *An Incurable Academic* (Pergamon Press, 1983), I did so as a social science generalist trained at the outset as a psychologist. This saved me from the professional disease of many educators, that of looking at educational problems from the narrow classroom perspective instead of from the wider, social one. The former perspective has been to the detriment of teacher preparation, something I had ample opportunity to observe as a professor at a teacher training institution for many years. Aspiring teachers are, in the courses given in education and psychology, often led to believe that educational and, in particular, psychological theory, are to make their teaching more efficient and, not least, help them "solve" their classroom problems with discipline and so on. The frustrations ensuing from such beliefs are bound to lead to disenchantment with the "foundations" delivered by education departments. If there is any pervasive message in the essays published here, it ought to be the emphasis put on the *social dimension* of educational problems.

The essays are grouped under half a dozen themes on which I have worked over the years. For each section a brief introduction has been prepared plus some references to publications in which the problems have been dealt with more in depth.

Most of the contributions here have been written over the last few years. Some have originally been given as papers at international meetings, others as guest lectures. About half of them have previously not been printed. All of them have been revised in order to remove repetitions and passages too obviously related to circumstances and events which are not any longer relevant. To what extent I have succeeded in these attempts is another matter.

I have to apologize for repetitions which simply are part of the particular contexts where they occur. For essays which (in earlier versions) have been published I have provided bibliographical references.*

Torsten Husén

* More detailed references can be obtained from Torsten Husén: *Tryckta Skrifter 1940–80* (Printed Publications 1940–80) Uppsala: Almqvist & Wiksell, 1981, which in 1981 was presented to the author by co-workers and former students.

Contents

I. Research and Policymaking

Educational Research and Policymaking (1968)*[1]
The Swedish School Reforms: A Case Study in Policy-oriented Research (1965)[2]
Educational Research and Policymaking: An International Perspective (1983)[3]
Policy Implications of Cross-national Education Surveys (1977)[4]

Introduction

As mentioned in the Preface, the author was involved in the 1950s and 1960s in conducting research relevant to the Swedish school reforms resulting in the comprehensive school. Most of these studies have been reported in Husén & Boalt: *Educational Research and Educational Change: The case of Sweden* (Stockholm and New York: Almqvist & Wiksell and John Wiley, 1968). More specifically, the Swedish experiences were communicated to American colleagues by an invited address at the Annual Meeting of the American Educational Research Association in 1965. The address was published the same year in *The School Review*. The first international mathematics study (Husén, ed. International Study of Achievement in Mathematics: A Comparison of Twelve Countries I-II. Stockholm and New York: Almqvist & Wiksell and Wiley, 1967) was carried out by IEA during a period of heightened awareness of the relative advantages and shortcomings of various national systems of education, particularly among educators and their critics in the United States. This study as well as the subsequent, so-called Six-Subject Survey, turned out to have repercussions on the policy debate in the participating countries. A paper on the policy implications was given at the IEA meeting in Rome 1977; another in the *Comparative Education Review* in 1986.

The relationship between research and policymaking, which has been dealt with here also with a historical perspective, is not as simple or "linear" as is often assumed. There is no straight "application" of what "research says". A clarification of the nature of this relationship ought to be conducive to more realistic expectations about what "research," in this case empirical

---

* The year in brackets refers in the case of an already published paper to the year of the publication of the original version, or – in case of an unpublished paper – to the year when it was presented.

research by social scientists, can contribute to educational practice and policy. The message conveyed in this section is that research mainly serves an "enlightment" purpose. It cannot provide any clear-cut recipes for policy action or "solutions" to practical problems encountered in the classroom or in educational planning and administration. Decisions about policy and practical action are taken under so many other considerations than those generated by scholarly studies.

Problems dealt with here can be further studied in T. Husén and M. Kogan (eds., 1984) *Educational Research and Policy: How Do They Relate?* (Oxford: Pergamon Press), which reports the proceedings of an international symposium in Stockholm-Lidingö in 1982.

Notes

1. Published in *Education and Culture* (Council of Europe, Strasbourg) 1968, No 7, 7–14.
2. Published in *The School Review* (University of Chicago Press), Vol. 73:3, 1965, 206–225.
3. Published in *Minerva* (London) Vol. XXI, No. 1 Spring 1983, 81–100.
4. Adapted from a paper presented at the Symposium on Current Findings of the IEA Six-Subject Survey and their consequences for educational policy and practice. The Symposium was sponsored jointly by the Italian Ministry of Education and the International Association for the Evaluation of Educational Achievement and was held at Frascati, Rome in March 1977. A revised version of the paper has been published in *Studies in Educational Evaluation* (Pergamon Press) Vol. 3:2, Summer 1977. An abbreviated version has also been published in the *New York University Education Quarterly*, Vol. VIII:3, Spring 1976, 2–9.

Educational Research and Policymaking*

LET ME begin with a true story relevant to my topic. A Swedish educational psychologist had been commissioned to conduct a study of pilot programs in which certain aspects of the comprehensive school and the traditional dualistic set-up were compared. One of the top officials of the National Board of Education, apparently somewhat bewildered by the technical jargon in the report submitted made the following comment: "I understand that we must try to find out how the two systems work, but is it really necessary to make it all that scientific!"

One certainly can understand the frustration that administrators and policymakers suffer when they try to penetrate the technicalities and the jargon of the researchers. This is, of course, a communication problem which cannot be solved simply by familiarizing the consumers with the terminology or by conveying to them the idea that simple *ad hoc* try-outs are not enough. Strictly scientific evaluations are also necessary. On the other hand, one might even raise the question whether some of the major policies regarding school structure would have been much different had there been no research at all prior to the decisions!

What kinds of relationships between researchers and policymakers provide the best possible setting both for good educational research and for good policy decisions? Before proceeding further with this, I should like to point out what kind of assistance relevant to school reforms researchers can provide.

Liaison Between Researchers and Policymakers

Social and behavioral scientists, in country after country, are called upon to help solve or at least to deal more effectively with problems pertaining to school structure, curriculum content, and methods of instruction. In some sectors they are apparently regarded as useful, but in what respects?

Firstly, the researcher can be helpful in tidying up the problems as they are first conceived by the policymaker.

The problems which are submitted to researchers are not only too broadly stated but, in most cases, they also need thorough reformulation in order to be susceptible to research methodology. Thus, for instance, in studying the relation between age and primary language teaching, the problem is not age

* Originally published in *Education and Culture* (Council of Europe) 1968, No. 7, 7–14.

but the methods of instruction. In 1941, some Swedish professors replied that the age of eleven would seem most appropriate, thus tacitly assuming that the traditional grammar approach should be used. Since then we have started to teach all children English at the age of 10 and even at 8, a decision which four decades ago would have been regarded as a pedagogical sacrilege. The comparisons between the comprehensive and the selective school structure in Sweden during most of the 1950's were naïvely carried out in terms of the conventional end products. Thus, the "grammar school" students in both structures were compared without consideration of the fact that, at least partly, they pursued different objectives and that they differed considerably in terms of grade-repeaters and drop-outs – i.e. without reference to differences in the price paid for the end-products. Therefore, at an early stage of a research project it is of great importance to establish at least occasional contacts between researchers and policymakers. The dialogue between them will, we hope, be conducive to more articulate conceptions of the problems and their implications.

Secondly, more close at hand and certainly more obvious than the tidying-up task, is the know-how or the technical craftsmanship that the researchers are expected to bring to bear on problems which the administrator and/or policymaker with (or, as a rule, without) the help of the researcher, is trying to formulate. The researcher is called upon to do the fact-finding, to carry out the surveys whereby the descriptive picture of a certain educational phenomenon is clarified. One fully appreciates the technique the researcher is applying when he, for instance, carries out sample surveys. The various Royal Commissions in England, such as the Robbins and the Plowden Committees, are cases in point.

Thirdly, the researcher can be called upon to assist in interpreting more adequately data which have already been collected. As part of the routine administrative procedures within all ministries of education, hosts of statistical information are collected. These data are particularly useful in order to improve the planning function within the ministry. The researcher can assist not only in interpreting data already gathered but also in advising what might be collected so that more relevant aspects of the educational reality are covered by the statistics.

The planning function has grown rapidly, to the extent that research has become part and parcel of planning. In this connection, I am not thinking primarily of fancy mathematical models which seem to shun encounters with empirical reality but rather the basic surveys that are needed.

Two Types of Educational Research

It would be useful to distinguish between two types of educational reseach, which by their very nature, call upon different relationships between researchers and policymakers. Here, I am not thinking of research versus development or "pure" research versus "applied" research but rather of the type of problems which are tackled.

The first type of problems deal with the school structure. At what age should children enter the regular compulsory school? At what age is it appropriate to differentiate with regard to variation in ability and performance? What is the total "yield" of a retentive system compared with a selective one? These problems are particularly pertinent in countries where decisions about them are taken by Parliaments and/or top ranking policymakers. In this connection, it would suffice to refer to the debate that has been going on in many European countries about the relative merits and drawbacks of the comprehensive or retentive school *vis-à-vis* the dualistic or selective one.

The structure of the school system of a country is not only a reflection of pious and abstract political principles, it also mirrors fairly closely the social class composition and the economic structure of the society it is supposed to serve. By no means does the school operate in a social vacuum, even if the opposite impression sometimes is conveyed by the conception certain educators express of its proper role.

Some years ago I gave a lecture in Germany about a topic similar to the one I am dealing with here. When questions were invited from the floor, one *Gymnasium* teacher, in full seriousness, contended that it would be quite necessary to differentiate between the academic and the non-academic pupils at the age of 10 as had traditionally been the case. Otherwise, it would not be possible to cover the syllabus in Latin before the graduation at the age of 19. As soon as changes in the basic school structure are contemplated, important vested interests are at stake, not least in a society where ability and education more and more tend to be the democratic substitute for inherited status and fortune.

The second type of problem is, in a wide sense, related to classroom exercises, such as methods of instruction, the use of teaching aids, guidance of pupils, etc. I am fully aware that problems pertaining to *what* should be taught, particularly in terms of what subjects should be taught, at what level, when, and with what objectives, occupy an intermediate position and that the policymakers both at the central, regional and local levels would like to have the decisive word to say. For instance, in Sweden it is up to the Parliament to determine the overall objectives of the school system and to decide upon the timetable which defines the subjects and their respective number of periods, since it then makes the appropriations which follow from these features of the curriculum. But, by and large, within the set framework, it is left almost entirely to the educators to decide on syllabus and on classroom practices.

Before proceeding to report further on my own experiences and thinking of the relationship between the academic man – be he of the ivory tower species or not – and the policymakers contemplating commissioning him to assist in solving problems requiring action, let me point out differences in their approach, evident, but nevertheless worth mentioning. The researcher, particularly if he thinks he is confidently playing the role of a good one, makes the undogmatic approach to problems a virtue. Faced with hardcore facts, his approach is not "What can I do?" but "How can they be explained?".

His is the meditative and inquiring life. The policymaker, by definition, is a pragmatist and an activist. Facts are for him material for decision and sometimes immediate action. He would not be a real policymaker unless most of the problems he deals with required action. All the caveats, "ifs" and "it depends" of the academic man imply postponement of action. The mere encounter of these two modes of life carries some germs of conflict.

In my own country and in other countries, I have encountered some confusion about the proper role of the researcher in the decision-making process. For instance, it has been argued that decisions about the school structure should not be made on the basis of "pure political deliberations". When in 1962 the Swedish Parliament passed legislation which made the introduction of the nine-year, undifferentiated comprehensive school mandatory all over the country, the objection was raised that this was a political and not an expert decision. The majority of the secondary school teachers who had been trained for an elitist system resented that their "expert" opinion was overruled. A colleague of mine referring to that opposition has contended that likewise the research evidence for the new set-up was either not available or even contrary. It seems to me that he and others had in mind some kind of Plato's republic of wise men and philosopher kings, be they university professors or not, who ought to have the final and decisive word in human and social affairs.

It has often been stated that the military is too important to be run by the generals. It has less often been emphasized that the schools are too important to be run by the educators, be they teachers, school administrators or professors of education. The appropriate role of the educator in the decision-making process is primarily to provide information and expert judgments and thereby to help to broaden the base upon which decisions are taken by those who, in a representative democratic system, have been elected to make these decisions. If the educator is a researcher, it becomes even more important that he should play his role according to the rules, i.e. confine it to professional performance as long as he wears his researcher's hat. Of course, the educator, teacher or researcher, like all other citizens is obviously entitled as a private person to advance opinions or make statements about policy issues. Equally self-evidently, he should try to keep these personal statements clearly separated from the generalizations drawn from his scholarly inquiries.

The "Ivory Tower" Philosophy

The nature of the research problems affects the relationship between the researcher and the policymaker. Problems pertaining to school structure are indeed in this part of the world hot issues which easily can cause rising political temperatures and even overthrow governments. This, then, brings considerable pressure to bear upon the researcher. The directive given to him might be confined to study certain aspects of a problem and not others. The temptation to spread a certain type of "gospel," whether or not he deeply believes in it, is particularly strong if the researcher or the institution to which he belongs is more or less entirely dependent on financial support for their operations from the agency that has commissioned the project. Instead of confining his role to research, i.e. study of the problem in order to increase understanding, he can easily become an evangelist who tours the country selling ideas. In order to function appropriately, the researcher has to be what Professor Cronbach of Stanford University has called the "eternal sceptic," the one to whom the slogan of the day or the policy statement is an hypothesis which, at best, lends itself to scientific inquiry. Before embarking on a discussion of where various types of educational research ought to be located and the relationships between producers and consumers of research that follow from that, I shall briefly draw upon my Swedish experiences.

Before 1950 there were no institutionalized settings for policy-oriented educational research in Sweden. The so-called Royal Commissions, commit- tees appointed by the government to inquire into and advance proposals pertaining to areas which needed reform, are a conspicuous and unique feature of Swedish political life, since the political parties and various interest groups are usually represented on these committees. Their reports are submit- ted to a wide range of bodies for review and evaluation before the results of these operations are used as a basis for drafting legislation. Before 1950, several of these committees commissioned *ad hoc* research from individual university researchers who could take or leave these offers without jeopardiz- ing their existence. This was the first time that the social sciences at large started to examine problems such as the development of abilities during school age, the size of the so-called reserve of ability, or the social class structure of the enrollment in various types of schools. The mere fact that research had some bearing on policy problems might have been even more shocking to the professors than to the policymakers. Those who were at that time still incurably ingrained with the ivory tower philosophy sometimes regarded the application of their respective sciences as at best dubious and at worst, dirty.

In countries where the university departments of education have not been interested in, or have been incompetent to respond to, obvious research needs, institutions outside the university framework have been created.

The 1950 Swedish Education Act made provisions for the organization of a Bureau of School Experimentation within the National Board of Education. The main task of the bureau was to administer the try-out of the comprehen- sive school during the early 1950's. But, since the Parliament had emphasized the necessity to make "continuous" evaluation of the new type of school and compare it with the old structure, a considerable part of the time of the permanent research staff was devoted to surveys. The experiences with research within a ministry were not too encouraging, because the researchers tended to be more and more absorbed in the day-to-day operations.

The 1954 Parliament passed legislation on a provisional reform of teacher training to match the new school structure then under experiment. The first School of Education (*Lärarhögskola*) was established in Stockholm in 1955 as an initial step of implementation. An Institute of Educational Research with a clear mandate to carry out research relating to school problems was an essential part of the new organization.

"Individualization," "Activation," "Motivation"

In 1962, a Bureau of Research and Development was established within the National Board of Education as part of the new Education Act which made a decision about the structure of the nine-year basic school for the foreseeable future. This, then, meant a shift in emphasis of research activities from school structure to problems of curriculum and methods of instruction. Another step in the implementation of the Act was that the National Board, which is the central administrative and planning agency under the Ministry of Education, issued a new curriculum full of cheerful prescriptions. Three of the honored words were "individualization," "activation" and "motivation."

The pious hopes of changing school practices (for instance, a more individualized and activating teaching) could not be achieved unless steps were taken by the central school authorities to change the total instructional situation. The observation that the textbook, hopefully apart from the teacher, tends to be the most powerful factor in the classroom, is commonplace. A radical individualization, that would replace class instruction and introduce an approach which would cater for the increased range of ability and interests required adequate instructional material to be prepared on a large scale. Piecemeal improvements by introducing single aids or attempts by individual teachers would not suffice in a situation when a change all along the line required the mobilization of expert groups for several years and a level of financial support unheard of before in developmental work.

In the 1962 Educational Bill, the Minister of Education approved of the new approach in principle and funds were made available. This was the starting point for a series of large scale projects which involved not only behavioral scientists but also subject matter and methods experts. Since part of the "packages" which emerge from these projects, consists of products – hardware or software material – it has turned out to be necessary to involve producers at a rather early stage, before the first set of prototypes has been finished. Both the development of the material and its production required a tremendous investment. This, then, has raised two questions. Firstly, to what extent should private producers be involved in producing materials which have been developed by public institutions? In order to be able to carry the costs from the beginning up to the first set of materials, the private producers would have to pool their efforts. Secondly, to what extent is it possible to prescribe the new methods-material packages, which at the same time would be a prescription of a completely new teaching-learning approach all over the country? The temptation to answer the latter question in the affirmative is great in a highly centralized system.

This was the era of educational technology when Swedish school authorities, not least under American influence, adopted the R & D approach originally developed in industry. But school education is not a manufacturing industry. The "products" cannot be planned and foreseen. The package approach was abandoned after a decade of setbacks.

It has repeatedly been stated that education as a discipline (if a discipline can be defined by its problems and not by its methodology which in itself is a dubious proposition) is located at the bottom of the academic pecking order, particularly in the United States but also in some European universities. One important reason for the sad state of affairs is the isolation of education from other fields of inquiry, particularly from the behavioral sciences. Solid training in one of the social, behavioral or humanistic disciplines is a necessary prerequisite for fruitful research endeavors in education.

Thus, if education as an academic discipline has suffered from provincial isolation, until recently this applied even more to its role on the international scene. School structure, historic and socio-economic roots and classroom practices vary from country to country. If we want to conduct research which meets the criterion of good inquiry, which is better understanding, we are obliged to advance better concepts and theoretical models and to establish at the international level the same cross-disciplinary research in education that is now emerging at the national level. This could then be conducive to an international community of educational researchers which has long been a reality in the natural sciences.

Three Different Purposes

In conclusion, I conceive of educational research at three different levels and for three different purposes.

(1) The universities should pursue their genuine and unique function, namely, basic research. This does not imply a complete withdrawal into the ivory tower, but simply that their researchers should be given sufficient time and resources to develop the new concepts and models without which further research, particularly the short-range and expensive developmental work, could not be productive. It is not up to the university scholar to spend his time in developing instructional systems or introducing new classroom practices. His role is properly fulfilled if he stays aloof and indulges in "irresponsible" thinking that precedes the developmental work.

(2) Large-scale surveys which aim at evaluating new organizational set-ups introduced by the central or local authorities ought to be carried on outside the universities. Since quite a lot of this research deals with the evaluation of new structures or curricula, it is evidently important that the evaluation be carried out by independent research bodies. Apart from the fact that it would ethically seem more fitting if a governmental or semi-governmental agency were not evaluating its own operations, reseach within a bureaucratic setting can easily become a nightmare to the researcher. His work is by definition anti-bureaucratic, i.e. informal, innovative, and unguided by time-tables.

(3) Obviously, certain administrative functions within the central or regional educational agencies cannot be successfully performed unless use is made of certain research techniques to secure routine data needed for appropriate action. I am thinking of the planning function which has to be guided by collection of information on pupils, teachers, schools, finance, etc. In some instances, regular sample surveys will have to be conducted. In recent years, research actions in some countries have been focussed on massive attempts to improve curricula and instructional methods. In countries where a central ministry of education more decisively influences the curriculum, one has begun to realize the possibilities of changing practices by preparing teacher aids or packages. The mere size of such an enterprise and its financial implications makes it a task for a ministry.

We can draw up a continuum which is located between two poles: on the one side, complete aloofness in the ivory tower, and, on the other, total immersion in the noise of actions and issues in the educational market place. It is the problem of striking a proper balance, to establish good liaison with the policymakers without becoming evangelists and without scaring the other partner into withdrawing his support.

The educational researcher today cannot avoid being brought into the process of action. It depends upon his ability to preserve a certain aloofness and integrity whether the healthy criticism, which in the long run is the prime mover of productive change and innovation in an educational system, will be kept alive.

The Swedish School Reforms: A Case Study in Policy-oriented Research*

THE Swedish academic man back in the early 1960s had little realization of how fortunate he was to find a ready listener for his studies bearing upon major topics of public policy. I once guided a British colleague around the Swedish National Board of Education. His puzzlement was explained in the relaxed atmosphere of a Stockholm lunch: "It's funny," he said, "you seem to take education seriously in Sweden." Since I knew him well, I concluded that he found us lacking in detachment; he did not see those furtive smiles of the Roman augurs. Anyhow, I gather that he saw that we had a certain faith in education as a major affair in our welfare state.

But it was my turn to be baffled when a few years later I was invited by another British colleague to see some members of the London County Council. The purpose of bringing us together, I found out, was to convey to the politicians the idea that (1) it might be a good thing to apply educational research techniques in evaluating the comprehensive secondary schools which had been set up in certain districts by the Council and (2) that such evaluations ought to be the responsibility of the Council. I had not discovered until then that selling the idea that educational research could make a significant contribution both in framing educational policy and in evaluating its products would in some quarters turn out to be a problem. We had taken it as self-evident that educational research would have to form part of the base upon which important rational policy decisions on educational matters are founded. In fact, we had come to believe in educational research as a necessary prerequisite to long range planning of our school system.

In ruminating upon a gracious invitation of the President of the American Educational Research Association to discuss the role of educational research in the course of the Swedish school reforms, I decided to highlight the relationships of research workers and legislators. A good deal of the following is therefore about bridge-building.

Some pieces of information about Sweden and the Swedish school system may serve as a framework for a story about how communication was established between policymaking bodies and researchers and how it came about that research and development is now conceived as one important function of our National Board of Education. Sweden, with a population of about

* Originally published in *The School Review*, Vol. 73:3, 1965, 206–225. Reproduced by permission of the University of Chicago Press.

8,000,000 people, is socially, economically, and religiously a homogeneous country. It is a parliamentary democracy, and the Social-Democratic party has been in power since 1932. The prime minister held office from 1946 until 1969. The Social Democratic party has consistently viewed educational reform as a prerequisite to creation of a social-welfare state and as an implementation of it. The rapidly rising standard of living explains much of the force behind the educational explosion at secondary and university levels. Even the minister of finance accepts the doctrine that education is a productive investment for both the individual and society. Educational planning is diligently pursued by the school administration and other public agencies. More than half the recurrent costs of education flow from parliamentary grants. Within the budget, the National Board of Education decides where and how to build new schools and meets nearly all the capital costs. Teacher's salaries are on a uniform schedule and are appropriated by Parliament. There is virtually no private education in Sweden.

Planning was for a long time carried out by *ad hoc* committees, so-called Royal Commissions, which constitute a unique element in Swedish policymaking and, as I shall spell out later, which account for the role educational research has played in this connection. There were three major committees after the war. The first was constituted in 1946, the second in 1957, and the third in 1960. They represented three continuous steps in the reorganization of the Swedish school system. The 1946 committee drew up the plans for an experimental period to try out a nine-year comprehensive school. The 1957 committee launched an extensive research program in evaluating the pilot program and, on the basis of this laid down guidelines for the future organization and curriculum in compulsory schooling. The 1960 committee worked out the consequences of this for the next stage in the school system, namely the *gymnasium* level. Each committee profited from the experiences of the previous committees, and each initiated research pertaining to the basic issues with which they were dealing.

The fact that planning on the national level is part and parcel of administration should be kept in mind, because realistic planning in many instances cannot be carried out without studies that go beyond simple fact-finding. Let me give only one illustration. Class size has been a much debated issue both in connection with the school reform and in negotiations between the teacher associations and the government. There has been strong pressure from certain quarters to introduce a bill according to which class size would gradually be reduced. Such a step would of course considerably affect the teacher-demand and, in its turn, the planning for teacher training. An investigation based upon a national survey of classes was therefore conducted. The outcomes did not give support to the belief that the proposed reductions would improve the standard of instruction. I shall have to come back to this study later.

What is, then, the basic change that has occurred? Until the beginning of the 1950s Sweden's schools were a reflection of the traditional European dualistic pattern. We had a seven- or eight-year compulsory elementary school from which, after the fourth grade, the students could transfer to the lower section of a selective academic secondary school. The number of transfers increased from 10 per cent at the beginning of the 1930s to more than 40 per cent in the fifties. In 1950 Parliament passed an education act providing for the compulsory part of the school system according to which the nine-year comprehensive school was to be introduced on a pilot basis during the fifties and thus replace the previous parallel school structure at this level. It was envisaged that a continuous evaluation should take place during the tryout period. A division of school experimentation was set up within the National Board. The government in 1957 appointed a committee which, among its terms of reference, had to consider the experiences gained during the pilot-scheme period and to make more definitive proposals about the organization and curriculum of the compulsory nine-year school that would cater for all the young people of the age range seven to sixteen. The 1962 Education Act then made provisions for the introduction of the comprehensive school all over the country.

This act, then, implied drastic changes whereby Sweden radically broke with the traditional dualistic pattern. In the case of the "eleven-plus" examinations in England and the selection at the age of ten for the nine-year German pre-university school, the *Gymnasium*, the selection decides not only who is going to receive academic education but also, with few exceptions, who is a potential professional and who is not.

In 1960 the Swedish Government appointed a so-called *Gymnasium* Committee which, according to its terms of reference, should investigate and make proposals for the revision of the previous *Gymnasium*. The intention was to take into account the situation created by the new, basic common nine-year school and also the explosive increase in enrollment at the preuniversity level. The committee also had to revise the curriculum of the *Gymnasium* in the light of the current and future needs of Swedish society.

Why, then, has the situation emerged in Sweden that educational research, together with planning and governmental *ad hoc* committees, has, more and more, been recognized as one of the instruments for bringing about educational change?

In the first place, it should be pointed out that since 1940 the school system has been under permanent revision by so-called royal commissions, that is, by committees appointed by the government. I shall briefly indicate some of the problems with which these committees were faced and how they tried to set about their tasks by means of research among other things. This might give an idea of how a liaison was established and reinforced between researchers and policymakers

These committees were chaired by the minister of education in office. It might not be irrelevant to indicate that the Prime Minister from 1946 to 1969, Mr Erlander, was the first chairman of the 1946 committee. He participated in the initial work of the committee when among other things, its research program was planned. Lines of communication for both research tasks and advisory work gradually evolved. Since the committees receive their mandate as well as their authorization from government, the Ministry of Education, through the committees, enjoys regular and prolonged contact with the researchers. The parliamentary budget committee, or an *ad hoc* committee to consider budget implications of education bills sometimes called for testimony by technical witnesses.

The National Board of Education, in common with other administrative boards, enjoys greater autonomy than the staff of either an American or a British department in anticipating, planning for, or implementing legislation or government decisions. This board had during the 1950s a standing research program relating to the emerging system of comprehensive schools as part of its regular operations. By a 1962 act, its Bureau of Research and Development is not itself to carry out research but is authorized to contract research assignments to educational research institutions. In the 1962 act the minister of education affirmed the policy that the bureau would pay particular attention to problems arising from implementation of the school reform.

The 1962 act also provided for inaugurating an advisory council to the Board, appointed by the government. The membership includes four research men in educational psychology and sociology, two representatives of teachers' associations, and one each for the parent-teacher association, management association, and labor unions.

The best way as indicated earlier, to illustrate how the lines of communication were opened up and reinforced would be to give a brief description of how the relations between research workers and policymakers (school administrators within the Ministry of Education and members of Parliament) developed after 1940.

The 1940 school committee, composed mainly of educators and charged with the task of contemplating what changes were called for in the national school system, approached the four holders of the chairs of education and psychology at the Swedish universities and asked for their evaluation of "the present conception of psychological research on mental development in children and adolescents." Much time was spent on the problem of how to connect primary and secondary education, that is to say how to deal with the dualism indicated above. The committee split into two groups, one in favor of a common six-year elementary school, upon which all types of further schooling should build, and one in favor of so-called double transfer, that is, one connection after the fourth and another after the sixth year in the elementary school. The issue boiled down to the problem of the "effectiveness" of the four-plus-five and the six-plus-four systems, respectively. The committee made extensive evaluations of the two systems in terms of actual number of school years to graduation, number of grade-repeaters, social background of students, school marks, and age of graduation.

The issue which during decades was a dominant preoccupation of Swedish secondary school teachers, who were used to teaching an intellectually and socially select group, could somewhat schematically be stated like this: At what age would it be necessary to differentiate between the academic goats and the practical sheep? Using an American vocabulary the problem might be phrased as that of at what age homogeneous grouping should be introduced, or when the college-bound pupils should be separated from the rest.

The 1940 committee wanted the professors to give the evidence of psychological research pertaining to this problem. On the whole, the professors' testimony tended to favor early "creaming off"; children should transfer to preuniversity secondary schools at age eleven. Except for the limited evaluation inquiries mentioned above, no research was conducted by the committee. The professors relied heavily upon the general literature on developmental research and for the rest fell back upon "the depth of their consciousness." At that time European professors were evidently still deemed to be the custodians of accumulated wisdom.

The appointment of the 1946 School Commission, which consisted mainly of members of Parliament, in various respects implied a turning point. Apart from the fact that the commission politically, and not least in school policy, held rather radical views, it also launched an extensive research program which was geared to elucidate the development of "practical" and "academic" aptitudes and their inter-relations at various age levels. Furthermore, the development of varous intellectual factors was studied.

The committee expressed a strong belief in educational research in its main report that was turned in to the government in 1948: "The findings of educational and psychological research have to be alloted a decisive role as concerns problems which have been subjected to rigid investigations."

The research program was assigned to Professor John Elmgren at the University of Gothenburg, who called it the study of "ability structure and factorial maturity in Swedish school children." His investigation, which was reported by the 1946 School Committee in a separate monograph entitled "School and Psychology," (1952) was based on cross-sectional surveys of school children from seven to sixteen. Elmgren found, like his predecessors, that so-called practical and theoretical aptitudes were positively correlated. Furthermore, according to the factor analyses, "practical" aptitude did not seem to be "as simple and unitary in its structure as general intelligence" (the latter being apparently equated with "theoretical" aptitude). The committee drew two conclusions in its report in 1948. The earlier conception of "theoretical" and "practical" aptitudes as being in a compensatory way related to each other was not valid. That finding certainly did not support a parallel school structure; and early differentiation by the transfer of the "academics" to a selective secondary school was not justified. In the first place, since the "greatest comprehensiveness" of abilities was to be found in pupils of high general ability, and early transfer would imply that the practical vocations would not then get their share of people of high general ability and would thereby suffer a great loss of prestige. This would then in the long run widen gaps between the social classes.

The interesting feature so far of the expectations put by the policymakers upon the researchers was that they should give generalized answers pertaining to school structure and organizational differentiation. They were expected to specify when children's ability structure had reached the level of differentiation that made a separation into different types of schools a sound measure from an educational point of view. They were supposed to be able to state the appropriate age, in general, for introducing instruction in foreign languages, etc.

Even though the interaction between school and society was appreciated, this process was thought of in a rather static way. Factors such as social-class differences in the choice of educational and/or vocational careers were hardly yet realized by the policymakers, and researchers were just beginning to study these problems. Irrespective of whether those involved had a conservative or radical outlook upon school organizations, they thought that there was a fixed number of students able to profit from academic instruction at the preuniversity and university level. The changing, dynamic society was still not recognized as an important factor having an insatiable demand for education, nor was education conceived of as an investment in human capital.

The major argument in favor of a reform of secondary schools and higher education was that of equal opportunity. The essence of democratizing the schools was that everybody, irrespective of social, economic, or geographical factors, should be on equal footing to realize his or her potentialities. This initiated two new lines of inquiry, the study of the "reserve of ability" and the influence of social factors which, in a selective educational system, acted as barriers against the realization of the principle of equality of opportunity.

One attack on the "reserve of talent" problem was made by me, utilizing data on conscripts; virtually every young man by the age of twenty had at that time to undergo a psychological and medical examination before being considered for military service. Since their records include mental tests, school history and marks, as well as social background, estimates similar to those later made by Dael Wolf in his book *America's Resources of Specialized Talent* (New York, 1954) for the United States were made. These estimates were quoted by the minister of education when he introduced the 1950 education act before Parliament. My colleague Kjell Härnqvist pursued the problem under the auspices of the royal commission on universities. He followed a fourth of the 1945 fourth-grade pupils up to 1956 or to the age of twenty. By holding initial ability (i.e. fourth-grade marks) constant and by comparing pupils who did or did not transfer to the academic stream at the end of the fourth year, he was able to estimate "talent loss" of the lower-class children by virtue of their lower rate of entry to the academic ladder. Relying upon these estimates of the untapped reserve of talent, strong support was given to more generous policies of student grants and loans for university study.

An investigation of the effects of "social handicap" was started in the middle forties, some of it being part of projects taken up by the institutions of education and sociology, part of it sponsored by *ad hoc* governmental committees. My colleague Gunnar Boalt, investigated the role of what he called social handicaps in the school careers of a complete age group of youngsters in Stockholm, following them up from the age of ten to twenty. Jonas Orring (who was secretary of the 1957 School Committee and later director general of education) studied the problem of grade repeating and dropout in the academic secondary school. I re-analyzed his data and related failure to social background. Studies of this type led me to question the alleged superiority of a selective and competitive school system in a society with an expanding economy and a strong need for mass education at the upper secondary level. When the relative merits of a selective and comprehensive system are weighed against each other, one must consider the price that is paid for the quality of the minority that reaches the top of the ladder. Social bias in the selection and screening procedures was obvious. But the system was apparently also biased against those who had certain special abilities. The high demands on performances in foreign languages obviously favored the more linguistically talented and were barriers for those whose assets were anchored more in mathematics and science, because people were not admitted to institutions of higher learning without qualifications in three foreign languages.

These investigations played an important role when the 1957 School Committee prepared its report which was submitted to the government in 1961 and when the 1962 Education Bill introducing the common nine-year school all over the country was drafted. Similar considerations were also behind the 1964 Education Act on *Gymnasium* education.

The main issue in Swedish school policy from 1940 to 1962 was, as indicated before, the problem of differentiation. It could briefly be stated like this: At what age should the students considered to be academically talented be separated from their non-intellectual classmates? They could transfer to another program in a separate school, to another program taught within the school, or simply to separate classes within the same program in the same school. The theory held by most Swedish secondary-school teachers was that both categories of students would gain from an early separation. The theoretically geared would not be hampered by their slow-learning classmates, and the latter would be saved the feeling of inferiority that would be caused by the constant confrontation with their bright peers.

This problem was investigated by the 1957 School Committee which sponsored an extensive research project was reported in a monograph, *Ability Grouping and Scholastic Achievement*, by one of my former co-workers, Nils-Eric Svensson. When the study was designed we took advantage of a unique situation. The City Council of Stockholm in 1955 decided to embark upon a program with a transitory organization of the nine-year compulsory school in the southern part of the city. Stockholm was thereby divided into two sectors, a situation which provided some cartoonists with a natural parallel to Berlin; a poster on one cartoon read: "You are now leaving the free school sector." In brief, in the southern sector no separation whatsoever took place during the first six school years and in some districts not until the ninth grade. In the northern sector the dual or parallel system was still kept for a short time, which meant transfer for an "elite" to the selective academic school after the fourth grade. Both the northern and southern sectors had similar social-class distributions. Since social background and initial ability measured by tests and school marks were kept under control we could take advantage of the situation and carry out a five-year follow-up. Comparisons were made between students of all ranges of ability in the two systems. By means of analysis of covariance we could compare outcomes taking initial social and achievement status into consideration. The main findings could, with some oversimplification, be stated as follows. First, when comparing the two systems and holding social background and initial ability of pupils under control, it was found that the comprehensive system had a greater total yield by the age of fifteen than the selective one. On the whole, bright pupils performed better in the selective system at an early age, but by the age of fifteen there was no difference whereas poorer-ability pupils performed better thoughout in the comprehensive system.

Another co-worker, Sixten Marklund, carried out a study on class structure and class size, based upon national survey data. Since school marks all over the country were equalized by means of achievement-tests in Swedish, mathematics, and English that are constructed at the University of Stockholm's Institute of Education Research and given uniformly to all students at certain grade levels, we were provided with survey material which has turned out to be useful for various research purposes. Marklund took advantage of these data and drew representative samples from the entire country. Homogeneity (as defined by IQ, school marks, and achievement tests) was studied keeping class size under control and vice versa, an approach that had not been taken by the numerous researchers who had tackled the problem of class size, for instance.

Svensson's study was reported to the 1957 School Committee successively as the results emerged from the follow-up through various grades. Most of the reporting was then made orally, directly to the committee consisting, as pointed out earlier, of the minister of education in the chair and outstanding representatives of the political parties. We met several times with the committee and discussed at length the possible interpretations of Svensson's findings. These deliberations even included discussions on problems of methodology.

Marklund's study on the school class offers an interesting illustration of how previously evolved lines of communication to policymakers were used and reinforced. Bridges that had been built to individual members of Parliament were utilized. The Finance Committee in Parliament, which has to examine educational bills and proposals, had over the years several times summoned me or my co-workers to appear before the committee to provide information.

Marklund's monograph happened to be published a few weeks before the Finance Committee had to consider a move made by some members of Parliament making provisions for a successive reduction of class size which, by the way, at that time averaged about twenty-five.

The rationale spelled out in the motion was that such a reduction would increase the educational productivity. Marklund was able to make it quite clear that within the range under consideration there was no evidence to support such a prediction.

After reading about the research projects that some of our institutions have carried out for governmental *ad hoc* committees or for the National Board of Education some questions about academic freedom may seem justified. What about the investigator's own interest and conception of what is important to study? If the problems are set forth by the policymakers this not only would hamper the influence of the creative scientific mind but also would contribute to superficiality in the sense that immediate tasks which are seemingly "productive" are preferred to fundamental ones, those that imply promise and fruitfulness for the future.

The best guaranty against such dangers is good liaison with the policymakers in two of the phases of research. In the first place, researchers would have to help policymakers in advancing fruitful problems, in formulating questions which not only can be expected to be relevant to the policy they are expected to frame but which also are precise and specific enough to be tackled by the methodology at hand. Second, investigators would have to help policymakers in interpreting the outcomes of a project and in particular, to indicate the limitations of the research.

As far as research pertaining to the school reforms is concerned there has been no single case when the specific problems have been assigned by the Ministry of Education or its committees. This has always been a matter of thorough discussion between the committees or the Ministry and representatives of the research institution to which they have turned.

Futhermore, the kind of relationship between investigators and policymakers that has been described here is often conducive to basic research which otherwise never would have been started.

A Bureau of Research and Development which was instituted at the National Board of Education in the Swedish 1962 Education Act. The role of the bureau is, as pointed out above, conceived of as a contract- or assignment-giving agency. Parliament every year appropriates a grant for its program. The board then, on the basis of a policy framed as a result of discussions with its advisory council, allocates money to research institutions which have been approached by the bureau or which, less frequently, have submitted proposals.

Policy-oriented educational research today, in order to yield something useful, should be centered around comprehensive programs carried out by research teams that can be kept together for several years. The experiences gained in Sweden point in the same direction as Lazarsfeld and Sieber do in their investigation on organizing educational research.* A research director has been assigned to each project, and the members of the team have been offered the opportunity of utilizing their work as part of their graduate studies.

Nobody would deny the obvious fact that the problem of setting up a national policy in education is a matter of growing concern not only in the United States but all over the world. In the 1950s the phrase "educational planning" had no place in the educator's vocabulary. Planning has to go together with continuous fact-finding and research by means of which one can get answers to problems for which facts are collected. An example of a failure to plan was the Federal Republic of Germany, where there was until 1970 no central ministry of education but complete decentralization to the various *Laender*. Today no country can afford to neglect long-range plans taking into account state and national needs. The establishment of nationwide machinery for the framing and implementation of educational policy would not suffice unless the machinery included bodies for research and planning. The experts should have close liaison with policymakers. However, to safeguard against corruption, the research bodies should be independent which implies that they should either belong to university institutions or be civil servants whose tenure would be unaffected by changing tides on the political scene.

Harper's Magazine in its December issue 1964 carried an article about a professor of psychology (Jerome Bruner) who had moved into education where according to the author, he spread "yeasty" ideas. As an interested observer of what is happening on the American scene, I have noticed that these ideas, yeasty or not, have permeated the intellectual bread in certain circles. The research worker has to promote a spirit of scepticism and inquiry into a system that tends to be dominated by self-sufficient schoolmasters who are suffering from the professional disease of regarding education as a self-contained pedagogical enterprise.

---

* Paul F. Lazarsfeld & Sam D. Sieber, *Organizing Educational Research: An Exploration* (Englewood Cliffs: Prentice Hall, 1967).

Educational Research and Policy-making: An International Perspective*

RESEARCH in education orientated towards the making of policy covers a very short period indeed. Research deliberately and systematically intended to provide an extended basis of knowledge for the reform and improvement of education initiated by persons responsible for educational policy is hardly more than twenty-five years old. The relations between educational research and the making of educational policy are dependent both on the "intra-scientific" or internal conditions of the work of research and on "extra-scientific" or external conditions. The intra-scientific conditions are the prevailing modes of doing research, prevailing schools of thought, the qualities of influential theorists or research workers. The extra-scientific conditions are the availability of research funds and institutions, the "market" for research, and the outlook of the government as it is expressed in its propensity for social intervention. They include also the liaison between research workers and policymakers.

The intra-scientific conditions are on the whole determined by the community of research workers. In the United States, Great Britain, Sweden and the Federal Republic of Germany, the ideas which affect educational research are either humanistic or the empirical-positivistic.

In the development of the intellectual community of educational research and the disciplines that formed the basis for scholarly studies in education, there is a marked break between the period before and the period after the Second World War. In the extra-scientific conditions which affect educational research, mainly, the willingness of governments to support and utilize research in education, the dividing line should perhaps be drawn at least a decade later. Studies in education commissioned and supported by governments in the belief that they would be useful for the making and carrying out of educational policy began to become more frequent in the late 1950s and early 1960s. No doubt, the 1960s were the "golden years" of educational research on both sides of the Atlantic.

Internal Conditions: Before 1945

In Germany the two overriding models of educational research for a long

* Originally published in *Minerva* (London), Vol. 21:1, 1983, 81–100. Reproduced by permission.

time operated side by side. The philosophical approach to the study of educational problems emerged in German universities in the late eighteenth century, when education began to be studied as a separate academic discipline with its own university chairs. The professors holding these chairs came mainly from philosophy, and later in some cases from history. As late as 1950, most university professors of education – there were not many – had their background in the humanities.

In 1910, there was at all German universities still only one *Ordinarius* and three *Extraordinarien* with the title of professor. By 1931, the number of *Ordinarien* had increased to five and the *Extraordinarien* to seven. By 1953-54, in the Federal Republic of Germany there were at the 18 universities some ten professorships at the level of the *Ordinarius* and seven *Extraordinarien*. Less than half of these were *habilitiert*, that is to say, had taken the more advanced qualification which was usually necessary for a professorial career. In addition there were at the *Hochschulen* of technology and business some ten professors of education at the level of *Ordinarius*.

The *pädagogische Hochschulen*, created in the 1920s by the liberal Minister of Education, C. H. Becker, prepared teachers for the primary schools and for what was later called the lower secondary stage – *Sekundarstufe I*. The *pädagogische Hochschulen* were established first in Prussia and later in the other *Länder*. Their integration into the universities in the late 1960s considerably increased the number of professors of education.

From 1953 until the late 1970s, the number of academic staff at universities and *Hochschulen* increased considerably. Thus the number of professors grew from 26 in 1953 to 518 in 1976, and the number of other staff in education – mostly *Assistenten* – increased from 75 to 3,600 over the same period.

Education – pedagogics and didactics – had great difficulty in establishing itself as a separate academic discipline. Demands for theoretical preparation in education originally manifested themselves in the context of training teachers for grammar schools on the European continent and in Scandinavia. Usually, professors in established academic disciplines gave lectures in pedagogics to prospective teachers. Thus, Friedrich August Wolf, who in 1783 became the second professor of education at the University of Halle in Germany, had his background in classical philology. At the University of Lund in southern Sweden, the professor of philosophy Matthias Fremling from 1803 lectured in education, and so a year later did his colleague in philosophy at the University of Uppsala, Daniel Boëthius. But education was not considered to be an independent scholarly discipline. The rector of the University of Uppsala, Henrik Schück, himself a professor of esthetics and literature, in the brochure of invitation to the inauguration of the first professor of education at the university in 1910 expressed doubts about the worthwhileness of the academic study of the art of teaching. But, he added, it would be up to the new professor to disprove this!

Around the turn of the century, empirical educational studies were conducted at several institutes of psychology. The most striking case is Ernst

Meumann, a student of Wilhelm Wundt, who founded "experimental peda-gogics" and in 1907 published *Einführung in die experimentalle Pädagogik* in three impressive volumes which still were on reading lists for graduates in Sweden in the 1930s. There were other leading research workers in educa-tional problems attached to institutes of psychology, such as William Stern, professor of psychology first in Breslau, and then in Hamburg; a pioneer in educational psychology, he made major contributions before 1914 both to differential and developmental psychology.

In the United States, from the late nineteenth century when education began to be taught at American universities, one approach predominated – the empirical. It must suffice here to point out two or three pioneers. G. Stanley Hall, the first head of the psychology department at Johns Hopkins and later the first president of Clark University, like many others, had his training in research in Germany. His *Life and Confessions of a Psychologist* gave a very concrete picture of how educational psychology was established in the United States and under what intellectual auspices this took place. Other leading figures in the United States scene were Edward Lee Thorndike at Teachers College, Columbia University, Lewis Terman at the Leland Stanford Jr. University, and Charles Judd at the University of Chicago. The last, who took his doctorate under Wilhelm Wundt in 1896, made a case for education as a science in its own right in his book on *The Science of Education* published in 1918. William James had already in the 1890s in his *Talks to Teachers on Psychology* emphatically maintained that teaching was not a science but "an art."

The low prestige of the study of education as an academic endeavour in the universities of the United States partly derived from the fact that the intellectual base for educational research tended to be established outside the departments of education; educational research could not acquire the aca-demic dignity of the disciplines on which it drew. In many places in Europe, it was established within the counterparts to these departments or in close contact with the chairs of education, some of which were combined chairs in education and psychology.

However, education as an academic endeavor did not enjoy a much higher status in Europe than in the United States. Even a basic course in education for prospective teachers was often met with resistance, because it was consi-dered to be a "practical pursuit" that had no place at a university, at least not within the faculty of philosophy where scientific endeavors were conceived of as purely "theoretical." But by having closer ties with its mother disci-plines, for instance philosophy and psychology, education did manage to be held in somewhat higher esteem in Europe.

On the British scene the study of education before 1945 was throughout dominated by a straightforward practicality. British universities had for a long time very few chairs in education. At Oxford and Cambridge, the practice was long established of appointing experienced schoolmasters to these chairs, which were expected to give prospective teachers some practical grounding in the art of teaching.

Educational research in Great Britain was deeply influenced by the Galtonian tradition with its focus on studies of individual differences. Sir Francis Galton, inspired by his interest in mental inheritance, documented in his book *Hereditary Genius*, proposed extensive surveys on mental capacities. Galton conceived of testing as an instrument of eugenics which he founded as an academic discipline at the laboratory he established at University College, London. Karl Pearson who took over the laboratory after Galton, pursued in his tradition further studies of "intelligence as a graded character." Pearson, and the statistical methods he developed, such as the correlation coefficient that carries his name, had a strong influence on differential psychology on both sides of the Atlantic.

Several of the leading figures in the British research on testing, such as Cyril Burt and Charles Spearman, were either trained or worked in the laboratory founded by Francis Galton, and then led by Karl Pearson. Large-scale surveys by means of group tests were largely inspired by the eugenics movement that emanated from Galton. Beginning in 1933, surveys of all eleven-year-olds were conducted at regular intervals in Scotland.

In Sweden, until 1937, there were only three university chairs of education; a fourth was then added. Three of the incumbents were primarily trained as experimental psychologists, thus representing the empirical approach. Axel Herrlin in Lund, Rudolf Anderberg in Uppsala and David Katz in Stockholm, had studied with Georg Elias Müller in Göttingen, who had been a student of Wilhelm Wundt. A fourth incumbent, John Landquist, with a background in philosophy, had studied with Bergson in Paris and Windelband in Heidelberg; in 1920, he wrote a book, *Människokunskap* (Psychological Knowledge), on the epistemology of psychology, in the spirit of Wilhelm Dilthey.

After 1940, when a governmental commission of inquiry preparatory to a reform of Swedish education was appointed, research in education gradually came to be much in demand. Expectations were very high, both in the commission of 1940 and a subsequent one appointed in 1946, that research could provide extensive bases in scientific knowledge for the proposals that eventually led to the introduction of the common basic and comprehensive school.

The predominant influences on Swedish research in the 1940s shifted from Europe to the United States. The latter country became the Mecca not only of Swedish students in the behavioral sciences but in particular for those wanting to absorb ideas about how to achieve progressive educational reforms.

Internal Conditions: After 1945

There was a slow reorientation of educational research in Germany after the disasters of Nazi rule and the Second World War. In the 1930s many of the leading students of human behavior had been forced to leave, most of them going to the United States. During the Occupation, the United States High Commissioner's Office made deliberate attempts to promote a change in the educational system. In 1952, the High Commissioner sponsored a six-week workshop on problems of educational research at the Hochschule für internationale pädagogische Forschung which had just been established jointly by American and German authorities with the purpose of serving German schools by cross-disciplinary research in education, and by long "in-service" training courses for teachers who wanted to learn the techniques of research which were appropriate to deal with the important problems of German education.

The first director of the institute was Professor Erich Hylla, who as early as the 1920s had worked in the construction of tests and whose background was mainly in educational psychology. The executive secretary of the course, Dr. Walter Schultze, also came from educational psychology, in Hamburg, and had been developing scholastic aptitude tests. By and large, the experts who were invited from abroad represented the psychological and empirical approach to educational problems.

The majority of the participants in the workshop were Germans, but there were about a dozen from other countries, most of them educational psychologists who were expected to provide inspiring ideas. The sponsors wished the workshop to serve as a "refresher course" for German educationists who had been out of contact with developments outside the country since the Nazi accession to power.

In the early 1960s, thanks to the initiative and the persuasive powers of Professor Hellmut Becker, a lawyer turned educator, the Max-Planck-Institut für Bildungsforschung was founded in Berlin. The explicitly formulated task of the institute was to conduct fundamental cross-disciplinary research relevant to German educational problems, since it was firmly believed that German education was in urgent need of reform. There were those who at that time spoke of about "twenty years of non-reform." Leading scholars at the institute, such as Hellmut Becker himself and one of the pioneers of the economics of education, Professor Friedrich Edding, later became very important in the *Bildungsrat* which was instituted to make recommendations for the planning of the educational system. There was in West Germany until 1970 no ministry of education; the *Länder* retained jurisdiction over educational matters.

When the *Grundgesetz* – the constitutional or fundamental law – of the Federal Republic was amended to make the planning of education a federal prerogative and when a Ministry of Education was created, federal financial support for educational research became rather abundant, at least in comparison with its previous scale. The *Bildungsbericht '70*, which drew up a blueprint for the reform of German education, devoted a separate chapter to educational research and recommended a substantial increase in the resources to be allocated for such research. The *Länder* followed suit and provided their share of funds for educational research and educational planning.

The pendulum of educational research began to swing towards a quantitatively orientated approach, led by young persons with a background in psychology and sociology and with training in the United States and Great Britain. For instance, young psychologists trained by the leading American psychometrician L. L. Thurstone at the University of Chicago came back and applied sophisticated methods of statistical analysis to psychological data. Others stayed for some time in the United States and on their return became the leaders in German studies inspired by ideas from "behavioral science."

Then, in the 1960s, the pendulum began to swing back from the quantitative scientific approach to an interest in hermeneutics. This change "from measurement to understanding" drew upon the tradition of Wilhelm Dilthey, Edmund Husserl and Martin Heidegger. The deliberate turning of their backs on the "neo-positivist" conception of knowledge was so fervently adopted by some young German educational research workers that "positivist" even became a pejorative term.

The scale of educational research in the United States after the Second World War is too great to describe in a short compass. The volume of publications has been extraordinary and very diverse. The psychologists with their empirical approach have dominated in terms of numbers, volume of publications, and recognition by the academic community. Leading scholars, such as Professors Lee J. Cronbach, Benjamin S. Bloom, N. L. Gage and Robert Glaser, were all trained in educational psychology. Curricular development, partly based on sophisticated methods of classroom observation, had earlier become an important field of study at schools and colleges of education.

Connections were established between behavioristic psychology – mainly the Skinner variant of operant conditioning – and didactics, a marriage which resulted in "programmed learning" with or without devices referred to as teaching machines.

In the 1950s, the federal government began to support projects on educational research through the Cooperative Research Program for which more than five million dollars were appropriated. The National Defense Education Act 1958 provided large sums, not least for curricular development and improvements in teaching of science. Finally, the Elementary and Secondary Act of 1965 almost overnight increased the resources for educational research many-fold. Title 4 of the Elementary and Secondary Education Act increased funds for research to more than one hundred million dollars. Research and development centers with huge resources for work in particular fields were established at leading universities. Regional laboratories which were expected to be even closer to the needs of the classroom were established.

In the early 1970s, the responsibility for the research and development centers was moved from the United States Office of Education to the new National Institute of Education, without any substantial increase in resources. Several evaluation-studies of both the centers and the regional laboratories took place. The fact that resources ceased to increase was a result, not only of financial constraints, which were functions of the state of the economy, but also of disappointment with some of these centers and laboratories which did not live up to the highly-pitched expectations.

Given the rapidly growing support for educational research, persons active in disciplines other than education entered the field. An increasing number of psychologists were attracted, as were – almost for the first time – sociologists, political scientists, and economists. Cross-disciplinary fields of inquiry were established, such as comparative education and the economics of education.

Educational research workers in Great Britain had, in the Galtonian tradition, for a long time been preoccupied by studies of individual differences, test construction, and surveys of intelligence; the leading figures were Cyril Burt, Godfrey Thompson, and Philip Vernon. Under the auspices of the Education Act of 1944 and the "eleven-plus examinations," research on how to diagnose scholastic aptitude and predict achievement in school became a major task for educational research. The social implications of the reform of 1944 were investigated by sociologists, such as Mrs. Jean Floud and Professor A. H. Halsey, who began to study the effects of the reform on equality of opportunity and the extent to which "parity of esteem" between various secondary educational programs had been achieved.

Since it was felt by the educational authorities that the universities did not meet the immediate needs of the practitioners, the National Foundation for Education Research in England and Wales was established as a private organization. At the beginning, it was mainly a test-developing institute which also conducted research on how the tests worked in schools.

In Sweden, educational research from 1945 to the early 1970s was predominantly conducted by persons trained in psychology. Typical was the series of major studies within the framework of the school reform leading up to the Education Act of 1962 (1962 års skollag), which made provision for a basic comprehensive school over the entire country. Prior to the commission of 1957 (1957 års skolkommission), which prepared the legislation, there had been studies on the "reservoir of ability" and its social background. Other studies included large-scale surveys which dealt with curricular content. A crucial issue which loomed large in the debate on reform, that of structural and pedagogical differentation at the lower secondary level, was dealt with in several major studies of which one was directly commissioned by the commission of 1957.

Most of this work was done in the dominant Anglo-American mode, with great reverence for experimental design in the empirical-positivist tradition. Experimental design was the ideal, surveys second best, and observational description was regarded as an unsatisfactory substitute. But a more humanistic, hermeneutic approach, more or less closely associated with Marxist ideology – the so-called "rosy wave" – in educational research began the early 1970s and was carried by a young generation of research workers.

External Conditions: The Interventionist Policies of the Welfare State

Over the last few decades, the state has increasingly played an interventionist role in promulgating and carrying out policies in health and education as well as in welfare in general. In order to conduct planning successfully, not least in education, an extensive body of knowledge is required, in terms of routinely collected data and also more specific information gathered by means of surveys, quasi-experiments and analytical studies and the secondary analysis of existing data.

Thus, something quite new happened after 1945 to the social sciences in several countries. Government agencies turned to research workers for "answers" to what were considered to be basically the "scientific" problems involved in the planning of educational reforms. Royal commissions in England and Sweden did the same. Behavioral or social scientists were expected to achieve the same things that natural scientists had accomplished during the Second World War. For example, in 1942, the Swedish school commission of inquiry of 1940 turned to the professors of psychology for reports on the "state-of-the-art" in the psychological development of young persons, hoping that the answers in the reports submitted to the commission would provide a firm scientific basis for a rational resolution of the problem of the proper structure of the common school. The crucial issue was at what age the academic goats would have to be differentiated from the non-academic sheep.

In all four countries the decades after 1945 saw a great increase in "policy-orientated" research, not least research commissioned by governments or by special governmental commissions. The Plowden Committee in Great Britain, the *Bildungsrat* in the Federal Republic of Germany and the 1957 school commission in Sweden are cases in point. Most of the studies were conducted by educational psychologists, although sociologists became more prominent in dealing with educational problems.

Before the early 1950s, educational planning was in some places regarded as almost tantamount to socialism, particularly since systematic "central planning" had so far only been attempted in the Soviet Union. Nevertheless the steady promotion by international bodies, like UNESCO with its affiliated International Institute for Educational Planning (IIEP) and the Organization for Economic Cooperation and Development (OECD), both led governments to establish organs for educational planning within or outside the ministries of education.

Both the international bodies – the IIEP and the OECD – with the World Bank, were instrumental in promoting the institutional establishment of educational planning. The IIEP was created mainly to serve the less-developed countries, where "planning" after the attainment of independence was expected to be a major instrument of bringing about rapid development.

In any case, certain educational policies which came to the forefront in the 1960s, such as provisions for greater equality of educational opportunity, bilingual education and the education of the handicapped could not be properly framed and realized without the information provided by surveys and evaluation studies.

Rising Expectations

The greatly increased scale of governmental financial support for educational research in the United States, Great Britain, Sweden, and the Federal Republic of Germany took place in the 1960s and the early 1970s. It was assumed that concerted and amply financed research in education would be able to achieve what it had achieved in industry, namely an increase of efficiency and productivity. Expectations were high among both educational research workers and the makers of governmental policy. In 1971, the Select Subcommittee on Education of the United States House of Representatives toured Europe in order to find out what had been achieved through educational research in certain European countries. In the introduction to the report based on the observations made by the committee, its chairman, John Brademas, quoted Charles Silberman's *Crisis in the Classroom:* "The degree of ignorance about the process of education is far greater than I had thought. Research results are far more meager and contradictory, and progress toward the development of viable theories of learning and instruction is far slower." Brademas pointed out that about 10 per cent of the budget in defense was spent on research and development, and in health 4.6 per cent.

"Yet when we come to education, as important to the life of the mind as is defense to the Nation or health to the body, we find at all levels of education in America spending an aggregate of less than one-third of one per cent of their budgets on the processes of research, innovation and planned renewal."

The subcommittee conducted its investigation in connection with the legislation for the establishment of the National Institute of Education (NIE). The Institute was thought of as a better instrument for improving American education than the system of research grants and centers for research and development previously conducted by the United States Office of Education.

Yet the 1970s culminated in sharp criticism, even disenchantment, about education in general and about educational research in particular. This was accompanied by the cessation in the growth of funds assigned to educational research; indeed, resources diminished.

Educational research chiefly conducted by social scientists had been expected to provide an extensive body of knowledge for educational practice and policy, in the same was as research in the physical sciences had done for industrial technology. There were some differences among the countries studied in accordance with the beliefs held by the political elite and the general public regarding the potentialities of science.

In Western Germany, there was much talk about the *wissenschaftliche Begleitung*, i.e. the "scientific accompaniment" of educational reforms. Although there were academics who, in the spirit of the philosopher-kings, thought that educational research could produce complete answers to educational problems, in most cases the makers of policy only expected that research would broaden the knowledge in the light of which they made their "decisions." Great Britain is a particularly interesting case in this respect. As in the other countries, the government greatly increased the resources available to social sciences, with the aim of increasing the stock of knowledge thought necessary for welfare and educational policies and their realization. A British political scientist, Professor Maurice Kogan, who had worked in the Department of Education and Science in London, some years later conducted long interviews with Edward Boyle and Anthony Crosland, two of the most articulate ministers of education Great Britain ever had.

Professor Kogan characterized Edward Boyle as a "reluctant conservative," and Anthony Crosland as a "cautious revolutionary." Although a leading member of the Conservative Party, Boyle was somewhat lukewarm about the program of "comprehensive" schools, whereas "going comprehensive" was regarded by Crosland, who took office as minister of education in 1964, as of the highest priority.

Both ministers referred to the research that I and my collaborators had been conducting on the Swedish school reform. Boyle deplored the short time-span available for a minister in Britain who usually held office only for a very brief period. He said that Swedish planning was possible because its Social Democratic government was able to cover "a cycle of twenty years over which a major piece of social engineering was achieved:" first five years of planning, then "five years of research by Husén." Boyle seems to have thought that research played a crucial role in the Swedish school reform and regretted that the short term of any one party's period in power rendered this impossible in Great Britain. Crosland, as is clear from Professor Kogan's interview, held educational research in high esteem. He esteemed it so highly that he invited me to come to London in 1965 in order to spend a full day with him when he was considering the issuing of his Circular 10/65 to local educational authorities requesting their submission of plans for the reorganization of secondary education. But he had a more realistic conception of the role and capacity of research. In response to Kogan's question why the circular was not preceded by research, he said:

> It implied that research can tell you what your objectives ought to be. But it can't. Our belief in comprehensive re-organization was a product of fundamental value judgments about equity and equal opportunity and social division as well as about education. Research can help you to achieve your objectives, and I did in fact set going a large research project, against strong opposition from all kinds of people, to assess and monitor the process of going comprehensive.

But research cannot tell you whether you should go comprehensive or not – that's basic value judgement.

The great expectations about the "solutions" educational research could give to basic educational problems and the consequent improvements in educational practice were not met. Disappointment and misgivings were the results. In the mid-1970s, I travelled on the same aircraft as a former German minister of education, who in the Brandt government had been instrumental in increasing federal support for educational research. During our long journey, he expressed his misgivings very emphatically about the "uselessness" of educational research. He had before entering politics been a professor of mining technology and he seemed to have expected that the "linear" model of research and development, which went straightforwardly from research through development metallurgy, would succeed in education as well.

Educational Technology

Another belief of the 1960s was that educational technology based on fundamental research on the learning process would be able to make school teaching more efficient. Television, programmed learning with teaching machines and computer-based instruction in turn came on the agenda as panaceas for inefficient teaching. They uniformly, and by a large margin, failed to live up to their promises. The fundamental reason for their failure is, of course, that education is not a manufacturing industry. In manufacturing, a process is chosen in accordance with a definite expectation of what product will result from it. But in education there is a wide margin of uncertainty, because the educational "raw material," the individual child, has a wide, and largely unknown, range of potentialities. It is in the nature of the educative process that it moves in a field of multiple possibilities. Technology can therefore replace teachers only to a very limited extent.

The establishment of the centers for educational research and development at some leading universities in the United States, with support from the federal government, was impelled by the anticipation that immense investments in research on a particular complex of problems, in the way in which it is done in industry, would yield results that could be converted into the equivalent of industrial products, namely, improved methods of school teaching.

The Support of Research

Policy-oriented research in education was practically non-existent before 1950. The next two decades saw an enormous increase of financial resources for research in education by direct governmental support for educational research projects, and by funds made available by research councils. The arrangements varied from country to country. In Sweden, the *Samhällsvetenskapliga forskningsrådet* – the social science research council –

was given considerably increased appropriations to support research of a fundamental nature. Its resources quadrupled over a decade. In the 1960s, at the two national boards of education, the *Skolöverstyrelsen* – the national board of school education – and *Universitets- och högskoleämbetet* – the national board of colleges and universities – bureaux of research and development with considerable resources were established. In the Federal Republic of Germany, several central agencies for the promotion of research provided financial support. In Great Britain, a considerable part of the governmental support for educational research went through the Social Science Research Council. In the United States, the federal government took the lead.

Private philanthropic foundations, such as the Carnegie Corporation and the Ford Foundation, have also supported research with the expectation that it would bear fruitfully on crucial educational issues. Foundations, by providing initial grants to educational research projects which they thought promised scientifically and practically useful results, have given research workers an opportunity to investigate hitherto unstudied problems. They have also been active in attempts to win public opinion to the support of equality of educational opportunity. There are several broad subjects in the field of educational research where the American foundations took initiatives which were subsequently followed by financial support by the federal government.

In the mid-1960s, the Bank of Sweden created *Riksbankens Jubileumsfond* – the Bank of Sweden tercentenary foundation – a semi-private body with a board of directors consisting of professors and parliamentarians; it has, for instance, supported the work of the International Association for the Evaluation of Educational Achievement (IEA).

The Expanded Labor-Market for Educational Research Workers

Multiplied resources led to a multiplication of workers engaged in educational research. Previously, a great deal of such research had been done by teachers who were not very interested in it but who felt compelled to do it in order to fulfill the requirements for the degrees which were often needed to qualify for advancement to administrative positions. With increased financial resources, young persons were encouraged to try to enter upon careers in which educational research was a major part. This led to a vast expansion of graduate studies in education. Those who completed their work in the graduate schools entered upon academic careers made possible by the enormous expansion of teacher-training institutions, careers as administrators in various public bodies, and careers in research in which they made surveys and other studies directly related to current educational activities. A new professional category of "staff policy-analysts" appeared, particularly in the

United States, and functioned as links between research workers and the makers of policy.

Academic departments of education in the period after the Second World War began increasingly to draw on the whole range of social sciences. Earlier, most departments of education in universities had suffered from an exclusive and very narrow focus on teaching problems and processes. They were ready to seek the help of departments of psychology, but had little contact with the other social sciences. But in the 1950s, the University of Chicago and Stanford University began to make "joint appointments" in their graduate schools of education for outstanding sociologists, psychologists and political scientists; other institutions followed their precedent. This substantially contributed to raising the quality and prestige of educational research among social scientists.

The impact of such a policy was less pronounced in European universities, where academic disciplines were organized around professorial chairs rather than around academic and professional courses of study, as was the case in the establishment of schools of education in the United States. There were two German institutions which, however, were established outside universities, namely the *Deutsches Institut für internationale pädagogische Forschung* and the *Max-Planck-Institut für Bildungsforschung*. In both institutes educational problems were investigated without regard for the boundaries of academic disciplines. In these institutions, economists, lawyers, political scientists and sociologists were appointed to senior posts.

The Relationship between Research Workers and "Users" of Research

The "users" of the results of educational research are in the first place practitioners in the field, the makers of policy in various central bodies, and the administrators or bureaucrats who are expected to provide "background material" upon which decisions are ostensibly to be based.

The relationships between research and the making of policy of course vary tremendously in the four countries under consideration. The relationships are affected by the size of the populations, and, not least, by the degree of centralization of the societies in question. Sweden is a special case in both respects. It has a small population of about eight million, and consequently the opportunities for personal contacts among members of the political, administrative and academic elite are much more favorable than in a country, such as the United States, with more than 200 million inhabitants. It is not difficult for the ministry or for the central agencies in Sweden to bring together or to communicate with most of the professors in a particular academic field in Swedish institutions of higher education. Furthermore, the role played by the central government and parliament in initiating and promoting educational changes differs, of course, strikingly from the situation in the two federal countries, the United States and Germany. In Great Britain, local educational authorities have more influence than those in Sweden.

The relationship between research and the making of central policy is differently arranged in each of the four countries. One arrangement is the "blue-ribbon" governmental commission of inquiry, such as the royal commissions in Great Britain and Sweden, which in both countries have been highly influential in the preparation of educational reforms. Another arrangement which is followed in a federal regime, like Western Germany, is the establishment of *ad hoc* bodies, such as the *Wissenschaftsrat* and the *Bildungsrat*, with both academic and political members who are expected to work out jointly within each council recommendations for policies; normally, these recommendations are for the separate states but in reality they are intended to achieve a uniform national policy. In the United States, "White House conferences" have been held to direct attention to important problems in education. President Johnson in 1964 appointed a task force chaired by John Gardner which drew up the main lines for a federal policy for education for the years to come. Another arrangement in the United States has been the panel of scientific advisers in the President's office.

In Great Britain and Sweden, royal commissions have had an important influence on the formation of educational policy. They are initiated when opinion becomes preoccupied with a particular public issue, such as broadened access to higher education or more equitable taxes. Representatives and advocates of the various pressure groups begin to call on the minister responsible for the particular field of policy, demanding that the issue should be subjected to an intensive inquiry by a royal commission. Simultaneously, the issue is taken up by the media; it is discussed in newspaper editorials and in other organs of mass communication. Finally, the government accedes to demands which have been put forward as public opinion in its various forms. The government might decide that it would be politically convenient to remove the issue from prominence by "burying" it through holding a commission of inquiry. Such a body is usually composed of representatives of the various political parties in the parliament, spokesmen for organizations on the labor market, i.e., trade unions and employers' associations, and other civic and interest groups who are preoccupied with the issue. The government gives the commission certain terms of reference for its work; these direct the commission's inquiry either towards a particular solution of the problem or leave the field open for whatever recommendations the commission might arrive at. The commission is given a secretariat and often conducts its own systematic inquiries or research or both.

In Sweden, a considerable body of social research over the last forty years has been conducted at the request of governmental commissions. After the commission has submitted its main report to the government, the latter, before considering any draft of legislation, circulates the report for consideration and review to various public agencies which might be affected by the recommendations of the report, and to private bodies, such as the central organs of the trade unions. These reviews are submitted to the government which may decide, if the general reactions are not too negative, to prepare legislation on the basis of the recommendations and the responses these have evoked. Thus, the material provided by the commission and the responses of the reviewing bodies are part of the preparation of the legislation for a bill that is finally submitted for the consideration of parliament; often the draft bill quotes directly from the responses by the reviewing bodies.

I have gone into some detail about the particular means of the formation of policy represented by a Swedish royal commission in order to illustrate the process of arriving at a proposal for a particular policy which finally is adopted by the government and the parliament; this process also includes research. When there is a reasonable amount of consensus and little political polarization, the outstanding issues in a particular field of policy about which there is conflict are resolved by these extended deliberations in royal commissions. The proponents of conflicting views have to "fight it out" over a certain period; they usually arrive at compromises. In cases where the recommendations are supported only by a majority within the commission, the minority puts its dissenting opinion on record. Jonas Orring, secretary general of the school commission of 1957 which prepared the comprehensive educational reform in Sweden, also prepared the draft of the education bill in the Ministry of Education; he also served as secretary to the parliamentary select committee which dealt with the bill before it came up for plenary debate!

The reform of the Swedish educational system was prepared during a period of more than twenty years, from the mid-1940s to the late 1960s. The school commission of 1946 consisted mainly of representatives of the political parties which nominated members of parliament who had a particular interest in educational problems. Its work was preceded by that of a commission which had been working since 1940 and which consisted mainly of professional educators, some of them representing the teachers' unions. The commission of 1946, which had to frame a policy on the basis of, among other things, the results of the findings of the previous commission, conducted a comprehensive study on the development of mental abilities from seven – the age of school entry – to sixteen – the envisaged school-leaving age. The work of the commission of 1946 was carried into the legislation for a pilot program of comprehensive schooling over a ten-year period for which provisions were made in the Education Act of 1950. It was envisaged that the final form of the nine-year common basic school should depend on the outcomes of the pilot program, which expanded rapidly as more and more municipalities joined it. Thus the work of the commission of 1957 had to consider these outcomes as well as the findings of the several studies of school differentiation which it sponsored or which were conducted under its own auspices.

In the 1960s, two bodies for the provision of advice regarding the reform of education and promotion of research were created in the Federal Republic of Germany: the *Bildungsrat* and the *Wissenschaftsrat*. In order to ensure that they gave independent advice, both were organized into two "chambers:" one "chamber" of academics and the other with governmental representatives. The chamber of academics of the *Bildungsrat* could arrive at decisions only after having consulted the other chamber in the *Wissenschaftsrat*; the two chambers had to arrive at decisions jointly.

The *Bildungsrat* had very wide terms of reference for its work. It was expected to draw up plans for education taking into account the trends of German society, including the demand for vocational and professional training. Furthermore, it made recommendations about the structure of the German educational system which had been hitherto a system of schools differentiated from each other in accordance with the social classes from which the pupils were drawn.

Another arrangement for liaison between academics and politicians and officials at the highest level has been the establishment of panels to advise on specific matters or on research policy in general. In 1962 the Swedish prime minister took the initiative in establishing what explicitly was labeled a panel of liaison between the Cabinet and the academic/scientific community. This body consisted of between 20 and 25 highly-regarded scientists representing the whole range of scientific faculties and disciplines, and half a dozen Cabinet members who had ministerial responsibility for various fields of scientific research. The entire panel was convened once or twice a year, although an inner circle met more frequently to deal with more specific tasks. The secretariat was located in the office of the prime minister. Relatively little attention was paid to social science and humanistic research, including educational research. This body tended, however, to fade away as a result of the range of other tasks facing the Cabinet members of the panel and the growing diversity of issues with which the panel had to deal. It has, however, recently been resuscitated.

In the early 1970s, I had a personal experience of the Panel on Youth in the Executive Office of the President of the United States where a group of experts under Professor James Coleman's chairmanship produced the report on *Youth: Transition to Adulthood*. This group was, of course, far more remote from the concerns of the makers of policy at the highest level of the American government than the Swedish panel which operated in a small country with a more closely-knit pattern of personal contacts.

The relationships between academic research workers more or less separated in their universities and makers of policy in adminstrative or legislative bodies have changed somewhat since the arrival of two new categories of "middle-men:" research administrators in central government bodies and the policy-analysts who are assigned to government and legislative offices. As appropriations for research have increased, the quest for efficient management of these funds as well as for accountability for their use have become more demanding. Thus, in all the four countries, a new category of research administrators has emerged with academic backgrounds in the field of research with which they are dealing. They serve as advisers to heads of administrative bodies as well as links with the research workers; this is a delicate position. The policy analysts are instrumental in following the research conducted in a particular field. They are expected to digest it for the makers of policy and to draw out the implications for policy.

Concluding Remarks and – Perhaps – Some Lessons for the Future

What conclusions do I draw from having been one of the actors on the scene of policy-oriented educational research since the 1940s, and having recently devoted some studies to it?

In the first place, there is a tendency towards neglect in financial provision for the fundamental research on which studies of more practical problems have to draw heavily. In times of financial constraints, there is a tendency to reduce the resources going to the study of more basic problems, because the reduction of funds in this sector is in the short run not as noticeable as are diminishing resources for research and development. A better balance has to be established between the fundamental research that forms the disciplinary basis for successful studies of a more "mission-oriented" character.

There has been a tendency in most countries, where educational research is supported by public funds, to develop project-research in an *ad hoc* manner as a response to availability of funds for investigating certain problems. By a grant for research an institute or a research group within an institute can be kept alive for a few more years. The shortcomings of such a system are, of course, lack of continuity and a narrow conception of problems.

There has been a growing realization that educational research is effective primarily in so far as it has an illuminating effect on public opinion. It has recently been asserted that there simply is no such thing as the precise application of the specific results of a given piece or project of research to a given "decision" regarding policy. Makers of policy who I have interviewed could point only in a few, exceptional cases, to how a given piece of research had affected their views in making a particular decision. Decisions are seldom "made," they emerge out of a complicated tug-of-war of pressures and influences of interest and civic groups; it is a process which often operates over an extended period in which there is no particular moment when a "decision" is made. (This has by Carol Weiss at Harvard been called "decision accretion.")

The knowledge relevant to a particular issue of policy most often derive from a multitude of particular investigations each of which contributes a tiny bit – either general or specific – to the "knowledge creep". Educational research workers must learn that they have a modest but appropriate role which is far removed from that of a philosopher-king or scientist-king. They lack the competence to play the latter role and the social conditions which would be necessary for it do not exist. At the basis of most problems of a policy with which educational research deals are value-judgments and political ideals and outlooks. Thus the problems of policy cannot by their very nature be solved exclusively on the basis of the results of research, however sound that research may be from a rigorously scientific point of view. The knowledge coming out of social science investigations is often not precise enough and the "users" are not able to generalize it properly, even if the results are valid and reliable enough. In taking decisions on social matters, those who make policy also have to resort to their experience and not least to consider the political objectives they want to achieve.

But educational research workers can in a more modest way still make important contributions to the accretion of knowledge. In the first place, they can by means of their analytical training and methodological competence reformulate the practical problems of making policy by selecting those aspects that are accessible to scientific educational research. On the basis of such research, their studies and their experience and reflection can make clear erroneous assumptions in the proposed policies. Second, they can "enlighten" the makers of policy, practitioners and the general public by heightening their sensitivity to features of the situations with which they must deal. Third, and perhaps foremost, the research workers can serve as informed and responsible critics. Those of them who enjoy the security of tenure which academic freedom and the autonomy of universities confer on them, and the prestige of being university teachers and scientists, can serve as responsible critics of existing policies and proposals for new policies, making clear the evaluative postulates of those policies and examining them for their likely effectiveness in achieving their ostensible ends. There is no reason why they should not render judgments of existing and proposed policies based on their own evaluative postulates and their knowledge based on careful educational research. They should do so, however, only with awareness that evaluative postulates and ideals are not the same as scientific knowledge, however scientific, sound and reliable that knowledge may be.

Policy Implications of Cross-national Education Surveys*

LARGE-SCALE sample surveys of multi-national systems of education, such as those conducted by the International Association for the Evaluation of Education Achievements (IEA), provide new information from which policy-makers in any single country can draw inferences about the state of affairs in their own schools.

In my view, three education policy perspectives could be enriched by cross-national empirical evidence that permits comparison of educational outcomes in the school systems of different countries. These concern the role schools can play in effecting social change; the extent to which the secondary school program should be the same for all students, and the relationship between school resource factors or "inputs" and student achievement.

Policy Domains

1. With school costs soaring, policymakers ask how much school *per se* can accomplish in achieving changes in cognitive competence and inculcating attitudes, and how much of the achieved competence is simply a reflection of the society in which the school operates. The perspective on the *relationship between educational policy and social and economic policy* can be broadened by cross-national comparisons of cognitive and affective outcomes, particularly with regard to special provisions for culturally or socially handicapped students and how resources are allocated. Multi-national studies provide a unique opportunity to disentangle the relative importance of the factors that the child brings to school – the pattern of social influences at large and his home background in particular – from the major factors identified in the school situation.

A glance at the purely descriptive statistics will suffice to convince us that schooling does not achieve education all alone; it must operate within the larger socioeconomic structure. However, it is important that we arrive at a realistic estimation of the role that school can play in bringing about worthwhile societal changes.

2. Questions pivoting on *the structure of basic schooling* can be answered in light of solid evidence comparing various systems. The pervasive issue in

* First published in *New York University Quarterly*, Vol. 8:3, 1976. Adapted by permission from *Studies in Educational Evaluation* (Pergamon Press), Vol. 3:2, 1977.

countries that have during the last few decades discussed the "democratization" of secondary education has been the issue of elitism or selectivity vs.
comprehensiveness. The basic school, when established on a universal basis,
was supposed to bring about literacy, docility, and discipline among workers
in an industrialized society with mass manufacturing as well as contributing
to nation-building. The selective secondary school in an ascriptive society,
where roles are assigned rather than won, served a social elite.

A translation of the principle of equality of opportunity to the operational
level is this: To what extent should a common school for everybody and a
school preparing students for the university run parallel to each other? Or
should there be a unified school catering to all young people throughout their
years of compulsory education? In research terms: Would an increase of the
intake to the pre-university school lower the standards not only of secondary
but also of university education, as has been claimed? The IEA surveys,
because they include countries with widely different school structures and
social systems, provide definitive answers to the policy issues raised here.

3. Originally the IEA surveys were designed with ambitious hopes of
determining with some accuracy *the relative importance of various factors in the
instructional processes and in the school resources.* It belongs to shared common
sense that factors such as school size, per-pupil expenditure, number of
periods of instruction, subject-matter competence of the teacher, availability
of various teaching aids, and the extent to which student-activating methods
are employed, all have an impact. It is equally obvious that the relative
impact of all such factors depends very much on the level of operation and
the setting in which they operate. This refers to the socioeconomic structure
at large within which a given national system of education functions, to the
pattern of resources, and to the instructional strategies employed. Increased
resources and/or improved instruction in one setting with initially poor
resources might enhance the quality of outcomes considerably, whereas the
effects in an affluent system of the same additional resources might be
marginal or nonexistent. These commonplace observations should be kept in
mind by the layman who attempts to interpret the results of the technically
sophisticated multivariate analyses conducted by IEA.

The identification and assessment of factors that relate to objectives,
content, and resources of school instruction in the perception of policy
planners tend to boil down to francs, pounds, and dollars, and marks. The
per-pupil expenditure during the 1960s, in constant prices, increased by
about 10 per cent a year in the high-GNP countries. At the same time, the
number of students who had to be accommodated (particularly at the secondary level) also went up considerably, with the result that the school expenditures grew two to three times more rapidly than the GNP. No wonder, then
that a pertinent question for policymakers and planners and educational
researchers is this: Given the objectives in a certain subject area, say science,
or English as a foreign language, what steps should be taken in order to
optimize the available resources?

The main resource translatable into money is the *time* in terms of number of years and number of periods per week that the teacher spends in instructing the student. The amount of subject-matter preparation at the university on the part of the teacher and the main instructional strategy, including teaching aids, are also a major source of expenditure. Omitted from this account is the time that the students spend on learning the subject matter, which economists refer to as opportunity costs and about which they have different opinions as to the justification of taking it into account.

Caveats

Social background interacts with school factors in such a complicated way that our present analytical techniques, e.g., multiple regression analyses or path analyses, sometimes fall short of disentangling them. This applies even more so to the attempts to sort out the relative importance of school resources and instructional factors. But in accounting for IEA failures to explain between-student, between-school, and between-system differences, we should also keep in mind the quality of the data that have been subjected to these sophisticated analyses. The main source of information about what goes on in the classroom has been the teacher and, to some extent, the student.

The information provided by teachers and students at best reflects their perceptions of the instructional process. Furthermore, in order to enlist the cooperation of the teachers, we had to promise not to link the information provided by a particular teacher directly to the student taught by that teacher. Therefore, the association we have is the one between the students from a particular school and an aggregate of teachers who taught a particular subject in the particular school we had included. Evidently, such an arrangement dilutes the correlations between student achievement and the methods of instruction. It should be pointed out, however, that information about school resources was provided by the school principals. Thus, the correlations between student achievement and resources are not affected by the same dilution as the ones between instruction and achievement.

It is in the nature of things that such studies must rely on extensive methods of inquiry that sometimes yield data of doubtful quality. I have in mind the limitations of large questionnaire studies which depend upon the motivation of the respondents and which, sometimes, by the nature of cross-national studies, entail distorting elements when the same questions have to be framed in many different languages.

Relative Achievement of Various Countries

In spite of the somewhat meager overall outcomes of the ambitiously planned IEA "fishing expedition" that set out to identify crucial pedagogical factors, I shall proceed to point out some findings that hold important national policy implications. Offered first for consideration are multi-national survey findings that are relevant to national educational policy in a wide social context, for they measure student competence in one country or region as compared to students in other areas.

The IEA Mathematics Survey gave rise to a spirited debate on the relative standards achieved by the students in some countries. This applied particularly to the United States and Sweden, where the mean performance of the 13-year-olds was conspicuously below that of, for example, England and the Federal Republic of Germany – not to speak of Japan. The mean scores were interpreted as indicators of the efficiency of the school systems in the respective countries. In the United States congressmen and newspaper editorials asked whether all the money spent on the overhaul of the mathematics curriculum and on research in mathematics education had been wasted. Persistent critics of American education saw the low mean performance as an indication of the low quality of American education in general. The same kind of criticism was leveled in Sweden, where comprehensive education through grade 9 was in the process of being introduced.

Few people realized that the massive investment in improving the content and methods of teaching mathematics that had occurred in the United States during the early 1960s could hardly have had time to affect significantly the level of competence by 1964, when the data were collected. In Sweden the relatively low level of mathematics performance among 13-year-olds was attributed to the change in school structure from a parallel or elitist system to a comprehensive system. It readily confirmed the misgivings of staunch critics that the abolition of the structural differentiation between academic goats and nonacademic sheep would lead to a lowering of standards. The mathematics performance of the 13-year-olds became an issue in the 1970 election campaign for the parliament.

As usual, divergent political perceptions and vested interests tended to confuse the issue. In interpreting the differences between countries, very few people took into account that in both Sweden and the United States students in the age range ten through thirteen attended more or less comprehensive schools, whereas in England and the Federal Republic of Germany, for example, they were divided between academic schools for a selected minority and common elementary schools for the remaining majority. This meant that certain abstract topics in mathematics, such as algebra and geometry, were not introduced into the American and Swedish mathematics curriculum until after the age of thirteen, whereas they were taught to the academic elite in the latter countries. Thus, a considerable, but by no means the whole, part of the mean difference in the mathematics performance in question was accounted for by differences in opportunity to learn.

The publication of the IEA survey reports on science and mother tongue showed that Swedish students, in terms of academic standards, belonged to the mainstream of the highly industrialized countries. Since the data included in this part of the surveys were collected after the comprehensive school reform had been implemented all over the country, the findings in science and mother tongue, as well as in English and French as foreign languages, were interpreted as an evaluation of the comprehensive system. The publication of the science and mother-tongue reports, and the attendant publicity, had the effect of removing the issue of the standard of the students from the agenda of the election campaign in the same year.

IEA has, sometimes in vain, tried to play down the conception of the project as a kind of academic Olympic Games, primarily because only to a limited extent can differences in student competence be attributed to purely scholastic factors. They are to a large extent attributable to socioeconomic factors and, therefore, are not only reflections of differences in quality between educational systems but of socioeconomic differences between countries as well. This, of course, applies with particular force to comparisons between highly industrialized and non-industrialized countries, where the mean difference in achievement scores amounted to between one and two standard deviations. The multivariate analyses consistently showed that home background accounted for more of the between-student variance than learning conditions at school. Thus, in the last run, educational improvements depend on social and economic improvements.

Regional Differences within Countries

In spite of the cautions issued by those who were in charge of the design and administration of the IEA project, in some cases differences between countries and even more so between regions within countries inspired heated debates on the relative quality of education in various areas. When the IEA Italian national report was published, the tremendous difference in student achievement between north and south Italy triggered a debate in Italian newspapers, where a deep concern was aired about the social and economic gap between the two regions. The Minister of Education, Mr. Malfatti, told me at a meeting in Venice in 1975 that IEA had administered an "electric shock" to the Italian people. One of the main questions was this: To what extent was the gap in student competence in Italy between the industrialized and urbanized areas on the one hand and the agricultural and rural on the other due to differences in socioeconomic level or to differences in allocation of school resources?

In the Federal Republic of Germany a spirited debate followed upon the publication of the mean scores in science and reading for the various *Länder*. Since the latter represented different school structures – Bavaria had, for instance, more of the traditional parallel school structure as compared to Hesse – conclusions were readily drawn about the "efficiency" of the two systems. Leaving aside that IEA data should not be used as scoreboards for international races, in the case of Germany the sample drawn at best represented the Federal Republic in its entirety. The number of schools drawn for each *Land* was generally too small to permit inferences about relative levels of competence without huge standard errors of estimation.

The national analyses of the data for India shed light on the influence of the socioeconomic structure on the competence achieved by the students in poor areas, where the majority of the parents had no or insignificant formal education and were about 60 per cent farm workers or farmers. About 20 per cent had never attended school and some 50 to 60 per cent had less than 4 to 5 years of formal schooling. The verbal milieu at home was poor; and there was no access to printed material, such as newspapers and books, or no radios or TV sets. Since the children as a rule represented the first generation in formal education, parents could provide little guidance or stimulation in regard to the academic pursuits of their children. Thus, home background accounted for relatively little (1.4 to 4.0 per cent) of the variance in reading competence between students as compared to 7.2 to 16.1 per cent in the industrialized countries. On the other hand, school-related learning conditions accounted for two to three times as much of the variance in India as in the industrialized countries.

Elitist vs. Egalitarian School Systems

In asking what are the policy implications of the IEA surveys, we are compelled to raise the question of what policy objectives are at issue. It would be preposterous to try to present an exhaustive list of the major policy issues in the participating countries, the more so since the IEA countries represent the entire spectrum of social and economic systems. One pervasive issue, however, as indicated above, concerns the productivity of selective and comprehensive school systems.

To be sure, in most social systems, even in those that are relatively ascriptive and show little social mobility, lip service is paid to the principle of equality, particularly with regard to access to further education after mandatory schooling. In the industrialized IEA countries practically 100 per cent of the 14-year-olds were in full-time schooling, which meant that the enrollment by and large reflected the social composition of the entire population. At the age of 18 or 19 the proportion of the age group still in full-time schooling varied from 3 to 76 per cent, an enrollment that throughout showed a much higher representation of the social strata that were better off. Even if differences between strata are partly accounted for by hereditary factors, the imbalance between strata in participation in some countries are so striking that they would to a considerable extent have to be explained by a built-in bias in the system as such. Thus, planners and policymakers can get important leads by comparing various national systems with regard to

structure, selection practices, and ensuing social bias in the secondary education enrollment.

The IEA data have quite a lot to offer with respect to policy issues related
to the *structure* and *selectivity* of educational systems, particularly at the
secondary level, for the IEA surveys have been an assessment of the effects
of mass education at that level. In some countries universal or close-to-
universal secondary education has been achieved, whereas in others there is
still a sorting and sifting of the students at the age of 11 in order to select
those who are supposed to be academically oriented for university-preparing
schools. The crucial issues could be stated as follows: Those in favor of elitist
sorting at an early age maintain that broadening of access to quality secondary
education would lower the standards. In other words, more would mean
worse. Those in favor of a more comprehensive system maintain that the
opening of opportunities would infuse new blood into the academic elite by
taking care of talent from lower social strata.

The analyses conducted on both mathematics and science data unequivocally showed that the ablest students, say the top 5 to 10 per cent, do as well
or even better in an egalitarian system as they do in an elitist system. In other
words, the cream of talent seems to be of the same quality in both types of
systems. In addition, the mass systems show a significantly lower degree of
social bias in the enrollment at the pre-university level.

A Belgian minister raised the question of how the able students were taken
care of at the secondary level. Since the tests in literature were the same for
the 14-year-olds and the pre-university students in the terminal year of
their secondary program, the achievements in the two populations could be
compared. It was noted that there was a general decline in the percentage of
high achievers from the first to the second age level. The main explanation
advanced was that many of the high achievers dropped out between the ages
of 14 and 18, which seemed to account for the low Belgian achievement
level according to the international standard in the second population. An
interesting observation, however, was that there was no decline – on the
contrary, there was an increase – in the number of high scorers in the
comprehensive system, which indicated that it carried even the elite better
than the selective system did.

A final example will show how IEA findings definitely resolved a national
policy issue that combined questions of student selectivity and teaching
methods. At the end of the 1960s there was in Sweden a spirited debate
referred to by Dunlop as the "foreign language teaching controversy." On
the surface, the issue was the proper method of teaching English. But in a
deeper sense the value of teaching foreign languages to undifferentiated
classes was at issue. The critics maintained that the curriculum and the
concomitant methods of teaching recommended by the Swedish National
Board of Education unduly favored a "direct" approach and discouraged the
use of the mother tongue, orally or in print, as a medium of instruction. It

was further contended that the complaints by the English departments at the universities about lack of basic knowledge of grammar among university entrants could be attributed to the extremist approach in teaching English in school as recommended by the central authorities. Finally, and this was the most serious accusation, it was maintained that the standards in English in secondary schools had been considerably lowered as a result of the allegedly prescribed methods of instruction.

The scrutiny of Swedish data on the methods of teaching English showed that very few teachers employed the extreme direct method that the critics said dominated. The great majority employed what Dunlop referred to as a modified grammar approach. Secondly, in all four skill areas – listening, reading, speaking, and writing – Swedish students at both the 14- and 18-year-old levels tended to perform at least as well and often even better than their age mates in other countries. Thus, there was no empirical evidence proving that the standards were lower either due to the employment of inappropriate methods or to the teaching of English to all the students, which was said to hold the able Swedish students back in comparison with countries where foreign languages are taught only to selected students in academic schools or tracks.

One must realize that in small countries with a national language that is spoken only by a limited population, students are exposed to the dominant international languages by TV, movies, travel, and other personal contacts. We cannot possibly give school the whole credit for the level of excellence achieved in countries such as the Netherlands or Sweden. But the main issues in the case of Sweden, namely that alleged changes in methods of instruction or in the structure of the schools had brought about a considerably low standard in English, could be dismissed.

Science-Humanities Gap?

In the 1960s Lord Snow published his essay "The Two Cultures and the Scientific Revolution," which expressed his concern about the lack of communication and understanding between natural scientists and men of letters. The main reason for the gap between the two categories was said to be the narrow specialization required in either a science or a classical-humanities track in the upper secondary school. Since IEA tested science, reading comprehension, and literature on the same students in a number of countries, a unique opportunity was offered in testing the "two-culture" hypothesis multi-nationally. This was done by Richard Wolf of Teachers College, Columbia University, using a special analysis. Not surprisingly, the data from England, where there is extensive specialization in the upper secondary school, supported the hypothesis, whereas there was little support for it in most other countries.

Sex Differences in Achievement

The policy implications of multi-national surveys based on representative samples can be illustrated by another example, sex differences in achievements and attitudes. When we planned the mathematics survey, we were keenly aware of the fact that a multi-national approach to the study of sex differences in scholastic achievement could be a fruitful one, simply because the conditions were rather uniform within countries but much more varied between them.

In the mathematics study, it was hypothesized that sex differences in achievement would be related to both the degree of coeducation and the role of women in professional science and technology. The first hypothesis was strongly supported by our data. Countries with almost complete coeducation tended to have the smallest sex differences in achievement, whereas those that were highly sex segregated had large differences. Because of lack of adequate data, the second hypothesis could be tested only imperfectly and was not confirmed.

In science, sex differences in achievement over countries consistently varied between the three major branches of the subject. Thus, differences in biology scores were relatively small, whereas the male lead was extremely large in physics, with chemistry taking an intermediate position. Furthermore, the differences in all branches tended to increase by age. Since the responses of each student to each single item in the tests are available in the IEA data bank, it would certainly be a worthwhile exercise to try to find out cross-nationally if, and to what extent, the subject matter as such is sex biased.

Time as an Instructional Resource

Rosier tried by means of multivariate analyses to identify learning conditions that were most important for Australia in accounting for between-student differences. He came out with four factors: Grade level; hours of studying science; hours of homework; and hours of teacher preparation of lessons. All four factors are in one way or another related to time.

To say that time is important in learning would seem to state the obvious. But it is not as trivial as it might appear. Time may mean many different things, such as the age or grade level when the student begins and finishes a particular school subject; the number of years he takes the subject; the number of periods per week instruction is given in the subject; and the number of hours devoted to homework. One of the researchers on the IEA team, John B. Carroll, who is the author of the international report *The Teaching of French as a Foreign Language in Eight Countries*, has developed a model of school learning in which time is the cardinal variable. Most of the time variables of the kind that we have exemplified above show very little spread within a given country because of tendencies to employ a uniform national curriculum. But the variability between countries is the more striking. Thus, the IEA foreign language studies offered a unique opportunity to elucidate the effect of time in the acquisition of skills that constitute mastery of a foreign language.

When the national mean scores in reading, listening, speaking, and writing of French were plotted against the adjusted means of the number of years that French was taken, high correlations were obtained. The overwhelming portion of the between-country variance in performances in French was accounted for by the number of years of study. In the United States, where French at the high school level as a rule is taken for only two years, the level of competence achieved is rather dismal. The same applies to Swedish students who take French as a so-called C-language for only two or three years. Carroll is able by his international comparisons and analyses to show very convincingly that for the majority of students it takes six or seven years of study to acquire satisfactory proficiency.

Evaluating Curriculum Revision

In England the IEA survey offered an opportunity to evaluate the Nuffield Science Curricula with regard to interest in science; understanding of basic scientific principles; and achievements in science. The Nuffield Foundation Science Teaching Project had been launched with objectives such as emphasizing science for understanding, learning through investigation, and fostering an inquiring mind. About half of the participating schools reported substantial modifications in their science teaching because of the introduction of Nuffield materials. By and large, the Nuffield program achieved what it set out to do. The students who were taught according to the new materials showed better competence in biology and chemistry but not in physics. The particular test devised for measuring understanding of science (TOUS) showed better scores for the Nuffield students. Also, Nuffield students held more favorable attitudes toward the subject than those taught according to the traditional programs.

In Hungary the ensuing national analyses of the IEA data had important policy repercussions on curriculum revision. The Hungarian students performed very well in science, whereas their standard in reading caused concern among teachers and policymakers. The regression analyses brought out the great importance of sociocultural handicaps, particularly in reading. A study of the teaching methods showed them to be rather old-fashioned, with reading aloud as a main approach. Little emphasis was put on comprehension. It was realized that curriculum planning could not be related only to textbook material but that it also had to take into account extra-school experiences provided by the immediate environment and the mass media. Analyses of the textbooks showed them to be insufficiently challenging and too easy for the later stage of the eight-year basic schooling. Three conclusions were drawn from the national analysis of the Hungarian reading data: More emphasis should be put on silent reading; textbooks should be graded for complexity; and the teaching of reading skills should go on for the entire period of eight-year basic schooling. Similar conclusions have been arrived at in other countries.

In connection with the extension of mandatory schooling, there has been a tendency to allocate the additional teaching time mainly to new subjects and topics and to limit formal instruction in reading to the first few years under the assumption that all students after that have acquired sufficient reading skills. This is, however, not the case, particularly among students from less educated homes.

When to Introduce Foreign Language

A long-standing issue among teachers and planners alike is the age at which the first foreign language – if any – should be introduced to the child in school. The 1940 School Commission appointed to recommend a complete overhaul of the entire school system in Sweden was divided in its opinion, among other things, as to the proper age of differentiating the academic from nonacademic students. Since most members of the Commission believed that a foreign language could be taught only to an elite, the proper age for introducing language teaching became a major policy issue by way of association. The Commission turned to the professors of education and psychology who held chairs at the four universities of the country and asked each of them to submit statements on the state of the art in educational and psychological research that had bearings on the issue. I have kept this episode of Swedish reform history in vivid memory, even though it occurred forty-five years ago, because I happened to be an assistant to one of the four wise men and was, therefore, involved in scanning the research literature and in drafting one of the statements. This involvement taught me something about the relationship between policymakers and researchers.

The Commission's question on the proper age of introducing the first foreign language was based on the tacit assumption that language teaching should employ the traditional grammar methodology. Therefore, a certain level of intellectual development had to be reached before the student could be expected to deal successfully with the grammatical rules. Being young and not too conventional, I irreverently suggested to my professor that we should advise the Commission that the first foreign language should be introduced from the first day the child entered the school. After all, German children learned German from the age of 2! Therefore – in theory – the same could apply to Swedish children. Needless to say, the professor did not follow my recommendation, realizing, of course, that a learning environment that enables German or British children to learn their mother tongues at preschool age could not be arranged for Swedish children. Not even the most extreme direct method and the most challenging gimmicks in the classroom can substitute for the kind of total immersion in the language to which a child is exposed in its mother culture.

The IEA French survey of eight countries covered widely varying practices with regard to the age level when French was introduced. A finding of great significance was that students starting at later ages or grade levels showed faster rates of learning than those who started early. It has been contended that by starting foreign language teaching in the primary grades, one could save time for the benefit of other subjects at the secondary level. Even if this were so, one should not forget that learning a foreign language could be made more challenging to a teenager than to a 10- or 11-year-old. At the primary level students find all kinds of learning challenging, whereas at the secondary level, say at the age range of 12 to 15, many find most of it a drudgery, particularly the grinding of subject matter they began to learn earlier in primary grades. The late start of a subject could entail some extra motivation because of its novelty.

In the case of Sweden, a sample of ninth-graders who had been taking French in grades 7 through 9 were tested as a national option and were compared with those who had taken French in grades 10 through 12. The latter group was by far superior to the former. This finding had important policy implications for the secondary school program.

So far, the IEA surveys in various subject areas have been "one-shot operations," that is to say, we have by the design employed been able to describe the level of competence achieved by students at various levels of the system according to international standards. Furthermore, we have been able to relate outcomes to certain "input" factors, such as student home background and school resources, for example, time, teacher competence, and methods of instruction. But evaluations of national systems, particularly if one wants to assess the effect of reforms pertaining to structure and/or curriculum, require availability of *longitudinal* data. If one sets out to assess not only changes over time (which is the main objective of National Assessment in the United States) but also wants to identify factors that are associated with these changes, then the application of the IEA design is necessary. This is what has been done in eight countries in the Second International Mathematics Study for which the field data were collected in 1980–81. By means of "bridge" items comparisons can also be made with student competence in mathematics in 1964 when data were collected for the first study.

II. Educational Reforms

Strategies of Implementing School Reforms (1980)[1]
Strategies of Educational Innovation (1972)[2]
Social Determinants of the Comprehensive School (1963)[3]
Why Comprehensive Education (1980)?[4]

Introduction

Educational reforms are part of or consequences of socioeconomic changes. They have, of course, a wider scope than just changes in classrooms. The debate on the pros and cons of a unitary or comprehensive school that has been going on in Western Europe for decades has been beset by arguments as if the school were operating in a social vacuum. Changing the school is conceived of as a matter of pedagogy that should better be left to the educators themselves. The reforms of the school structure that have been launched since the 1940s can be seen as attempts to "democratize" education, to achieve more equality of opportunity in access to higher education and to promote participation at the "grass-roots" level. To what extent expectations set for reforms have been met by outcomes will be discussed later in this book.

Two theses are advanced in the present section. In the first place, major reforms cannot be implemented overnight. Institutional changes take a long time to bring about. The preparation, tryout, and final implementation of the comprehensive school reform in Sweden took three decades. It was by and large a successful reform. The Swedish university reform legislated in 1975 was given much less than a decade and had some disastrous consequences. Secondly, a reform has to be anchored among those who are going to carry the brunt of the daily work: teachers and administrators. They must have the feeling of being active and responsible participants in the process and not just objects of arbitrary policy decisions over their heads.

The author has elaborated more on some of the problems dealt with in this section in *The School in Question* (Oxford University Press, 1979) and in *The Future of Formal Schooling: The Role of Institutional Schooling in Industrial Society* (Stockholm: Almqvist & Wiksell International, 1980). The latter is a report edited by the author from an international symposium held at the Royal Academy of Sciences in Stockholm in 1978. Both books give a critical analysis of the school as an institution in modern societies.

Notes

1. Presentation given at the 5th anniversary in 1980 of the *Stichtung voor Leerplanontwikkeling* (SLO) in Utrecht.
2. An earlier version of this paper was presented at the US National Academy of Education Meeting in Chicago, Spring 1968. *The Australian Journal of Education*, Vol. 16:2, June 1972, 125–135.
3. *International Review of Education*, Vol. 9:2, 1963, 158–174.
4. Presentation in Vienna 1980 at the invitation of the Renner Institute.

Strategies of Implementing School Reforms*

THERE are no universal paradigms for the conduct of educational reforms. Historical, cultural, social, and economic conditions vary so much both between and within countries that specific policy measures and tactics employed would have to be considered anew for each national and local school system. When comparative educators say that countries can learn from each other, this is, indeed, a truth subject to considerable modifications. There are no elaborate models or paradigms that unadapted could be borrowed from one country to another. But I would submit that there are some general and pervasive principles that constitute important elements in the specific strategy that in individual cases has to be contemplated in planning, implementing, and evaluating educational reforms. I further submit that these principles apply more or less to all planned efforts to bring about educational change.

I should like to advance six such principles which appear to be universal and therefore have to be considered in connection with educational reforms, particularly those pertaining to the structure of a national system of education.

First and foremost: educational reforms are *part and parcel of social reforms*. There is a corollary to this, namely that educational reforms cannot serve as substitutes for economic and social reforms. The statue of Danton on Boulevard St. Germain in Paris carries the inscription: *Après le pain l'éducation est le premier besoin du peuple*. Reforms affecting the structure and content of educational provisions have to be conceived within the larger framework of socioeconomic changes that affect public welfare and the standard of living. There seems to be a kind of lawful sequence inherent in reform work. It is striking to note the interaction that exists between improved standards of living and aspirations for more formal education. None of them takes precedence over the other. They are parts of the same change process.

One cannot avoid being struck by the fact that many educators conceive of the school as if it were operating in a social vacuum. This occurs so often that one is tempted to refer to this as a professional disease. Quite a few educators do not realize the wider context of their role. This explains an observation that I have made in many countries, including, of course, my own; that reforms emerging from decisions taken by relevant political bodies

* Presentation given at meeting of Dutch educators convened by the *Stichting voor Leerplanontwikkeling* (1980).

are regarded as undue "interference" on the part of politicians. We, the expert educators, we, the professors, possess the competence and the technical knowledge. We are in a way pretending to be the Platonic philosopher-kings to tell the politicians how it all has to be done. The politicians need only to implement the wise ideas that we advance. I am struck by the observation made in many places that educational reforms are regarded as implementable if they bear the hallmark of what is regarded as aloof and disinterested scientific inquiry and/or solid classroom experience.

There is another observation closely related to the one of conceiving education in a social vacuum, namely that educational reforms by themselves are expected to work wonders. We can trace two sets of influences behind this conception. In the first place, we have the time-honored liberal idea that education serves as an equalizer of opportunities. Secondly, social interventions in education appear less "dangerous" than in the domains of social welfare or employment. Educational reforms are more innocuous than interventions in the fabric of social and economic order, because the latter type of interventions smack of socialism, not to say revolution. By limiting interventions to education one would in some kind of mysterious way bring about the changes in the social and economic sphere that are less upsetting and revolutionary.

The second generalization relates to the *initiation of reforms*. With few exceptions sweeping reforms are initiated at the *national* level by means of pre-planning and planning within governmental agencies and by decisions taken by government and parliament. Such decisions usually affect the general framework of the educational system, for instance by bringing about structural changes and by putting financial resources at the disposal of local schools. They are thereby setting the framework for changes of a pedagogical nature. In some countries governmental commissions, such as the Royal Commissions in England, are set up and include representatives of the various interest and advocacy groups. In these commissions blueprints for the ensuing legislation are then worked out in a spirit of compromise. Usually these commissions try to achieve some kind of consensus that can form the basis for the preparatory legislative work that takes place in the Ministry before a bill is submitted to the Parliament.

Sometimes governmental policy documents are worked out without these commissions but with representatives of the various interest groups, for instance in the Federal Republic of Germany just before a Federal Ministry of Education was established. The Social Democratic Party and the Brandt government prepared what they called *Bildungsbericht 70*. This was a blueprint for educational change in the Federal Republic of Germany from 1970 on. The report envisaged through the mid-1980s rather thorough-going changes, not least, in terms of the financial resources being made available to the German schools. Furthermore, far-reaching structural changes were envisaged, changes that would make schooling during the compulsory school age comprehensive within a more unified system.

The move from initiation and decision to implementation usually implies a move from the center to the periphery, from the top to the grassroots. An often lacking prerequisite for successful implementation of a reform is the creation of sufficient motivation and commitment at the local or grassroot level. This commitment or motivation has in a way to be "stimulated" by central decisions, not least by the financial resources being made available from the center. Those who had followed the school reform in Sweden remember the stimulating effect that central government funds had on the willingness of the local school systems to jump on the band-wagon to join the pilot program of comprehensive schooling launched in the early 1950s. Thus, in a way, these funds were used to entice the municipalities to "join the club." I would, however, not maintain that they played a decisive part in promoting the introduction of comprehensive education.

Thirdly, changes in the educational system of the magnitude we are considering here, i.e., changes in the structural, administrative, and financial framework for what goes on in the schools, have to overcome strong traditions and deeply ingrained practices. Therefore, changes with such a scope have to occur *gradually* and *slowly*, in case they are not associated with what is virtually a political and/or social revolution. I am here referring to changes that occur within the existing social and economic framework. They occur when this entire framework is in a state of dynamic change. We can usually observe how the larger economic and social framework in a state of change calls for concomitant changes in the educational systems. My point here is simply that reforms in the educational system have to occur gradually and slowly if they are not going to fail completely, or, if they are not going to fade away, disappear without implementation.

Educational practices and structures by a long tradition have achieved a strong institutional rigidity. The fact that an act has been passed by Parliament and that new regulations have been issued does not automatically lead, say, to a completely new educational system by the beginning of the next fiscal year. It takes an awfully long time to achieve this. The illustrations I can offer are from Sweden. We had two government commissions of inquiry drawing up blue-prints for the school reform, one more expert-oriented at the beginning of the 1940s, and then a politically composed commission during the latter part of the 1940s. These two commissions put in ten years of work. Then ten more years passed with a pilot program that gradually included more and more municipalities. Finally, when the 1962 Education Act was passed, another ten years were allowed for the implementation at the local level. Thus, the change took place over a thirty-year period.

An example of a badly implemented reform is the one on higher education in Sweden. The Commission on Higher Education, the so-called U68, was appointed in 1968, worked for about four years and submitted its report by early 1973. Access, governance and structure of the system of higher education were radically changed. By 1975 the Parliament passed a new Act of Higher

Education, an Act that formally went into effect in 1977. I shall not elaborate on the bad consequences of such an instant reform. It certainly illustrates that deeply ingrained institutional patterns, such as the ones that have evolved over many centuries of university history, cannot be changed overnight.

These experiences have taught us certain lessons. In the first place, in planning a reform, pilot programs allowing sufficient time for evaluation have to be launched. Such programs should be used to test the feasibility and the soundness of the blueprint. Secondly, as early as possible attempts should be made to involve in various ways those whose status and working conditions are affected by the proposed reform. In launching a school reform one should in the first place consider in-service training, but also involve parents. Thirdly, a systematic attempt should be made to stimulate public discussion about the problems connected with the reform intentions, because very often there is naturally quite a lot of entrenchment on the part of those who have an interest in *status quo*. They flatly reject the reform and are hard to involve in a dialogue.

This leads me to the fourth general principle concerned with attempts to achieve *maximum participation* by those who are involved in a reform. Here one must make a distinction between nominal and responsible participation. The important thing here is, of course, that participation should be one under full responsibility. In reviewing for OECD the federal policy in the United States in the field of compensatory education I experienced one example of purely nominal participation. The legislation called for the setting up of Parental Advisory Councils at the local level. These councils appeared to me, in most places to be quite nominal bodies in the hands of the educational bureaucracy.

It is extremely important for a central body, be it a Commission or a Task Force within the Ministry of Education charged with planning, to achieve at an early stage of its work *maximum consultation* with those concerned in the field. I have a personal experience of this from my time as Chairman of the National Commission for Education in Botswana in Africa, where the Commission made it a point as soon as it began its work to invite in the first place written submissions by all interested parties on the issues dealt with. We also made it a point to hold hearings with representatives of the various interest groups and to visit as many schools as we possibly could. We visited schools in all provinces and consulted with those who took a keen interest in our work. We were particularly keen on talking to those whose "empires" would be affected by the recommendations that we envisaged. We were thereby able to achieve more consensus about our recommendations than would otherwise have been possible.

Thus, motivated and informal participation already at the first stage of the preparation of a reform is of extreme importance. Needless to say, the same kind of participation is of crucial importance when it comes to the implementation of a reform.

My fifth general point has to do with *resistance to change*. I have already indicated some participatory strategies that can be used to overcome this. In trying to introduce educational reforms we have to deal with people who have a strong interest in *status quo*. There are many examples on the international scene of how reform efforts have failed because those who had a vested interest in *status quo* were too powerful.

The 1957 School Commission in Sweden conducted a survey of the attitudes among teachers towards the reform, and of how much they knew about the reform. A reform process elicits, of course, a certain amount of insecurity among teachers, particularly among those whose status could be very much affected by the reform and who therefore tend to build up an emotional blockage against it. The interesting thing was that those who were against the reform – this applied particularly to secondary school teachers – knew less about the reform than those – mostly at the primary stage – who were in favor of it, in spite of the fact that there had been no difference in the amount or quality of the information to which both groups had been subjected. Such an emotional blockage can easily occur. We have also, of course, to consider the resistance among the emperors themselves, for instance administrators and union bosses at the central level. Those who are running empires of central federations of teacher unions see strong effects on their power, not least by structural changes in the system.

The sixth, and last, general observation I want to make relates to the necessity in launching a reform to build in right from the beginning an *evaluation and monitoring mechanism*. The most evident advantage of conducting an evaluation concomitant with the implementation of a reform is that one is forced to *make explicit the values* underlying the reform. In order to evaluate one is forced to operationalize the evaluation criteria. In such an exercise contradictions between blurred values or goals which are differently interpreted by the different parties are easily revealed.

When in 1950 legislation was passed on comprehensive education in Sweden, it also included a pilot program envisaged to run for about a decade. In the Education Act there was a paragraph stating that with certain qualifications the Parliament decided to introduce comprehensive education. The crucial phrase in the paragraph was that the parallel system should "according to the extent the planned experimental activities prove its suitability" be replaced by a comprehensive one at the end of the ten-year pilot period. This was so vaguely stated that those who were in favor of a change-over to comprehensive education interpreted it as a final decision to introduce the new structure. The modifications depending upon the outcomes of the pilot program were envisaged to be only minor ones. However, those who were against the reform said that the new type of school had to be compared with the existing school types, for example the selective and academic one. If the new system proved less efficient in terms of achieved pupil competence, if it did not prove to be a "better" one, then it would have to be abolished.

Nobody at the time of enactment made this ambiguity in the Act explicit, because of a reluctance to acknowledge that there were different values behind the two interest groups. An operationalization of the values of the two parties would have led to different types of criteria for the evaluation of the pilot programs which would have made comparisons between the old and the new system rather pointless.

Let me finish by making some suggestions about how comparative research could elucidate the mechanisms of educational reforms. It appears to me that it would be fruitful to conduct a series of national case studies, particularly in countries which are about to launch reforms. One could also contemplate going back to the recorded experiences that exist from reforms that have already been launched in other countries. In a series of such case studies, in which one looks at reforms that have already for some time been under way, one could look more closely at successful and unsuccessful reforms and try to identify the conditions determining successes or failures.

In studying a reform in a country, one has to ask questions, such as: Who benefits from the reform? Whose privileges are negatively affected? Who will gain or lose by the reform? Reforms are usually embedded in a lot of rhetoric. They are, for instance, said to equalize opportunities. Almost nobody follows up the actual effects in terms of equalization between, for instance, rural and urban areas. This can in many cases rather easily be done. One ought to look at the social and political forces behind the reforms, how they emerge and how they interact. Another aspect of a reform that one ought to look at is the interaction between on the one hand centrally issued directives, and on the other local initiatives and commitments. Going back to what was mentioned earlier: it would be profitable, in doing such case studies, to look at *what strategies* were employed in enlisting the support of the teachers and what conditions make teachers support or resist a reform.

The study of educational reforms and the mechanisms behind them is indeed, an extremely fascinating one. It appears to me to be one of the most fruitful ones in comparative education, a field where countries with different social and political systems have quite a lot to learn from each other but have to be very careful in borrowing from each other.

Strategies of Educational Innovation*

THE study of the innovative process and factors conducive to innovation is a fairly new undertaking. I cannot remember that I ever heard the word "innovation" being used in educational context until the mid-1960s. The term had been taken over by the educators from industrial technology, as has the entire conception of research and development as part of the implementation of innovative change. Sometimes innovation is preached with a fervor as if it represented a value *per se*. People are oblivious of the self-evident fact that significant innovations and persisting changes in education ought to represent adequate responses to fundamental transformations in culture and society. Therefore, not all innovations in education could be regarded as fitting responses to these transformations.

I need not spell out for what reasons it would be appropriate to talk about a "great mutation," when we are trying to describe the rapid transformation that the industrialized societies have been undergoing. The same applies to certain aspects of our educational systems, such as enrollments and organization, whereas others are strikingly lagging behind. To put it briefly, what are needed today are strategies whereby applicable knowledge and techniques could be incorporated into the content and organization of curriculum, the methods and materials of instruction and the procedures by which the educational enterprise is administered. The more stable an organization or an institution is – and the school is certainly one of the more stable – and the more deeply entrenched it is in the social matrix, the more difficult it becomes to make it respond to external changes. The so-called social lag is a well known, and sometimes frustrating, phenomenon in education.

One might ask to what extent a certain lag between the development of society at large and the educational sub-system is unavoidable. Is there any reason to believe, as did the Swedish School Commission in an optimistic report which it submitted to the Government in 1948, that the educational system can act "as a propelling and progressive force in our society," a kind of optimism that was aired by many people who represented the "new education" after the Second World War. There are ample reasons to believe that the schools are lagging behind because of the social mechanisms involved and that the problem faced by educational planners is to reduce the lag to a necessary minimum. Professor C. H. Beeby in his book *Quality of Education in Developing Countries* (Harvard University Press, Cambridge, Mass., 1966)

* Published in *The Australian Journal of Education*, Vol. 16:2 1972, 125–135.

has advanced a model of the growth of the primary school system as related to teacher education in which he distinguished four developmental stages. During the first stage, called the "dame school," teaching is relatively unorganized and to a large extent a play with meaningless symbols, with memorization being the important thing. The next stage is characterized by rigid organization and method, with "the one best way." Examinations and inspection are heavily stressed and discipline is strict. Memorization has become even more important. The third stage is that of transition. The fourth one, finally, is characterized by emphasis on meaning and understanding, problem-solving and pupil activity. Discipline is more relaxed and positive. More stress is put on the emotional life of the children. The main thesis that Beeby advances is that, by and large, we cannot have a more advanced educational system than the societal context under which it is operating. Attempts that have been made in developing countries to introduce advanced educational technology have often failed because such approaches require not only a certain level of competence in the teachers but also a certain socio-cultural level of parents to make the children responsive to the particular methods of instruction.

It would take me too far to pursue this problem further. I have, however, taken it up because I think that there is much evidence in support of the contention that education cannot serve as a substitute for social and economic reforms. The latter must to a large extent precede educational change. I think that we ought to be aware of the fact that we cannot change the basic pattern of a society or bring about an enhanced standard of living just by injecting more and better education. Education seems to have its proper place in an inherent sequence of cultural and social transformations. Sweden provides a case in point, how educational change has in the first place to be conceived within the framework of national priorities. The basic issue in the Swedish reform debate since the end of the nineteenth century was the parallelism or duality of the system, which meant that rather early on some children, as a rule from well-to-do homes, transferred from the early grades in the primary school to the secondary, university-preparing academic school. The Social Democratic party was quick to declare its allegiance to a comprehensive system which covered the entire compulsory school period. The attempts to establish a six-year basic school for all children during the 1920s failed because sufficient political backing in the Parliament could not be secured. Even within the Social Democratic party, a fraction of secondary school teachers were against the reform, which was said to "lower standards" in the secondary school. The legislation passed by the Swedish *Riksdag* in 1927 was a compromise between the dualistic and comprehensive camp, in so far that a "double transfer" from primary to academic secondary education was granted. When the Social Democrats came into political power, at the beginning of the 1930s, for a long period they took only a marginal interest in reforming education. Social and economic reforms aiming at full employment and social security were in the forefront. The unemployment among highly educated people led many radicals to a tacit acceptance of the dualistic or elitist system, provided that more lower class students could be granted access to higher levels of education. During the so-called "harvest time," after 1945, the Social Democrats again brought the reform of education into focus and it became one of the major political targets. The country embarked on twenty-five years of educational change which was successively enacted by an almost unanimous parliament. The lesson to be learned from the Swedish experiences is, among other things, that legislation and implementation of the Welfare State to a large extent has to precede commitments to educational change: first full employment and decent standards of living, and then education.

Resistance to Change

I pointed out that educational reforms, irrespective of whether they aim to bring the educational system in line with social and cultural transformations, are often running against well-established and deeply entrenched institutional forces. In a society where education increasingly tends to become the democratic substitute for inherited wealth and privileged background and where demands for equality of opportunity become vociferous, change tends to be regarded as a threat to the prerogatives of the establishment and is therefore strongly resisted. These forces are primarily operating at the political level. But resistance to change within the educational system itself can be even stronger because of the more pronounced vested interests in the *status quo* that many representatives of the system have. In 1958, when about one-fourth of the school districts in Sweden had introduced the nine-year comprehensive school on a trial basis, the Swedish Radio Corporation sponsored a public opinion poll pertaining to the changing school situation. The poll showed that between one-half and two-thirds of the public preferred the comprehensive system, about one-fourth was against it, and the rest was undecided. Thus, at a period when the overwhelming majority of the secondary school teachers, who were accustomed to an elitist system with pronounced selective features, rejected the blueprint for the educational system which was laid down in the 1950 Education Act, the majority of the electorate was in favor of it. In the *Riksdag* the backing of the reform was even more overwhelming. No votes had to be taken on major points in the education bills.

The basic issue on which controversy focussed was whether and to what extent the learned, academic, elitist, high-prestige, university preparing secondary school should be replaced by a unitary school to which all the children living in a certain catchment area should be assigned. Admission to the elitist secondary school was competitive and based on standardized marks obtained in the primary school. A considerable portion of those who were selected for the secondary school later either repeated one or more grades or dropped out. Thus, the teachers were instrumental in deciding the fate of the students and in fact served as a kind of gate-keeper to the establishment. Both selection to the academic schools and grade-repeating occurring during the course of study were not surprisingly related to student social background.

Even in a country with a social and ethnic homogeneity such as in Sweden a change-over from a dualistic and selective to a comprehensive and unitary system is quite an educational revolution. Teachers who were used to teach a select group of students, rather homogeneous in ability and even more so in social background, were suddenly faced with the task of teaching a group representing a much wider range with regard to scholastic ability, motivation and home background. They had been trained for and used to a system where a considerable attrition in terms of grade-repeating and drop-out took place, but were now compelled to take care of *all* the students and could not get rid of those who were considered unsuitable for academic exercises. Several euphemistic terms were invented for the non-academic students during the change-over period. They were labeled the "non-theoretical" as opposed to the "theoretical." A more picturesque label was "book-tired," which expressed lack of interest in academic pursuits.

The 1950 Education Act envisaged new teacher-training institutions, which were supposed to spread the germs of educational reform to new generations of teachers. The reform called for a new conception of the role of the teacher. Among other things, the reshaping implied a more individualized approach in teaching which would call for more work *with* the children than work *to* them or *for* them.

In 1960, four years after the first new School of Education had been put into operation, the 1957 Governmental School Commission sponsored a survey comprising all teacher candidates in all types of training institutions a few weeks before graduation. The survey had two major aims:

(i) To find out how informed the young teachers were about the school reform, its aims, its organizational set-up, the new instructional methods, and their implications for the role of the teachers.
(ii) To assess their attitudes toward these aspects of the reform.

Those who were trained at the new School of Education were significantly better informed than those who had been trained at the traditional institutions. The prospective middle-grade teachers were more favorable to the reform than were the prospective upper-grade teachers. For instance, twice as many of the upper-grade teachers endorsed the statement that a comprehensive system by and large best suits the students who do not intend to prepare for the university and are heading for vocational programs. The attitudes towards the reform were more favorable among the trainees at the School of Education. One could, of course, expect that teachers whose role was more deeply affected by the reform would take a less favorable attitude than those whose role was less affected. The drastic changes in the organizational structure occurred at the upper grades and caused serious concern among secondary school teachers.

It could also be hypothesized that information about and attitude toward the school reform were positively correlated, and more so for teachers at the upper grades. The correlation between information and attitude scores was 0.24 for middle-grade and 0.46 for upper-grade teachers. The correlation was higher for those whose working conditions were more profoundly affected by the reform and who therefore could be expected to be more strongly emotionally involved for or against a change.

What lessons could be learned from these findings and from the experiences at large in the educational scene in Sweden during the 1950s up to the legislation about the comprehensive school in 1962 and the *gymnasium* (the academic upper secondary school) in 1964? In the first place it should be emphasized that the structural change, the abolition of "differentiation," was the main issue and therefore was in the focus of interest until legislation put an end to open controversy. The so-called "inner reform," the adaptation of the instructional methods to the goals of the school had just begun. Secondly, a reform of teacher training should be concomitant to reforms of structure and curriculum because of the extremely extended time-lag between teacher preparation and the full stocktaking in the classroom. It is a matter of decades even if, as has been the case in Sweden, an intensive in-service training is put into operation. Thirdly, efforts to inform yield a substantial pay-off in terms of less defensive attitudes toward change.

Reforms of school structure, time-tables, etc. can nominally and superficially be accomplished by legislation and implemented by administrative decrees. The classroom effects of curriculum prescriptions, however, might be minimal. Most studies of teachers' classroom behavior indicate that the average teacher of the 1970s on both sides of the Atlantic seems to behave very much in the same way as he did twenty or forty years ago! Travers analyzed verbal behavior of 83 American teachers and found that about one-fourth of the behavior pertained to classroom administration, another fourth to assigning tasks, and one-third to instruction in which putting questions to the students was most prevalent. Similar findings are reported by Tausch in Germany and Stukát and Engström in Sweden. The main approach is the "frontal" one: the teacher turns to the entire class. He is controlling and teaching, in the first place, a *group* and not individual students.

Causes of Resistance to Change

One is certainly justified to ask, why time-honored practices prevail in spite of the fact that they are running contrary to basic notions of how children develop and learn. Why do instructional approaches frequently violate accepted psychological principles and findings of learning and differential psychology taught in the basic courses in general and/or educational psychology? For instance, grouping practices, for which there is no scientific support, are widely employed. Homogeneous grouping in terms of one criterion is far from perfectly correlated with grouping according to another criterion.

We can advance at least two major explanations which account for the sometimes frustrating experience that researchers repeatedly make, namely that their findings, even those which are highly conclusive, have a very small, if any, impact upon what is happening in the classroom.

I have already at some length dealt with the first explanation. Educational practices *are* indeed deeply entrenched, because they have prevailed for decades, not to say centuries. Even minor changes, for instance in the emphasis on different topics in teaching a given subject, might take quite a time. The teaching role is tied to heavy anchors. When we conducted a survey of the teaching of mother tongue in the upper section of the primary school at the end of the 1950s, we concluded that the curriculum that had been issued by the Government in 1919 had been universally implemented!

Secondly, and equally important, is the explanation that the major strategy in bringing about change and innovation has been to do things *to*, or at best *for*, the teachers and not *with* them. The point, which I am going to elaborate later in this paper, is that the framework, within which innovative actions so far have been taken, ought to be thoroughly reshaped. I shall therefore spend the major portion of the remainder of this paper in describing a framework within which I think that a flexible attitude could develop. The problem we continuously face as educators and researchers with innovative intentions is that changes cannot be introduced in a piecemeal way. Even the best practices can easily fail if they are imbedded in a traditional and static pattern. But before spelling out a philosophy of educational innovation in modern society, I shall for a while focus on the process of translating research findings into adopted classroom practices. We all know that this is a long and complicated process.

Paul Mort once stated that it takes fifty years until a new educational principle has been generally accepted and another fifty years until it has permeated the instruction, at a time when it has already become obsolete. Actual studies pertaining for instance to the use of new curricula, team teaching, and instructional material provide us, however, with the encouraging findings that innovation does not proceed so slowly.

In the first more comprehensive handbook on educational innovation, edited by Matthew Miles in 1964, the editor makes a distinction between two types of innovative strategies: (i) The change may be initiated by the target system itself (the school system to be changed), or (ii) by other systems in the environment of the target system. This might be a good distinction on the American scene, but in highly centralized systems, as is the case in many European countries, change is often not only initiated by central government, but also implemented by its administrative decrees.

From Basic Research to General Adoption

The translation of change from the isolated university setting to the schools in the field is a four-step operation. (1) Problems are subjected to scientific study whereby new knowledge is advanced. (2) Research findings are transformed into innovative practice, including testing and evaluation in real school settings. (3) Established practices are diffused to a considerable number of schools or school systems. (4) Adoption takes place. There are certain actions associated with each stage of this procedure.

Concepts derived from basic research findings would have to be subjected to feasibility research under "optimal" school conditions, for instance in a university laboratory school with a highly competent and research-minded teaching staff, which is in continuous touch with the researchers.

A small group of "ordinary" schools will have to be selected in order to serve as the testing ground with the aim of finding out whether the new concepts or set-ups really work under normal classroom conditions. This requires a certain amount of initial interest and willingness to co-operate on the part of these schools and on the other hand an openness and willingness to provide assistance on the part of the research center. Thus certain deviations within reasonable limits from general school practices are expected from the participating schools or school systems. The project center will have to provide consultants and conduct seminars and conferences and not to forget to give teachers who want to conduct graduate work in connection with the project opportunity to do so.

The third step, the diffusion of the new set of practices, is to put them into practice in a rather large group of demonstration schools spread all over the country or the region. These schools will then serve as the final bridge between research and actual school practice at the grass-root level. The contact with the research center is somewhat more attenuated than during the former step but at least some selected teachers will have to be brought to summer institutes or conferences.

Another Frame of Reference for Innovative Actions

There is, as indicated above, a serious problem of proper frame of reference involved here. So far, at least in Europe, the conception of innovation held by many state officials, top administrators and unfortunately even by researchers, has been rather authoritarian. If structural change is contemplated in a centralized system, a national committee of policymakers is appointed. They could be assisted by top experts who are also brooding in splendid seclusion. When changes in curriculum are contemplated, the central government appoints a group of experts at the national level. They are supposed to dream up the new ideas, eventually subject them to some testing by inviting criticism from selected educators, and then tell the teachers "how it all ought to be done." We always meet the same model: more or less rigidly-conceived plans are advanced and expected to be put not only into practice but also accepted by the teachers who carry the daily burden and toil.

But one need not be too sophisticated about how social systems change or resist change in order to understand that we cannot with reasonable success bring about change only by actions taken from above, by doing things *to* or *for* the system. If we want to achieve social (including educational) change, we are entitled to enter the system and to try strategies whereby we seek to change the system from *within*. The basic problem is thereby to make the system susceptible to change, to establish a climate which reacts positively to change. The psychological task is to make explicit changes or innovations that the system *wants*. We are certainly all familiar with the classical experiment which Kurt Lewin and his associates conducted during the Second World War as part of an attempt by the authorities to change consumer habits among American housewives. Sheer propaganda and intensive lecturing did not work. But once the wives were invited to small-group meetings, where they had an opportunity to discuss the problem with the experts and could even decide what they thought was good, considerable change occurred. Change was brought about by employing simple democratic procedure. The experts who over the years have told the teachers "how things ought to be done" have as a rule been protected from all the frustrating paraphernalia and toil involved in the proposed changes. Those of us who are experts seem to have the somewhat naïve conception that our great ideas, by some kind of inner dynamics, will materialize in perfect classroom practices. The resistance we have experienced has often been rationalized as procrastinating manoeuvers by reactionary teachers who lack the right kind of forward-looking attitude and creative imagination. We have seldom tried to get behind the unwillingness, where we meet fear of the new and untried and preference for the established and time-honored.

How could then a commitment to new practices be achieved in the individual teacher? The basic approach has already been pointed out. We must convey to the teacher in the field the idea that the experts are working with him. If we want the teacher to change basic instructional practices, we should not begin by telling him that what he has so far been doing is wrong, but by helping him to discover the consequences and outcomes of his practices and thus help him to discover what is wrong. What are, for instance, the consequences of a one-sided "frontal" instruction or class teaching? What is required could with a new expression be called sensitivity training. The teacher could thereby get a more detached and critical attitude toward his own practices instead of withdrawing behind defense barriers which protect him from the serious threats of the experts. Almost 40 per cent of the primary school teachers in the City of Stockholm in a survey conducted in 1955 maintained that the advice given by psychologists and other experts in the mass media had worsened instead of improved their task as educators.

Needless to say, innovative and creative change has to be introduced by voluntary action and not by expert preaching or governmental decrees, irrespective of whether the system is centralized or not. Much of the resistance to change stems from the approach whereby the experts or the administrators tell the teachers that they have so far been wrong and that "we," the experts, researchers or administrators are right; and that they, the teachers, therefore should follow our advice.

Why should we not try to build into our innovative strategies procedures which are strongly supported by findings from our own research? We need among other things proper positive reinforcement agents which will reward innovative behavior. So far innovative behavior has often been negatively reinforced. The teachers who try new practices have been punished by increased work load and disapproval on the part of their colleagues. Even the most ardent initial enthusiasm has often been extinguished under such pressures. On the contrary, the educational system in various ways reinforces static attitudes and practices. I need not spell out the major forces which tend to keep the system in equilibrium. Learning is supposed to occur only when the teacher gives something to the children. Work is regulated by a fixed timetable. The learning tasks are chopped up into standard assignments. Extra assignments are often given as punishments. Administrative procedures within and outside the classroom are authoritarian.

The core of the matter, then, is to help the teachers to organize the system in such a way as to reinforce innovative attitudes, creative participation and willingness to subject time-honored practices to critical scrutiny. We need to subject the reinforcers which affect teaching behavior to scrupulous analysis. What kind of teaching behaviors do we praise or support and what behaviors do we blame or discourage?

The simple conclusion drawn from this analysis is that the problem of introducing educational innovations has to be tackled mainly at the local level. We have to work *with* the teachers, try to teach them to think creatively, and thus innovatively. The implication of this is, among other things, that the administrative apparatus should be geared to support an innovative climate. A rigid and power-seeking bureaucracy easily develops into a cement-cover that bars innovative efforts instead of providing the service needed in order to support the teachers in the field.

Educational innovations certainly do not come about automatically. They have to be invented, planned, initiated, and implemented in a way that will make educational practices more adequately geared to the changing objectives of instruction and make them more consistent with the changing standards of instruction. A major problem then becomes: to what extent should these changes occur by arrangements taken within the hierarchy of public office or how much should they depend on actions taken by private groups and enterprises? The heart of the matter is how the aims of innovation should most easily be achieved and how a sufficient degree of flexibility could be built into the innovative process. In countries with strongly centralized national systems, change is put into motion from the national center through the channels of bureaucracy. I can see no possibility in relying on private initiative when changing organizational structure, financing or administrative procedures. The changes in school structure in most European countries provide cases in point. Such types of innovation must be backed by legal force and administrative decrees which follow suit on legislation passed by the national parliament. But when it comes to changes in methods of instruction, no law, force, or decree in the world can secure a more adequate instruction with regard to content and method. No central or local inspector will have any effective impact. Real influence at the grass-root level will have to depend on voluntary participation. No formal authority can impose cooperation.

A bureaucracy can achieve substantial changes in the organizational framework of an educational system, but is, by its very nature, alien to creative changes pertaining to learning itself. Innovation of this type cannot occur within a bureaucratic setting, where there is accountability up the line and supervision by those who occupy positions higher up and where the individuals at the bottom are referred to the top for decisions and where there is explication, formalization and uniform application of standards of work. But the introduction of new ways of learning in the classroom requires lateral instead of vertical delegation, voluntary instead of imposed actions. Cooperation and general agreement will work instead of close supervision.

I think that an important lesson can in this respect be learned from the work carried out by the Physical Science Study Committee (PSSC) in the United States and the cooperation that emerged between this and other private groups on the one side and public agencies on the other. Briefly, what happened when the physics curriculum was upgraded was a concerted action of a governmental agency and a non-profit research corporation which marvellously cut across the power structure of both the public agencies and the national organizations. The National Science Foundation, a semi-federal agency, subsidized a private group which took the initiative to curriculum construction that required funds of a size that no private publisher could venture. The PSSC prepared the material, consisting of an impressive package of tests, manuals, films, laboratory material, etc., and offered it to the textbook industry. Within a few years the material had been adopted to the extent that it was used by half the high school students who took physics. A sociologist, Burton Clark, who has studied how patterns of innovation worked in this case, thinks that "it is doubtful if a national ministry with full authority over a national curriculum could have changed the study of physics more in the same period."

My point is that the central or governmental agencies should financially support construction of for instance, instructional packages at schools of education, within publishing houses, and autonomous educational groups without bureaucratic formalism. This does by no means exclude a certain "steering" on the part of the sponsor. It seems to me that interesting national case-studies of alliances between governmental agencies, universities, educational organizations, committees, and publishing houses could be carried out. The aim of such studies would be to elucidate how innovations are brought about and how dissemination of them takes place outside the channels of formal bureaucracy but nevertheless influences its work.

The thesis advanced about grass-root changes is based on an optimistic conception of the human being. But the educational enterprise has long enough been run according to a motivational theory which says that students learn because they want to avoid unpleasurable consequences. This is one of all the conceptions that run contrary to what psychology says about how human beings react. My belief is that there are energies and creative elements *within* the individual that are essential and should be brought to bear on the innovative process. An open and continuous dialogue between the teacher, the student, and the expert can elicit these energies.

Social Determinants of the Comprehensive School*

THERE seems to be a certain, one would be inclined to say lawful, sequence inherent in reform work in our society. Universal suffrage and social security have been the precursors of educational change. The statue of Danton on the Boulevard St. Germain in Paris bears the following inscription: *Après le pain l'éducation est le premier besoin du peuple*. At the Library of Congress in Washington, D.C., a similar inscription may be read in the Thomas Jefferson Room: "Educate and inform the mass of the people, enable them to see that it is their interest to preserve peace and order and they will preserve them. Enlighten the people generally and tyranny and oppression will vanish like spirits at the dawn of the day."

School reforms pertaining to the obligatory and public school in our modern, economically expanding society have to be conceived within the framework of the Welfare State. After provision has been made for social security, the time has come to provide for a universal secondary education with goals over and above those of establishing an elementary literacy.

Educational changes, in their turn, seem to occur according to a similar rank order. Sweden affords a good illustration. The organizational structure of the compulsory school has been changed by political initiative, culminating in parliamentary legislation. The next step has been the issuance of newly constructed curricula by government agencies. After some time it becomes clear even on the parliamentary level that teacher training is not adequate for the new goals set up for a school providing general secondary education. It will evidently take some time before a reformed system of teacher training can affect the "inner work" of the school, relating to the organization of studies and the proper use of methods and teaching aids.

Tendencies in Reshaping Secondary Education

Before embarking upon an analysis of factors behind educational change, we shall give a general description of proposals in various European countries to re-organize and expand secondary education. It would be a challenging

* Originally a presentation at the 1962 meeting of the European Society for Comparative Education and subsequently published in the *International Review of Education*, Vol. 9:2, 1963. Reproduced by permission of the Unesco Institute for Education, Hamburg, FRG.

task to try to identify the economic, social, and political factors which have been decisive when reform plans have gone farther in some countries than in others. Why did a radical reform such as the Langevin-Wallon plan have great political difficulties in being accepted, whereas the same kind of school organization was passed by an overwhelming political majority in Sweden? This would be a key problem to comparative education. I shall briefly and tentatively analyze some of what I think to be the pertinent factors later in this paper.

In the matter of educational expansion and reorganization, the big difficulty with which most European countries have had to cope concerns the link-up between the elementary school, which is for the benefit of the people as a whole, and the academic secondary school, which prepares for university studies. Efforts to create a unified organization for the school pertaining to the compulsory attendance ages have run foul of those historical and social forces which assert that both school-types are intended for different social strata and command a different prestige.

No problem of that sort has existed in the United States or the Soviet Union. The American public school grew out of local endeavors to raise the popular educational level. Education beyond the elementary level never became, as it did in Europe, the sole or main gateway to a successful career. As for the Soviet Union, its revolution was so sweeping that the academic schools lost their social exclusiveness as they were merged with the rapidly expanding system of popular education.

For this reason the problems of differentiation in the United States and the Soviet Union have held to the purely pedagogical plane. There have been debates in both countries as to what extent and how far up in the grades classes can be kept undifferentiated. Thus the comprehensive high school in the United States has been excoriated by university professors; in trying to cater for all tastes, say these critics, the comprehensive high school is terribly wasteful of talent. In 1959 James B. Conant published an initial report on this school-type in *The American High School Today*, which pointed out that the situation was by no means as serious as some vociferous critics had portrayed it.

A decree issued in 1934 by the Central Committee of the Communist Party prescribed undifferentiated classes for the Soviet Union. Communist ideology does not recognize the existence of any differences of innate ability. Whenever Russsian educators are asked what is being done to solve the problem of heterogeneous classes, their usual answer is that it is the responsibility of teachers to ensure that all their pupils can keep pace. This entails extra instruction for some of the pupils. Frequent reference is made at the same time to the study groups at the Palace of Pioneers, where pupils can devote themselves to subjects of special interest to them during their spare time. The obligation of more successful pupils to help the poorer ones is also emphasized.

Assessment of Factors Conducive to Comprehensive School Reforms

It stands to reason that the organization and procedures of the school must be adapted to the conditions of a changing society. But this adaptation is a more difficult process than one imagines. Social policy is easier to implement in practice than educational policy. Actually, it takes longer to bring about change in education, mainly because the school, in the same way as the church and the judicial system, is strongly institutionalized. With centuries of tradition behind it, especially where learned academic education is concerned, the school cannot readily accommodate to new social conditions which have emerged during the course of only a few decades. Indeed, it is characteristic of the school as an institution that in most countries its spokesmen are sometimes inclined to disregard its social function. Some of them feel that the teacher's chief mission is to give pupils that measure of knowledge and skills which is fixed by the syllabus, or, more accurately, by textbooks. The relevance of these matters for the individual or for society usually does not induce any agonizing bouts of conscience.

Focus on change is inevitable when analyzing the present-day educational situation. Whatever quantitative criteria we choose, we cannot escape the fact that we live in a society which is growing and restructuring itself on an unprecedented scale. Within the space of a few decades the conditions of our existence have altered so radically that man himself has been left behind. We think the problems of adaptation confronting us in the industrial nations are formidable enough. They are even more formidable in the developing countries.

If we choose to confine ourselves to quantitative criteria of changeability, we can begin with education itself. In the United States by 1980 more than 80 per cent of the 17-18-year-olds were in school. About half of them go on to college or university. At the turn of the century these figures were 7 and 5 per cent respectively. In Western Europe, where in the 1930s only about one-tenth of the pupils went on to secondary education and less than 5 per cent entered the university, secondary education up to the age of 16 is now universal with more than 50 per cent going on to the university-preparing school. More than 20 per cent of the age group enters university. The portion of GNP going to education was in most industrial countries around 3 per cent in the 1950s. Now it is close to 9-10 per cent.

The educative society is distinguished by the rapid changes occurring in the structure of its job world. Mechanization, automation and rationalization are imposing new demands on production and distribution. New trades are emerging and old ones are passing by the board. Increasing rationalization means that the individual must be better qualified to cope with his job. Salaried employees also tend to increase rapidly their absolute and relative share of the labor force as compared with manual workers.

The service society has arrived on the scene. In all industries we find an ever growing proportion of people whose vocations call on them to render assistance to others in different ways. The social techniques demanded of service personnel differ from those imposed on "line" manpower. For the most part they are required to have communications skills, in other words the ability to communicate with others both in their own language and in one or more foreign languages.

Among the consequences of structural changes in the economy are a high degree of mobility between occupations and extensive programs of retraining and further training in all sectors of the working community.

Ejnar Neymark, an officer of the Swedish Labor Market Board, took a random sample of young men born in 1928 and followed their educational and vocational progress, as well as their geographic mobility, from their 14th to 28th year. He found that almost half the men switched from one "job family" to another between the ages of 20 and 28. (Neymark was not concerned with changes of employment or between specific jobs). Facts of this kind suggest that we must thoroughly revise our mental picture of how young people go about choosing their further education and their careers. An apparently widespread stereotype is that once teenagers have completed their secondary schooling and answered the question, "Where do we go from here?," to their satisfaction, they aim at a specific occupational field to which they then stick for all time (even when allowance is made for a large number of them who become turnover-prone). Actually, only a minority of school leavers in any technologically developing society stay true to the first occupation they enter. The principal cause of this mobility is simply the hastily changing structure of the job world itself.

Obviously, this fact is of the utmost importance for school planning, and especially so when it comes to striking a balance between general and vocational education. For my part, I can come to no other conclusion than that the school in a changing society must lay a broad foundation of such knowledge and skills which are diffusely called "general education." This is vitally important because of the conditions governing not only further education, but also retraining. Thus experience of unemployment induced by structural rationalization in the economy demonstrates that the persons unamenable to retraining are to a great extent identical with those whose formal educational background is poor, persons whose ability to read, write and count is so weak that they cannot be equipped with the new trade skills they need without first undergoing fundamental education. According to some spokesmen of the business community – and indeed of parent-guardian interests as well – prolonged compulsory schooling should be primarily exploited to give pupils vocational training, for instance with reference to those trades and industries which are located in the same community as the school. This is a shortsighted way of looking at things, but it also happens to appeal to young people who are "book-tired." In the long run a narrow vocational bias of education towards the end of the compulsory schooling period would prejudice both the young people and the business community; for the narrower the scope of general education and the less solidly rooted are the basic skills, the smaller the range of talents at the command of young people when confronted with the universal need of further education in adult years, as well as with the retraining for new jobs which will be forced on many of them.

The changing society with its expanding economy and its rising welfare for all citizens thus imposes new demands upon the individual, which entails new challenges to its educational system. It is my contention that these new demands justify the organization of a school around certain goals, which will of necessity materialize in a comprehensive and not a selective system.

When discussing the proper way of providing an education for all children in our society, most people are willing to pay lip service to the following two principles:

(1)   The principle of self-realization, so thoroughly spelled out by the Educational Policies Commission in the U.S. It should be an unalienable right of every growing individual to make a free choice among various educational paths and that everybody irrespective of place of residence or social origin should be given "equal opportunity." In sum: it is the duty of the school to see to it that everybody can develop their potentialities to the full.

(2) The principle of making adequate educational provisions for all kinds and degrees of ability that might contribute to enhanced production and the common welfare. From the point of view of political economy and the national productivity, ability is conceived as a natural resource that should be converted into useful things. Education from the point of view of a nation's economy might thus be regarded as a commitment of the Welfare State to its own growth.

But as soon as the discussion comes down to the specific problems of organizing the school according to these principles, one will find that they run contrary to certain dicta of teaching efficiency that most teachers take to be self-evident. The intricate and controversial problems as to which age and to what extent the academically gifted children should be spotted and taught in separation from their former classmates is loaded with such axiomatic assumptions. Thus most teachers hold that the less heterogeneous the class the more efficient the outcome of instruction. By the same token, the smaller the class the better the outcome. This would then mean that one should try to make an early separation of children of different ability, both from the qualitative and quantitative point of view.

But are all these purely pedagogical principles (for instance, that it requires much less work to teach a homogeneous class than a heterogeneous class) compatible in their practical consequences with the two superior principles of self-realization and utilization of all kinds and degrees of ability? I shall try to give an answer to this question in the following.

In Europe, the problem as reviewed previously has revolved around the extent to which the lower section of the learned academic school should be incorporated with the basic school. As the period of compulsory attendance increases, the longer the period that basic school (whether we call this elementary school or something else) runs parallel with the learned academic school. The age at which this parallelism starts varies from one country to another. In West Germany it begins at the age of 10, in England at 11.

Throughout the 1950s this whole complex of problems was subsumed in Sweden under the term *differentiation*. The key word back in the 1940s was "linkage," in reference to the transition from elementary school to lower secondary academic school *(realskola)*. Most of the arguments advanced in favor of retaining the system of parallel schools have been pedagogical. This line of reasoning claims that teaching is easier with separate provision for intellectual goats and the practical sheep. It has thereby been assumed that such a system is somehow more effective, that is, more economical and productive.

I do not propose here to examine in depth the Swedish debate on this matter. That would require a monograph unto itself, one that I have already written (Husén, *Problems of Differentation in Swedish Compulsory Schooling*, Stockholm 1962). Years of experience with problems under this head have moved me to recommend the abolition of the parallel-school system in favor of one comprehensive school offering a restricted system of electives in undifferentiated classes up to the age of 16. As I see it, an inevitable consequence of the principle of self-realization is to organize an "elective" school to replace the selective school which has increasingly come to characterize education at the upper academic levels.

Everyone is prepared to pay lip service to the principle that each pupil should receive the schooling for which he or she is best suited. But this begs other questions. What do we mean by the word "suited?" And who is to determine this: the school, the pupil, or parents? Since a vast body of research on differentiation has been conducted in Sweden since the end of the 1940s, I should like to cite illustrations from some of the studies.

When the 1946 Parliamentary School Commission, whose terms of reference were to submit recommendations on the future pattern of Swedish education, came to consider the linkage between basic and higher schools, it felt called upon to initiate a research program dealing with the development of ability. The Commission's starting point was the popular conception that there existed two kinds of such ability: an academic and a practical. The one was suited to book learning, while the other lent itself to vocational education. According to many educators, the academically inclined should be transferred at an early stage to a special school-type or to special classes, where their progress would not be impeded by their more practically inclined schoolmates.

The studies sponsored by the Commission showed that practical and academic achievements are positively correlated: that is, the academically inclined – or more precisely, those of verbal and book-learning aptitudes – tend on average to perform better in practical tasks than pupils of low academic ability, and vice versa. In other words, no compensating mechanism operates as between bookish and practical ability, so that a person endowed by Providence with reading skill is supposedly all thumbs when it comes to handling tools, let us say, while the class dullard is supposedly equipped with a greater practical gift.

The very existence of a positive correlation between practical and academic ability suggests that any attempt to separate pupils on this score is at best an extremely hazardous undertaking. Obviously, there are many pupils whose intellects, and even more whose personal interests, turn in a specific direction. The School Commission estimated their number at 50 per cent of the total. But the other half is more or less undecided. What does one do with these pupils? In the Commission's view, the academically gifted should not be already hived off at the ages of 11 and 12, because that would deprive the practical occupations, so called, of their share of academically qualified practitioners. For if selection for secondary schools is made at these ages, their classes will be attended not only by pupils of one-sided academic bent, but also by those who combine a good academic with a good practical talent.

At the beginning of the 1950s, in the discussions by interested persons and groups which followed the Commission's final report in 1948 and the experimental program with the nine-year comprehensive school, the opposing camps (that is, those in favor of late differentiation and those against) agreed that the age of 11-12 was satisfactory to permit determination of those who were academically gifted. This discussion suffered from one serious weakness: it mixed diagnosis with prognosis. Even if teachers can, on fully objective grounds, identify the 11-and-12-year-olds who were the best performers, or if this could be determined with the help of objective tests, it obviously does not follow that either teachers or tests can indicate which pupils will be able to cope with a certain school-type *in the future*. It is one thing to establish the current performance of pupils, and quite another to try to determine their potential performance, that is, their proficiency under future conditions of development and environment. Some educators contended that both the graduating and receiving schools would already be able at an early stage to identify those pupils who were especially well suited for academic studies. This thesis has been refuted by a study of Orring (reported in Husén and Boalt, *Educational Research and Educational Change,* New York 1968) on promotions, grade-repeating and dropping-out. Orring followed up a representative sample of pupils in academic secondary schools and related success or failure to marks received in the previous school. He found that about half the pupils who were competitively selected on the basis of their marks did not graduate from the academic secondary school within the regular period. The argument that this result was due to the fact that admission criteria were not strict enough is contradicted by the fact that a large part of the very best pupils at time of admission later repeated grades or dropped out. To this it may be objected that if authority to make selections is vested in the receiving school alone, then such a large "wastage" need not arise after admission. But Orring found that the number of repeaters and dropouts was far less upon completion of the first year of *realskola* than during the second and third years. This must be due either to poor diagnosis on the part of the receiving school or to changes within the pupils (meaning in effect that prognoses cannot be made), or to a combination of both factors.

We now know a great deal more about how pupils develop during their teens than in the 1940s. A number of studies dealing with the development of young people, not least in terms of their scholastic achievement, have been conducted. The researchers have all run into the difficulty of arriving at satisfactory correlations between on the one hand the criteria used for admissions to academic schools, such as teacher ratings, intelligence tests, achievement tests and marks, and the performances achieved several years later on by pupils in these schools on the other. In England, where a large part of educational research since the mid-forties has been committed to ascertaining the best possible methods for administering the "11+ examinations," it has to be admitted that a considerable number of pupils are unable to cope with grammar school even after the most scrupulous procedure. A fact-finding report issued in 1954 by the British Ministry of Education disclosed that more than one-third of the grammar school entrants did not reach what could reasonably be deemed the academic objective. This investigation suffered from one serious weakness: only in exceptional cases was it able to show how many pupils might have made the grade if they had been given a chance to gain admission later, but who were definitely excluded from an academic education because of the early selection date. I shall refer again to this matter below.

Thus pupils *do* change in different respects during the course of their teens. This not only means an increased range of variation in regard to achievements and interests, but also a change in the rank order of achievements. We have a category of "late bloomers." Obviously, the process also works in reverse. The years of puberty, with all that they imply in the way of psychosomatic revolution and changing social relationships, react powerfully on achievements in school. Young people begin to orient themselves to the adult role. In due course they become preoccupied with choice of further education and a career. They gradually come to be aware of their qualifications and may take an interest in trying these out, for instance during the phase of practical vocational orientation in the basic school. To suggest that young people can be made to commit themselves on an appreciable scale to a choice of career before they are 15-years-old is to indulge in an illusion. Any sorting-out or selection of pupils before that age is essentially a mirrored image of parent's ambitions and the extent to which teachers get on with their pupils.

This brings me around to what I regard as a highly neglected aspect of the differentiation issue. When the contention is made that pupils must have the opportunity to compete "on equal terms" for the limited number of places available in a learned academic school, it appears to be simply assumed that this competition is quite fair if based on marks and examination results. According to this line of reasoning, social background (such as the educational attainments and the economic position of parents) count for little or nothing in connection with a competitive selection for academic education or with the selection implicit in grade-repeating or dropping-out.

The procedure whereby pupils are selected for a "blocked" school – that is, a school which imposes certain requirements as to marks or which must select from among applicants because it cannot accommodate them all – is "loaded" with social factors. Evidence of this effect for Scandinavia was first produced by my colleague Gunnar Boalt in a monograph of 1947 which is summarized in Husén & Boalt, *Educational Research and Educational Change: the case of Sweden* (1968). After following one complete age-group in Stockholm from the fourth grade of elementary school to graduation from *Gymnasium*, he was able to show the existence of social handicaps both in selections for the *Realskola* and the *Gymnasium* and in the weeding-out of pupils in both school-types. Boalt defined social handicap as the degree of correlation between (say) socio-economic group and selection, with ability as shown by marks or tests held constant.

Examples of social handicap are given in the table below. The findings are quoted from Husén & Boalt, 1968. In the spring of 1955 all fourth-grade pupils in Stockholm were divided into nine ability levels of educational attainment according to their school marks and to their scores on standardized achievement tests. At each of these levels we determined the proportion of children from each of the three socio-economic groups (better-situated, middle class and working class) who applied for admission to an academic secondary school. In addition, we determined the frequencies of rejects at each level and within each socio-economic group. The number of rejects is given in parentheses after the number of applicants, both frequencies being shown as percentages.

Ability level:		9	8	7	6	5	4	3	2	1
Number of	1	87(6)	89(20)	82(18)	82(36)	70(52)	58(69)	47(69)	21(80)	14(10)
applicants										
(and rejects)	2	85(6)	77(23)	74(33)	59(50)	47(60)	36(68)	20(79)	13(100)	7 (75)
in % of socio-										
economic	3	66(13)	72(29)	45(31)	40(43)	24(57)	18(61)	8(82)	7(54)	5(100)
groups 1, 2 and 3.										

We consistently found that a smaller percentage of the most intellectually able pupils seek to enter secondary school from socio-economic group 3 than from group 1. These figures concern 11-year-olds and obviously reflect the choice of parents. Already when considering further-going education at this age, the children of parents having less normal schooling are handicapped by comparison with equally able peers who are more fortunately endowed in this respect.

It is also clear that grade-repeating and dropping-out, where these are common, correlate rather strongly with social background. The previously cited report of the British Ministry of Education showed that dropouts among the top one-third in the entrance examinations for grammar school were four times greater for pupils whose fathers performed relatively unskilled work than for equally able pupils whose parents were "professionals," usually university graduates or well-to-do holders of business positions.

This brings me to another argument that has been employed in the Swedish debate to justify early separation of the academically gifted from their schoolmates. What an awful waste of talent, so the argument runs, to have the superior pupils slowed up by the dullards. The brainy ones ought to have the opportunity to enroll in special schools or classes, where they can spread out to the best of their ability. It is further contended that the slowcoaches also benefit from differentiation, since they are spared the feelings of inferiority which might arise from the constant comparison of their poorer performances with those of their brighter fellows.

Let us briefly consider the first argument: society gains from giving separate instruction to children of outstanding intellectual ability. The correctness of this view is supposedly confirmed by comparing the high scholastic standards of *Gymnasium* graduates in Scandinavia with, say, the graduates of American high schools. But the comparison does not hold water for two reasons. In the first place, the Scandinavians who finish *Gymnasium* represent no more than one-tenth of their age-group, whereas about 80 per cent of American 17-18-year-olds graduate from high school. For the comparison to be valid, the top tenth of these Americans should be compared with their European counterparts. In the second place, no account is taken of the price paid under a system of never-ending selection for the product which reaches the graduation stage. If, as is true in many countries, more than half the pupils who are admitted to *realskola* and *gymnasium* on a competitive basis drop out along the way, then a very high price will have been paid for the quality product which finally emerges. For the inescapable fact is that the dropouts include not only the poor learners, but also a large proportion of superior pupils who have somehow fallen by the wayside because their social backgrounds did not have enough educational motivation to impel them towards graduation. When dropouts from the Swedish *realskola* are analyzed with reference to the scholastic achievements of pupils and their social origin, we find that these are correlated with socio-economic groups. Obviously, all kinds of children who drop out of school represent a national-economic loss, especially in the educative society with its shortage of trained manpower.

The high scholastic standard of those who passed the leaving examination in many European countries is attained at a very heavy cost. Were I to estimate the proportion of a country's potential academic talent that is left unnurtured when selections for secondary school are made at the ages of 10-12, and entrants are successively weeded out thereafter, I would say between 40 and 70 per cent. The selective school, i.e. the school which seeks to separate the book learners from the rest as soon as possible, inflicts a fearful wastage of talent; in my opinion, the wastage is much greater than would result from allowing pupils of different gifts to stay together in the same classes as long as possible.

In the light of the circumstances described above, I find that the educative society requires an *elective school,* not a selective school. By elective school I mean a type in which the pupils, by being permitted a phased choice of electives, can gradually focus their studies in a direction to which they are drawn by their abilities and interests. Such a system of restricted electives is flexible in the sense that a wrong choice need not be irreparable. Thus a pupil will not be definitely committing himself to an intellectual or manual occupation merely because of an elective made in school. In the last analysis, no selection of pupils in their compulsory-attendance years can be reconciled with the principle of self-realization.

By way of conclusion, I should like to narrate the following incident as typical of the way in which many educators react to the comprehensive school. At a meeting where I lectured, we reached the problem of reforming secondary education. The local school principal asked in a caustic voice, "What's behind this reform – pedagogy or politics?" My answer was, "Politics, of course." Like all other social reforms a school reform ultimately rests on political valuations, as expressed in a democratic society by parliament. Social workers do not decide the principles governing social reforms, nor do military officers determine our country's policy on national defense. The school is no exception to the rule that citizens must comply with the democratically arrived-at decisions of the community at large. Naturally, this in no way deters the teachers from giving voice to their opinions on the pedagogical aspects of school reform. And they have done so in abundant measure. No doubt they would have won a more sympathetic hearing had they generally realized that certain educational drawbacks cannot ever outweigh the national and individual benefits accruing from a school which caters for everybody.

Why Comprehensive Education?*

REFORMS affecting the structure of the basic school as well as access to further education at the secondary and tertiary level have, as pointed out earlier, to be conceived of within the larger framework of the Welfare State. After provisions have been made for social security, full or almost full employment and decent medical care, education gains in priority. After a certain minimum of social security has been ascertained, the time comes to provide for universal secondary education with goals over and above those of establishing elementary literacy. In the affluent society the possibility of universal tertiary education looms at the horizon.

Looking back on the debate on educational reforms in Western Europe over the past few decades one is struck by the observation that professional educators, teachers, tend to reason as if the school were operating in a social vacuum. Therefore, when parliamentary decisions that are at cross-purpose with strong teacher opinions are taken they are easily conceived by educators as "interference" on the part of the politicians into affairs which are not their business. Educational reforms are regarded as the proper domain of the "experts," including the professors, who readily assume the role of Platonic philosopher-kings.

The belief in educational reforms as substitutes for social and economic ones explains why educators and non-educators alike expect educational reforms to work wonders. Such reforms have been launched as "spearheads towards the future" and as heralds of a new society. Why has it been so? The optimism about what education can do by itself stems in my view from two sets of motives.

The first is a major feature of the liberal ideology since the end of the eighteenth century. The inscription in the Thomas Jefferson Room in the Library of Congress in Washington, D.C., has been cited above. The father of the universal public school in the State of Massachusetts, Horace Mann, in the 1840s labelled education as the Great Equalizer that would put people on par in their careers and remove poverty. "It does better than disarm the poor of their hostility toward the rich: It prevents being poor." The so-called Great Society Program launched by the Johnson administration in the 1960s built on the assumption that compensatory education would contribute to breaking what was referred to as the "poverty cycle." The logic behind the compensatory education programs was briefly as follows:

* Presentation given at the Renner Institute in Vienna in 1980 at the invitation of Chancellor Bruno Kreisky.

People are poor because of lack of competence.

Bad school attainments are due to poverty.

Ergo: compensatory education will, by improving their school attainments, improve their life chances.

Or put in another way: as President Johnson was saying when he signed the Elementary and Secondary Education Act of 1965: "We are going to teach them out of poverty."

I have in 1978-9 on behalf of OECD been reviewing the federal compensatory education programs and shall not try here even to summarize the findings of the review team. Suffice it to say that compensatory education has not improved the plight of the poor to an extent that matches the euphoria of those who sponsored the legislation in the early 1960s.

The second motive behind the propensity to conceive of educational problems in isolation is that social interventions in the educational domain are less controversial and therefore less dangerous than attempts to change the overall social and economic order. To be sure, changes in school structure, which tend to stir up violent political controversies and which educators tend to discuss as if they were merely didactic problems, constitute a marginal case. Here changes are threatening the prerogatives of the privileged.

When the idea of making the first nine years of public education comprehensive was introduced in the Swedish debate in the late 1940s and then subjected to an extensive pilot program in the 1950s, it was dealt with almost entirely as a pedagogical problem: how far up in the school would it be possible to teach all children with the enormous variation in background and innate ability in the same program or even in the classroom?

Before proceeding further, it would be in order to define what should be meant by comprehensive education. The main features of such an education are:

(1) The school types covering mandatory school age, say from 6 to 16, as a rule elementary and lower secondary school, are integrated into one common school which caters for all pupils in a given area. Thus, the parallelism at the lower secondary level between various types of schools with different purposes and serving pupils with different social class background is abolished.

(2) Flexibility in provisions is aimed at by bringing various programs, both "general" and "vocational" ones, together into one unified system. Transfer from one stream or program to another can take place. Choice of program does not imply definitive choice of a vocational career.

Why did Sweden "go comprehensive?" A strong force behind the quest for a unified, comprehensive school consisted of the popular movements characteristic of Swedish society after the turn of the century, particularly the labor movement and the workers' educational organization. The main motive for a structural reform was in their view to provide increased equality by providing equal access to further education irrespective of social class and place of residence. The inequalities existed not only between social classes but also, and to a glaring extent, between rural and urban areas.

Without pretending to analyze the Swedish situation in depth I would like just to indicate certain conditions that in this case were conducive to a reform that by and large was carried by political consensus.

In the first place, one should point out the political stability over several decades, with the same political party in power, which meant a consistency in planning and implementation that is not possible when frequent changes in government take place. The labor market has been comparatively peaceful with strong organizations and an efficient system of negotiations. Last, but by no means least, the social welfare reforms from the 1930s on laid the groundwork for the enhanced standard of living that in its turn determined an enhanced level of aspiration as far as education is concerned. A policy of full employment, and a system of basic and income-related pensions for all provided a framework of social security. The educational reforms were concomitant with the introduction of child allowances, school health programs, free school lunches, free teaching materials, study grants from the upper secondary school on, and state loans for university studies.

One did not at the outset realize that the parallelism in most European school systems prevailing in the age range 10 to 15 between those who were selected at the age of 10-11 for the academic university-preparing school and the remaining majority who completed the elementary school to a certain extent was a social segregation. It was discussed in terms of "differentiation" and "inherited abilities," which meant sorting out the students with regard to their capability to cope with academic subjects. Their scholastic aptitude had to be assessed which in terms of the criteria employed meant their ability to cope with the verbal tools and the abstract concepts they signify.

Let me further pursue the argument that the separation of academic from non-academic implies to some extent social class separation as well, the stronger the earlier the separation or differentiation takes place.

Everybody is, of course, ready to pay lip service to the principle that every single pupil should receive the kind and amount of formal schooling for which he or she is best suited. But this begs two crucial questions. What do we mean by "suited?" And who is to determine the suitability: the school, the pupils, or the parents? I shall try to shed some light on these problems by referring to the vast body of empirical research conducted particularly in Sweden, where the so-called differentiation problem for a long time was the pivotal issue.

When the 1946 Parliamentary Commission had to consider how the structure of Swedish formal schooling should be reshaped it initiated a research program on the development of abilities from the age of 7 to 16, the age range covering mandatory school attendance. The Commission shared the popular conception that man is equipped with two independent types of abilities: theoretical or academic on the one hand, and practical or vocational on the other. The former constitute the aptitude for book learning while the latter lend themselves to practical, or rather, manual pursuits. Thus, by finding out how human abilities develop during school age one would obtain a factual basis for a decision when it would be appropriate to separate the academically inclined from the more practical ones. According to the majority of secondary school teachers a transfer of the former to academically oriented school types, i.e. to university-preparing *lycées* or *gymnasia*, should take place as early as possible in order to let them develop to their full capacity and not be hampered by their slow-learning schoolmates. Such a policy would also benefit the latter, because they would not be discouraged by lagging behind all the time.

The studies on how the factorial structure of cognitive abilities developed from 7 to 16 showed in the first place that academic and practical achievements are positively correlated: that is, the academically inclined, or more precisely those of booklearning aptitudes, tend on average to perform better in practical tasks than pupils of low academic ability, and vice versa. There is no compensating mechanism that operates between bookish and practical abilities, so that a person of, let us say, high verbal ability fumbles when it comes to handling tools, while the class dullard is equipped with greater practical gifts. Furthermore, it appeared that the theoretical abilities "crystallized" earlier than practical ones. This suggested that scholastic aptitude could be assessed at an early age. This supported the notion among many teachers that the existing system where transfer to the academic secondary school occurred at the age of about 11 rested on hard psychological evidence. The Commission did not dispute this evidence, but rejected an early transfer for two reasons. In the first place, because of the correlation between verbal and practical ability, one could not successfully separate pupils with the former inclination from the latter. It was estimated that some 50 per cent of the pupils at the age of 11–12 were undecided with regard to both their cognitive and affective inclinations. Secondly, if the academically gifted were hived off at such an early age one would deprive the so-called practical occupations of their fair share of qualified incumbents. Even worse, it would also deprive the manual occupations of articulate spokesmen and be to the detriment of the working class.

The discussion some twenty-five to fifty years ago about the pros and cons for comprehensivization of mandatory schooling suffered as pointed out above from one pervasive weakness: both proponents and adversaries of a comprehensive structure confused diagnosis and prognosis. It is one thing to identify pupils at the age of 10-12 who are good and bad performers. It is quite another to *predict* how pupils are going to perform in particular pedagogical environments and under particular developmental conditions. Over many years pupils in Sweden had been admitted to the academic secondary school on the basis of standardized school marks. About half of those screened on the basis of marks at entry subsequently failed and became either dropouts or reached the final examination after having repeated one or more grades. The argument that this happened because the admission criteria were not applied strictly enough was contradicted by the fact that a considerable portion of the best pupils at the time of admission became either dropouts or grade-repeaters. One could then object that if one did not use grades given by the school which delivered the pupils but instead vested the receiving school with the authority to make the selection, such a "wastage" would not occur after admission. But a follow-up study conducted by the 1957 School Commission, which made the recommendations for the introduction of a comprehensive school all over the country, showed that the number of failures increased after the first year in the *realskola*. This must be due either to a poor diagnosis on the part of the receiving school or to changes within the pupils; or to a combination of both.

We know now more about how pupils change during their teens than we did some twenty-five years ago as well as more about both inter-individual and intra-individual differences. The years of puberty and adolescence with all that they imply of changing social relationships have their repercussions on school achievements. Young people begin to orient themselves to the adult role and become increasingly preoccupied with the choice of further education and more realistically turn their minds to what might follow that in terms of an occupational career. They gradually become aware of their qualifications and take an interest in trying these out. To suggest that young people can begin to make a responsible commitment to a career before the age of, say, 15-16, or maybe even 17-18, it to indulge in an illusion. Any sorting out or selection of pupils before 15-16 is essentially a reflection of parental ambitions and how well pupils get on with their teachers.

This brings us to the argument: society gains from giving separate instruction to children of outstanding intellectual ability instead of keeping them all together not only under the same roof but even under the ceiling of the same classroom for the entire period of mandatory schooling. The validity of the argument seems to be supported by a comparison of the high scholastic standards of, say, *Gymnasium* graduates in several European countries with those of, say, the high school graduates in the United States. But such a comparison is for two reasons not fair. In the first place, in some European countries not more than some 20 per cent of the relevant age group completes the university-preparing school as compared to some 80 per cent in the United States. In the second place, no account is taken of the price paid in a selective system for the product that reaches the graduation stage. If, as has been and still is the case in several countries, half or more than half of those admitted on a competitive basis to the *Gymnasium* or the *lycée* drop out along the way, then the price paid for the final products in terms of not only individual frustrations but social wastage as well is, indeed, very high. For the dropouts include not only poor learners of whom most have allegedly been screened out at admission, but also a large proportion of able pupils who have somehow fallen by the wayside because their social background was not schoolminded enough or did not have the supportive power to carry them through. There are, as has been shown by the French sociologist Pièrre Bourdieu and his co-workers, certain built-in sorting mechanisms which pervade the traditional school system.

The International Association for the Evaluation of Educational Achievement (IEA) was by its surveys able to elucidate the problem of what happens to top students in systems which are more comprehensive, retentive, and have more "holding power" as compared to those who are less retentive and have less holding power. IEA compared the top 1, 5, and 9 per cent of the total age group in some 15 countries with regard to mean achievements in mathematics and science. Furthermore, we compared the countries with regard to the social background of graduates from the university-preparing school.

The outcomes of these comparisons were clear-cut and consistent: for instance, the top 5 per cent of the pupils in countries with a high holding power and usually also with comprehensive features showed the same level of competence as those of countries with an early selection and a low holding power. The second finding was that the imbalance between upper and lower class representation among graduates was more pronounced in countries with early differentation of pupils than among those with a late differentation. I shall in a moment come back to this in reporting studies related to the try-out activities with nine-year comprehensive school that were conducted at the Stockholm School of Education in the late 1950s and early 1960s.

The Swedish Parliament in passing the 1950 Education Act made provisions for a ten-year pilot program of comprehensive education, where elementary and lower secondary schools had been merged during the entire nine-year time span of mandatory schooling. The municipalities were invited to launch local projects within the general framework of the decision taken by Parliament. The incentive consisted of central funds available to cover the extra costs. The City Council of Stockholm decided to join in these activities but to limit its participation to the area of the city south of the so-called Stream that divides Stockholm into two parts equal in size. I remember from that time a newspaper cartoon showing a person on a bridge separating the two halves passing a poster which read: "You are now leaving the non-comprehensive sector." (This, of course, alluded to the situation in Berlin before the construction of the wall, and reflected the political controversy around the introduction of the comprehensive school in spite of the fact that it was supported by a majority of the people.)

This offered a unique opportunity to obtain factual information on how the two systems, the comprehensive and the parallel one, operated. For some years the northern part of the city would keep a system of transfer, or rather, selection to academic secondary school after the fourth year in the elementary school, where the majority then spent the remaining four years of their mandatory school attendance. The facts that we were after were of two kinds, both crucial, indeed, in the debate on the relative advantages and disadvantages of the comprehensive and parallel systems respectively:

(1) How are the pupils developing cognitively in the two systems? Are the bright ones held back in the comprehensive system, and if this is true, by how much? To what extent is there a wastage of academic talent in the comprehensive system, as compared to the selective? This was in the debate going on in Sweden in the 1950s and later, on the continent and in England, considered to be the key problems, because the reform issue was conceived mainly in pedagogical terms and not as a social reform that would broaden the opportunity for the majority of the pupils to obtain further education.

(2) What kind of wastage of academic talent occurs in the traditional system as a result of selectivity at an early age? What price is paid in terms of non-admission, grade-repeating, and dropout among pupils from various social classes? Since comprehensivization at that time in Sweden, some twenty-five years ago, was conceived essentially as a problem in the domain of pedagogy, it was not even brought up in the debate. The Stockholm study reported by N. E. Svensson in *Ability Grouping and Scholastic Achievement* (Stockholm 1962), was crucial in directing the attention of the policy makers and some educators to this aspect of the comprehensivization issue at a time when politically the matter had reached a stalemate in the Commission that was charged to produce recommendations on how a comprehensive system should be introduced over the whole country.

The contention is made that the pupils who want to transfer from elementary to the academic secondary school compete on equal terms for a limited number of places. It has been assumed that the criteria employed, such as school marks or examinations, are independent of social background. But a massive body of research evidence from the last few decades shows that there are social handicaps both in the selection procedure for entry to the *Gymnasium* and in the screening that subsequently takes place. The social handicaps stem from the fact that whatever criteria used in the selection procedure they are all correlated with social background. This explains the finding from the Stockholm study that at a given level of ability according to marks or examination scores, pupils from working class background were much more frequently rejected than those of middle or upper class background. We also found that grade-repeating and dropout were related to home background. This is consistent with the study conducted within the British Ministry of Education in the 1950s that showed that the dropout rate among pupils of working class backgrounds was four times as high as among students of equal ability according to admission criteria but with professional home backgrounds.

What I have said so far could be regarded as an advocacy for a flexible and truly *elective* comprehensive education as opposed to the selective, traditional dual or parallel school. An elective system permits a phased, step by step, choice of programs and subjects. The pupils are allowed to focus their studies gradually in the direction of their abilities and interests. Such a system is flexible in the sense that the options are kept open as long as possible. A wrong choice need not be irreparable and does not have to be felt as a failure. The pupil need not commit himself definitively at an early age to an intellectual or manual occupation merely because of the school structure. Selection or sorting of pupils during the years of mandatory school attendance cannot be reconciled with the democratic principle of self-realization.

But it would be incumbent on me in my role as a social scientist and a critic of the school in my home country (see, e.g., Husén. *The School in Question,* London 1979) to finish on a cautious note. It is important to point out that comprehensivization does not mean gray uniformity in provisions of educative experiences. One has to watch carefully not least the school bureaucracy that easily acts according to simple and uniform formulas of finance and adminstration. We must be wary about guarding the principles of flexibility and electivity.

Furthermore comprehensivization is not a panacea against what appears to me to be a pervasive feature of modern industrial societies, irrespective of their social and economic order, namely the creeping "diploma disease" which reflects a growing element of meritocracy. There has been a growing tendency in the highly industrialized countries on the part of the employment system to leave it to the educational system to conduct the sorting and sifting of prospective workers. Former credentials are used as the prime criterion of selection. Young people at an early age become wary of this, and the increased competition has had serious repercussions in terms of distortion of genuine educative values and of school motivation. Absenteeism, discipline, and vandalism have become serious problems in the age range of 13 to 16 in several countries, including my own. Those who cannot meet the demands and are unable to "stick it out" by staying in school as long as possible give up. These problems cannot be solved by the school alone, because they stem from features inherent in our growth-oriented societies, some of which are governed by market forces, others by the bureaucratic elites.

Since educated ability in highly industrialized societies has increasingly become a vehicle of personal success as well as of economic growth, we are faced with a dilemma between equality and meritocracy. As long as educated intelligence on the part of society is regarded as an investment in economic growth, those who achieve merit in academic pursuits will be singled out for special reward, which means being better paid and elevated to positions of power and influence. This means that we would have to live with the equality-meritocracy dilemma in the school as long as the growth philosophy prevails. This does not in the long run augur well for comprehensive education. It is my firm conviction that a society with a true participatory democracy cannot be established without providing as far as possible equal opportunity by bringing the children from all walks of life under the same roof. But, even more important it cannot work without providing them with the shared experiences which constitute a common frame of reference and understanding.

III. Equality and Meritocracy

Second Thoughts on Equality in Education (1974)[1]
The Dilemma Between Equality and Excellence (1976)[2]
Implications for Educational Policy of Individual Differences in Learning
Ability: A Comparative Perspective (1978)[3]

Introduction

In the industrialized countries equality in education (*Chancengleichheit, égalité des chances*) has been a policy objective to which much lip service has been paid. It can be embraced by so much unanimity because of its vague character. What should we mean by equality in education? Only formal equality of opportunity or equality of results and life chances as well? Even though massive attempts have been made in our time to remove economic barriers and to broaden access to further education, there are still wide gaps between social classes in real participation in education at higher levels.

The thesis advanced here is that modern, growth-oriented, technological and complex society is beset with an inherent dilemma between equality and meritocracy, or between equality and excellence. There is a growing tendency for educated intelligence to become a major determinant in the life career. The employment system increasingly uses the amount of formal education as the first criterion of selection among job seekers. This dilemma is, however, seldom acknowledged in the public debate and among policymakers. It leads, however, to serious frustration among those who are unsuccessful in climbing the educational ladder, those who – in an expression used later in this book – constitute the "new educational underclass."

These problems and their ramifications have been dealt with more at length in Husén: *Social Background and Educational Attainment* (Paris: OECD, 1975) and in Husén: *Talent, Equality and Meritocracy* (The Hague: Nijhoff, 1974).

Notes

1. Paper presented at a summer seminar 1974 at the Aspen Institute for Humanistic Studies. The Equality-Meritocracy Dilemma in Higher Education. In: Philip G. Altbach (ed.) *The University's Response to Societal Demands*. New York: International Council for Educational Development. Published 1975.
2. Published in *Higher Education*, Vol. 5, 1976, 407–422.
3. Published in the *Scandinavian Journal of Educational Research*, Vol. 22:4, 1978, 173–191.

Second Thoughts on Equality in Education*

IN THE 1960s policymakers began to be obsessed by problems of equality in education. The liberal quest for equality of opportunity entered upon a euphoric period. The seemingly unlimited resources put at the disposal of those in educational research and practice who wanted to do something served as a stimulant. Surveys were conducted and experimental programs in compensatory and remedial education were launched. There was a strong belief in what education, given the needed resources, could do in improving society.

But at the very peak of its dazzling success, in the euphoric moment of being conceived of as the prime instrument of social progress and prosperity, doubts began to be raised and serious criticisms leveled. The school as an institution came under heavy attack from both left and right. Second thoughts and criticism also emerged with regard to something that had so far been regarded as an unassailable *credo*, namely equality of educational opportunity.

It would seem rather *passé* to deal with problems of equality in education that have been in the focus of educational debate since the Coleman equality of opportunity survey in the mid-1960s and fueled by Jenck's re-analysis published a few years later. But time has come to step back and try to account for some of the results of the debate. In the light of recent thinking and research there are social scientists who have begun to have second thoughts about the matter.

Conservative critics maintain that due consideration to socio-biological realities have not been made and that the educational system is not there primarily to bring about equality. On the contrary, it is there to create distinctions. The liberals have to their regret discovered that their policy formulas to bring about a better balance between social strata in participation in advanced education have not worked nearly as well as they anticipated. Neo-Marxist critics maintain and have, at least in Sweden, tried to show that schooling in the capitalist society serves the interests of the ruling class and is geared to reproduce already existing class differences.

Let me go back to the mid-eighteenth century and begin with Horace Mann as a typical example of eighteenth century optimism. He considered the common public school to hold promise of providing equality of opportunity

* A presentation given at an international seminar on higher education at the Aspen Institute of Humanistic Studies (1974).

and of shaping a society unaffected by social and economic inequalities. The school for children from all walks of life would serve as "a great equalizer of the conditions of men, the balance wheel of the social machinery . . . ." It would "do better than disarm the poor of their hostility toward the rich. It prevents being poor . . . ." Apart from being an equalizer, the school was seen as a prime instrument for individuals born in humble circumstances to move up the social ladder. Everybody should be given equal opportunity to achieve and to be promoted, provided he had the talent and the energy to go ahead. The school that prepares young people for the different positions in society was assumed to perform these functions in a spirit of justice and impartiality. Its selective function was assumed to occur strictly according to proven merits and not to social background, sex or race. The big individual differences in income, wealth and power that after all are highly conspicuous in a society that has realized the meritocratic principles, are to a large extent reflecting innate differences in ability to go ahead in life. Thus, in *one* sense a meritocratic society is "classless," because it provides in principle to every person an equal opportunity to become prosperous and influential.

The liberal vision of equal opportunity prevailed in most Western industrial countries well until the late 1960s. The rapid expansion of the educational systems in the 1950s and 1960s was due to two main circumstances. The rising standard of living stimulated a "social demand" for education. The conception of education as a capital investment with a high rate of return both to the individual and to society justified that the education sector in the late 1950s and during the 1960s was allowed to grow twice the rate of the growth of the economy. Policymakers were engulfed in a kind of equality euphoria. By removing economic barriers and making more places available in upper secondary and higher education and by increasing the length of attendance in the common school, ideal conditions could be created to implement the vision of equal opportunity, where everybody had access to the kind and amount of education that suited his inborn capacity.

The late 1960s, not least the traumatic upheaval of 1968, marked a turning point. The power of the formal school system to serve as an equalizer was brought into question by participation studies conducted during the 1960s in the OECD countries. Furthermore, the assumption that greater equalization of educational opportunities would in its wake have enhanced equalization of life chances turned out to be much less valid than the optimists had anticipated. In his keynote address to the OECD Conference in 1970 on Policies for Educational Growth the Swedish Minister of Education had the following to say about education as a promotor of social change:

> It is possible that we have been too optimistic, particularly perhaps concerning the time it takes to bring about changes. On the other hand, it is hardly possible to change society only through education. To equalize educational opportunities without influencing working conditions, the setting of wage rates, etc. in other ways, would easily become an empty gesture. The reforms in educational policy must go together with reforms in other fields: labour market policy, economic policy, social policy, fiscal policy, etc.

Referring to the optimistic statements made during the first OECD Policy Conference on Education in Washington, D.C. in 1961, Charles Frankel and A. H. Halsey in their summary report from the 1970 Conference conclude:

> Too much has been claimed for the power of educational systems as instruments for wholesale reform of societies which are characteristically hierarchical in their distribution of chances in life as between races, classes, the sexes and as between metropolitan/suburban and provincial/rural populations. The typical history of educational expansion in the 1950s and the 1960s for the OECD countries can be represented by a graph of inequality between the above-mentioned social categories which has shifted markedly upwards without changing its slope. In other words, relative chances have not altered materially despite expansion.

The whole debate on equalization of life chances, and on educational opportunities in particular, was still in the early 1960s rather unsophisticated, which explained the reason why it was conceived of only as a matter of simply removing social, economic and geographical obstacles to access to further education. During the next decade a much higher level of sophistication was achieved mainly due to three circumstances.

(1) The basic problem of how individual differences in educability emerge and develop came into focus in an intensive controversy in the wake of the famous article by Arthur Jensen in the *Harvard Educational Review* of 1969 and was further analyzed and empirically studied. Benjamin Bloom has questioned certain basic notions of how, for instance, individual differences are distributed, to the extent of regarding them as "a vanishing point" in organizing classroom work.

(2) A series of important surveys of how differences of educational attainments were related to socio-cultural background were conducted and by their policy-orientation inspired a debate which brought up basic technical as well as theoretical problems. The studies by Jencks and his associates (*Inequality*, New York: Basic Books, 1972) of the development of inequalities in life chances and the IEA cross-cultural investigations of the relative importance of home and school in accounting for differences between students and school in, for instance, reading and science achievements deserve to be mentioned here.

(3) The very concept of equality, for instance, equality of opportunity versus equality of results, became the subject of thorough philosophical analysis. Before the end of the 1960s James Coleman was the only one among educational researchers who had attempted to clarify the concept. But after that a more deepened and faceted debate on equality emerged with contributions from John Rawls, Charles Frankel and others.

I shall in the following comment on these three aspects of the setting in which the issue of equality is now conceived.

How Differences In Educational Attainments Occur

The nature-nurture problem was for a long time regarded mainly as an aloof, academic issue with almost no repercussions in the general public debate. That does not mean that the problem had no policy implications. On the contrary, it had strongly influenced eugenic policy, for instance, legislation on sterilization of persons with low IQ or on setting immigration quota in the United States in the early 1920s. But until the late 1960s the matter was treated in academic aloofness and did not cause the emotional outburst that followed in the wake of the Jensen article in the *Harvard Educational Review* or Herrnstein's article on IQ in the *Atlantic Monthly* a few years later.

In an address to the American Psychological Association in 1958 Anne Anastasi pointed out that the task that lay ahead for research in the area of heredity-environment was to explore the *modus operandi* of genetic and environmental factors. They cannot, as had been assumed by most researchers in the field, be regarded as acting in an additive way. Instead the two sets of factors interact along a continuum of directness. Anastasi cites Dobzhansky, a leading geneticist, who advances a striking illustration of how interaction can take place. Suppose that all persons with blood group AB are considered to be aristocrats, while those with blood group O are considered inferior and only suited for menial labor, then blood group genes will in the course of time artificially become "determiners" of certain types of behavior. A parallel example from the real world is the effect of discrimination against a particular social class or ethnic group. In the long run this will result in group differences which are correlated with genetic background without being causally affected by them.

Certain basic circumstances have seldom been considered. In the first place there is no indication that cognitive behavior of the type assessed by intelligence tests is monogenic. Secondly, endeavors to link genetic material, once identified, with concrete cognitive behavior has not yet begun. Thirdly, the concept of "heritability" which has played a key role in the Jensen debate does not apply to individuals but is, as pointed out by Dobzhansky, a characteristic of a *population* not of a particular individual. Estimates of heritability, in case they are valid, which in itself is a doubtful proposition, are applicable only to the particular population studied by particular instruments at a particular point in time. This is a special case of the general principle that heredity is not a status but a *process*. Furthermore, in the method employed by Cyril Burt, Arthur Jensen and others, who contend that the larger portion of individual differences is attributable to genetic factors, the research findings apply only to individual differences which are studied by means of identical twins, whereas policymakers are primarily interested in group differences which are more readily manipulated by policy measures.

The polarization that in the 1970s occurred in the scholarly world with regard to the heredity-environment issue could hardly have been predicted by the late 1950s. But a decade later the political development had added new dimensions of applicability to a research field that previously had been regarded to consist of rather aloof and "pure" academic exercises. Studies of the relative importance of heredity and environment were supposed to provide answers to problems such as, "Is compensatory education worthwhile?" or "Do ghetto children fail because of innate inadequacies or because of social handicaps?" An overriding problem was to what extent the educational system could rectify social handicaps in lower class children or among racial minorities.

Prior to the Jensen debate many social scientists had shown an almost euphoric optimism about the possibilities of a system of advanced mass education, an optimism that became only slightly affected by the criticism and quest for excellence that became vociferous in the wake of the Sputnik shock in the late 1950s. Robert Faris in a Presidential Address to the American Sociological Association in 1961 was a spokesman for this optimism. It does not suffice, he said, to have a "limited stock of geniuses at the top of the productivity organization." By improving society one can also improve the conditions which promote the development of abilities. He further notes, that "a society generates its level of ability, the upper limit of which is unknown and distant," and best of all, the process of achieving that level is potentially subject to intentional control. The "boom" in formal schooling could be seen as a "potent instrument for raising the ability level of the population." The nation was at present "quietly lifting itself by the bootstraps to an important higher level of general ability."

The task of the educator is to bring about worthwhile changes in the behavior of growing or grown-up individuals. Such changes are achieved by environmental and not by genetic means and are accessible to direct observation. Since, as pointed out above, no links between specific genes and concrete cognitive behavior have been identified, the burden of proof as to how genetic factors act as restraints to educative efforts rests with the hereditarians and not with the environmentalists. Environmental influences on mental development are the only ones that can be directly observed and measured with increasingly refined techniques developed within the behavioral sciences. What remains unexplained after the environmental influences have been assigned their "share" could conditionally be referred to as genetic factors, after reasonable consideration has been given to measurement error and to theoretically important but unmeasured environmental factors.

The need to clarify conceptually the heredity-environment issue is of utmost importance since otherwise quite wrong policy implications might be drawn. It cannot be emphasized strongly enough that heredity is not a status, a kind of fixed point, but a process. The hereditary component of a personality trait, say scholastic ability, can only be inferred from a process of development that is *not directly accessible to observation and/or measurement*.

Dobzhansky (in *Genetic Diversity and Human Equality*, N.Y., 1973) has attempted to bridge the gap between social philosophy and biology in bringing out the policy implications with regard to equality of the heredity-environment issue. He emphasizes that equality should not be confused with identity. Equality is a social and not a biological concept.

Equality between various social, racial and ethnic groups has often been confused with equal representation. Over the last few decades extensive survey research has consistently found big differences between upper and lower social strata in the portion of the relevant age group that has gone to upper secondary school and university. Such imbalances provide ample justification to hypothesize that a large portion of talented youth of lower class background does not get the opportunity to enter further education and therefore belongs to the "ability reserve." But one cannot therefore immediately jump to the conclusion that any imbalance, however small it may be, is entirely due to inequality of opportunity. Dobzhansky points out that a model of full representational equality between social classes implies that *all* cognitive characteristics are determined by home background and randomly distributed over social strata. But even if we assume that genetically determined intelligence has the same distribution in all social strata, we still have to consider the "residual" factors that account for some 50 per cent of the differences in scholastic attainment and which have consistently been shown to be determined by home background, including such factors as parental education, verbal stimulation and motivational support. Individuals vary not only in their intellectual capacity but also in their ability to take advantage of opportunities offered to them. There is reason to assume that both these capacities to some extent are genetically conditioned.

Finally, equality has two aspects. It is usually conceived in terms of social Darwinism: as the right to compete with everybody else for access through the educational system to the various social positions according to the same formal conditions. That is to say, everybody should have the right to strive and compete on equal terms. Secondly, equality should also be conceived of as the right to be treated differently according to one's particular abilities and interests. Different inherited capacities require different environments if they are to develop to the satisfaction of the individual. Equality of opportunity does therefore not mean identity of treatment.

The Limited Role of the School in the "Ecology of Education"

Some thirty to forty years ago hopes were high on both sides of the Atlantic for what the school could do in what George Counts referred to as "building a new social order." After the First World War a reformist wave swept education in the industrialized world, under the auspices of among others the New Education Fellowship. The Progressive Education Association, in which Counts was playing a leading role, expected the school to assume increased responsibilities for the education of young people and for bringing about social reforms. Similar views were held by the politicians who were behind the main report of 1948 submitted by the Swedish 1946 School Commission, charged with a radical reform of the compulsory school system in the direction of comprehensivization.

> The main task of the school is to educate democratic human beings . . . . Only by means of free education can the school lay the foundations for a development of society shaped by the insight and free will of its citizens . . . . The school in a democratic society must . . . constitute a milieu for the free development of children. The individuality and the personal assets of the pupil ought not only to be considered and respected but should form the starting point for how instruction and education of the child is laid out. The work in the school ought to aim at promoting a free and harmonious development of all aspects of the personality of the pupil but should at the same time develop what is unique and special with him.

It would seem useful in this context to consider some important constraints on what the school can do and deal briefly with what Lawrence Cremin refers to as the "ecology of education." Education in the first place cannot be identified with formal schooling only. Furthermore, non-formal education is occurring in the context of other educational institutions, such as the family and mass media, whose role and impact over a short period have changed considerably. The contribution of the family to the outcomes of formal schooling has been in the focus of interest among educational researchers and policymakers on both sides of the Atlantic since the mid-1960s when the strategy of compensatory education was developed. Parents, siblings and peers, as well as churches, libraries, museums, summer camps, factories, radio stations and television networks, relate to each other what Cremin calls "configurations of education." Educational institutions and configurations have to be viewed in relation to each other and to "the larger society that sustains them and is in turn affected by them . . . ."

Profound changes in the composition of the family have over the last few years taken place in the industrialized countries, changes that have had strong repercussions on its educative functions. In the first place, the average number of children per family has declined, a change that has been particularly drastic after mid-1960s, when the pill began to have its impact. This unexpected demographic downtrend has dramatically affected the demand for teachers. After a long period of shortage, countries like England, the Federal Republic of Germany and the United States now tend to have a surplus of teachers. The great majority of families have only one child or two children. The number of single-parent families has increased rapidly and so has the number of mothers working outside the home. For example, by 1955 in Stockholm only some 15 per cent of mothers living with their husbands and having children of primary school age had full-time jobs outside the home. Two decades later their number had increased to almost 60 per cent. Three-generation families have almost disappeared. In recent years several countries have experienced a dramatic decline in birthrate that not only affects the ecology of their educational systems but also the enrollment pattern and the planning of teacher training.

All these changes in the "ecology" of education in some respects imply a broadening of the tasks of the school, but in other respects a narrowing of them. The school is supposed to take care of the children for an increased number of years during an increased part of the day. Its educative functions in a wide sense have been widened. But what about the traditional tasks of imparting certain cognitive skills: the three Rs and orientation knowledge? Relative to other institutions its role has been diminished. The school does not any longer, as was the case in the pre-industrial or neo-industrial society, possess a monopoly on imparting certain cognitive competencies. It has to compete with other institutions, such as the mass media. Out-of-school learning has gained in importance.

The survey research conducted after the mid-1960s has given rise to a lively debate about whether "school makes any difference." The Coleman survey of 1966 on equality of educational opportunity was commissioned by the United States Congress in order to evaluate the programs launched to provide education to the handicapped and ethnic minorities. The survey on 11-year-olds conducted in England by the Plowden Commission a year later aimed at disentangling the relative influences of school and home on school attainments. Jencks and his associates re-analyzed data set from other surveys in order to study the impact of IQ, home background and formal education on adult income. They concluded that the school is of marginal importance only in explaining differences in adult earnings. Finally, we could cite the IEA surveys which comprized some 20 countries with students at three levels, 10-year-olds, 14-year-olds, and 18-year-olds respectively.

We shall not enter here upon a discussion of the highly intricate technical problems, not to mention the difficult interpretation problems one encounters in studies of this kind. Suffice it to say that individual differences in educational attainments to a large extent are accounted for by non-scholastic factors. The amount of variance explained by such factors varies of course between subject areas. Thus, a large portion of the variance in reading is accounted for by home background whereas in the case of performance in a foreign language only a small portion is explained by background factors. This does not, however, justify the conclusion that the school "does not make much difference." Evidently, the laying off of the school would have catastrophic consequences in a highly complex, technological society with its complicated interaction between the school, home and other agencies within the global environment that constitutes the educational ecology. The more advanced the education of parents and the more developed their consciousness about the value of education, the greater the likelihood that their children will take advantage of school instruction.

In the light of the investigations cited above and the debates ensuing from them, we shall have to reappraise the role of the school as a competence-imparting institution in relation to other institutions, such as the family, mass media, and voluntary organizations. Such a reappraisal will help us to understand the crises that has been triggered by the discrepancy between the expectations of what the school should perform and what it is actually able to perform.

A More Faceted Conception of Equality

The roots of the classical liberal conception of quality of educational opportunity are in the eighteenth century with Locke, Helvetius, and, most important of all, Jean Jacques Rousseau. In *Le Contrat Social* of 1762 he spells out how in the "natural" state men are born equal with the rights within the framework of the "general will." There are innate differences in personal qualities but these do not jeopardize social equality as long as society rewards people according to their merits and not according to birth and wealth. A "natural aristocracy" (Jefferson) emerges in a society that dissolves the privileges that form a basis for "artificial aristocracy," an expression that means the same as "ascriptive" aristocracy in modern sociology.

The famous Preamble of the American Declaration of Independence of 1776 was first drafted by Thomas Jefferson who was strongly influenced by Helvetius and Rousseau. When he and the other Founding Fathers said that "all men are created equal" they meant that all are born with the same moral and political rights but not that they are endowed with equal capacities and qualifications. When Jefferson used the expression "natural aristocracy" he meant the same as Rousseau, namely that no artificial barriers should prevent the natural aristocracy to achieve the social status that matched their talents.

The founder of the common public school in the United States, Horace Mann, belonged to the same tradition. He saw the school as an instrument for an open society to achieve social justice, remove poverty, and achieve equality of opportunity. He is often quoted as labeling the school as the "Great Equalizer." Similar strains of thought are to be found among many of the European liberals who fought for a common basic school that would put young people on equal footing in realizing their different talents.

Equality of opportunity was by many implicitly conceived in terms of social Darwinism. As Peter Schrag put it in an article in *The Saturday Review* of 1970:

> Everyone in the jungle (or in society, or in school) was to be treated equally: one standard, one set of books, one fiscal formula for children everywhere, regardless of race, creed and color. Success went to the resourceful, the ambitious, the bright, the strong. Those who failed were stupid or shiftless, but whatever the reason, failure was the responsibility of the individual (or perhaps of his parents, poor fellow) but certainly not that of the school or the society.

The rethinking about the equality problem that has been going on in recent years has widened the perspective on the consequences of social Darwinism. The question was asked whether one should not also consider what comes out of the system, that is to say whether equality of *results* is not more important than equality of initial opportunity. The practical implication of this is that extra resources should be provided to those who are socially and culturally deprived. This has, for instance, been the philosophy behind what in the 1960s emerged as programs of "compensatory education," most well known of which has been the Headstart Program. In his 1966 report to the United States Office of Education, Coleman points out that "equality of educational opportunity implies not only 'equal' schools but equally effective schools, whose influence will overcome the differences in the starting point of children from different social groups."

The implication in terms of policy that ensues from the rethinking of the concept of equal opportunity is that it is rather pointless to put the final responsibility for scholastic success or failure on the individual. One has to shift the burden of responsibility to the system – to the educational system and/or society at large.

Dilemmas in Achieving Equality in Education

As has become increasingly evident, the traditional mode of conceiving equality in education and of framing policy to achieve equality of opportunity is beset with certain dilemmas that have seldom been made explicit.

The basic dilemma lies in the fact that the educational system is there to impart competencies and therefore by necessity creates differences. The school cannot at the same time serve as an equalizer and as an instrument that establishes, reinforces and legitimizes distinctions. As long as there is only one approved avenue to the "mainstream of dignity" for which some are selected according to one single, linear standard (bright, average, stupid) which implies that some are destined to fail, people are lured to aspire for something they are unable to achieve. To parody Orwell: those who from the outset are more equal than others will take particular advantage. In his review of the report submitted in 1973 by the Panel of Youth chaired by James Coleman, Martin Trow in discussing the policies proposed by the Panel points out the dilemma of diversity versus equality. By making a broader spectrum of formal options available to the young people for what they may want to pursue one also introduces forces that work in the direction of inequality. He says: ". . . the very qualities that make special schools attractive to voluntary choice makes them inappropriate for forced choice. Looked at the other way, the more schools are the same, the less complaint can be made there is an educational loss arising from forced assignment . . . The commitment to diversity and free choice makes an implicit assumption that all choices are equally good if they are free."

Therefore, the problem of achieving real equality of opportunity is to provide multiple options based on different values that are *not* ranked along only one dimension. We have begun to realize that uniform provision within education is not a single solution to a more equal society. As Dobzhansky has shown: equality in biological assets calls for pluralism, not identity, in treatment.

A third basic dilemma is the one between equality and meritocracy. We submit that it has become more acute in the technological complex society. It was first made explicit in a drastic way by Michael Young in his 1958 diatribe *The Rise of Meritocracy*.

T. H. Fitzgerald in his review of the report of the Panel on 'Youth' states the case very succinctly:

> We live in a country which has wanted to be equal but has also wanted to be efficient. We have believed, in a general way, in freedom for the individual, but we also wanted order, and to reward merit. We have utilized schools not only as an instrument for increasing equality (and therefore freedom), but also as a system for sorting, credentialing, and tracking, along with inculcating the values appropriate for such arrangements. A society organized around the principle of merit (or the presumption thereof) will tend to accumulate differences in life chances among its citizens. If it is to be efficient, it must set up gatekeeping and succession functions. If it is to distribute differentially whatever rewards are valued, it must enjoy legitimacy or maintain a constrained order to deal with resultant tensions. We are now more aware of how these divergent objectives and incompatible values pull us apart, but the schools are only one ground for this encounter.

The egalitarian-meritocratic dilemma cuts across various types of economies and social orders. It emerges with forcefulness in all highly industrialized countries, be they capitalist or socialist. In his book on *Coming of Post-Industrial Society*, Daniel Bell foresees a growing element of meritocracy. The movement toward the "new centrality of theoretical knowledge, the primacy of theory over empiricism, and the codification of knowledge into abstract systems of symbols that can be translated into many different and varied circumstances" means that rationality and systematized knowledge rather than property and political status become the basis of influence and power. Bell sees the ascendence of technology and increased bureaucratic controls which increase the influence of professional and scientific elites, as salient features of the post-industrial society.

The equality-meritocracy dilemma is not just one of increased power of educated intelligence. It is not just that the highly educated will become more prestigious, more influential and better paid. There is also a tendency for meritocratic prerogatives to be passed on from one generation to the next.

In the liberal conception of meritocracy a high degree of intergenerational mobility in social status due to intra-familial variation in capacity is assumed. A "just reshuffling" takes place between the social classes according to inborn capacity. Those who are born into privileged circumstances, but genetically are "regressions" towards the mean, will also regress in social status, whereas those of high genetic potential in lower classes will move upwards in status. But the notion that the social classes will "sort themselves out" according to inborn capacity between generations is not supported by particularly convincing evidence. One finds in different social orders that those who "made it" to advanced positions (not least by means of advanced education) tend to pass on their privileges to the next generation. In a society where the inheritance of wealth is nil or close to nil, the best parents in privileged positions can do is to try hard to support their children in getting access to attractive and higher education.

In the meritocratic society the passing on of achieved status from one generation to the next is a substitute for the inherited privileges of the ascriptive society. All industrial countries are very far from the inter-generational "reshuffling" of statuses believed in by those who advocate systematic meritocracy based on intellect and effort. The "new intelligentsia" in countries which have recently gained independence and/or have gone through a rapid process of modernization spearheaded by the new educated class have a vested interest in preserving the privileges that have often been won with much work and sacrifice. Lipset concludes, after having reviewed the literature on social mobility, that "advanced Communist countries have not been more successful in removing all barriers to upward social mobility than the advanced Western countries . . . . And despite the efforts of many societies to ensure that educational resources are equally available to all, everywhere lower-class children seem unable to take full advantage of them."

There is in my view an intrinsic element of meritocracy in the social fabric of advanced industrialization. It is connected with a strong demand for expertise with advanced training in fields such as administration, technology, science, and communication (in a wide sense, including teaching). The necessity during the "take-off" period towards modernization to recruit a new intelligentsia makes the social status system somewhat more fluid. Ascriptive status determined by birth and social background is partly replaced by achieved status for which education becomes increasingly important. In societies with universal secondary education and in transition to mass higher education, further education gains in importance not primarily for acquiring particular job competencies but for maintaining one's competitive power on the labor market. The employment system expects the educational system to do the sifting and sorting which in its turn makes the educational system more competitive. With job recruitment increasingly being done on the basis of certificates and degrees, the better educated have better chances of climbing the social ladder than the less educated or, at least, do not run the same risk of slipping down. Questions of examinations and grades have become increasingly controversial as a result of this development.

The impact that meritocratic factors has on a society depends upon the value attached to economic growth as a worthwhile goal and how one sees its compatibility with subjective indicators of the "quality of life." Since economic growth so closely depends on efficient utilization of modern technology and management techniques, a new premium will be put on those competencies which will guarantee success in the competition for prestigious positions and high social status.

The solution to the equality problem is in my opinion inseparably connected with how the problem of economic growth is resolved.

The Dilemma Between Equality and Excellence*†

The Changing Concept of Higher Education

A review of problems related to equality of access to higher education would make little sense if the key concepts were not spelled out. What do we mean by "higher education" and by "equality?" I have in an article in *Minerva* (Vol. 14:4, 1976-77) raised the question of the adequacy of the term "higher education". In an era when educational provision after secondary school is in some quarters conceived of as a civil right, it would seem more appropriate to define this continuing education in terms of an age or stage bracket and call it "post-secondary" or "tertiary" education. Martin Trow has advanced a taxonomy which distinguishes between three types of higher education. The first is the elitist-selective one where a small percentage, typically 5 per cent of the relevant age groups, continues formal education at the university after completing upper secondary school. This size of enrollment was characteristic of the traditional university. The next stage is mass higher education when 15 to 50 per cent of the age groups enter higher education. The third type is universal higher education when the majority of adults in one way or another enter this type of education. It appears to me self-evident that the expression "universal higher education" is a *contradictio in adjecto*, because it begs the question, "Higher than what?" Once a policy of universal access has been proclaimed, at least in theory, no great problems of equality are entailed. "Universal" is by definition equal. Access becomes everyone's birthright although even the most thoroughgoing proponents of such a system might not subscribe to Hutchins's ironic suggestion that a Bachelor's Degree should be entered on to everyone's birth certificate!

The rapidly increasing demand for higher education has to be viewed in the context of two important social forces. In the first place, it has been part and parcel of what I have referred to elsewhere as the liberal conception of equality: everyone should be given equal formal opportunity to go ahead in education. The most important opportunity in life is that of obtaining a good

* Invited address to the Third International Conference on Higher Education, University of Lancaster, England 1975, published in *Higher Education*, Vol. 5, 1976.

† Originally published as "Problems of Securing Equal Access to Higher Education: the Dilemma Between Equality and Excellence," in *Higher Education*, Vol. 5, 1976, 407–422.

education, of getting into a good school. (In the United States civil rights have legally been spelled out as equality of opportunity.) Secondly, the increased standard of living associated with the advent of the information society with its, at least until now, insatiable need for highly trained manpower has been a powerful force behind university expansion.

The very concept of higher education has considerably widened during the last two decades. It encompasses not only the type of studies to which formerly a matriculation examination from the upper-secondary, selective school granted access. Institutions of higher education now tend increasingly to become continuation schools for adults with some years of vocational experience and service stations in a system of training and retraining which has become a necessary element in a rapidly changing society with a workforce which is consequently being restructured. Since the widened opportunities and participation have almost exclusively been privileges enjoyed by the young people who came directly from secondary school, an increasing "generation gap" has emerged in regard to level of education achieved. Therefore a strategy of "recurrent education," which in some countries has been formulated as educational policy (for example by the U68 Royal Commission in Sweden) has been proposed by organizations such as the Organization for Economic Co-operation and Development (OECD). In Sweden, the new Bill on Higher Education sets aside a certain quota of places for adults above 25 with work experience.

Research-oriented and research-related higher education is in some institutions in the process of giving way to a more vocationally oriented higher education, in which undergraduate education takes the form of a "training camp." In Europe, universities were until the 1950s relatively small institutions which enrolled a select social and intellectual elite of secondary-school leavers. Some students entered professional programs in order to become doctors, lawyers, and ministers. The remainder embarked upon the rather unstructured curriculum of the faculties of philosophy which was supposed to provide not only subject-matter preparation for prospective secondary-school teachers but also the disciplinary grounding for prospective graduate students. The majority of the teaching staff consisted of chairholders, called *Ordinarien* in Germany and referred to as *baroni* in Italy. This meant that the relatively small numbers of undergraduates had quite a lot of formal and informal contact with their professors.

The research going on consisted mainly of small individual projects which were regarded by outsiders as esoteric and harmless pursuits that professors and a handful of graduate students should be free to indulge in. The ritualistic exercises in pure research were looked upon with awe by the ignorant populace and were not expected to be of any practical or social relevance. Applied research was in many instances looked upon with suspicion by the academics themselves. But this changed during and after the Second World War, when the university researchers were called upon to take on their share of the war effort. This led to a marriage between government (which provided the bulk of the research funds) and universities which has not been without friction.

Thus, the universities were dragged out of their protected sanctuary of academic obscurity. Their products became increasingly important in the planning and implementation of national policies. At the same time they became enormously expensive, which provided the stimulus for vociferous demands by political bodies of accountability.

The growth of the university in terms of both quantity of enrollment during the transition from an elite to a mass system and of diversity of functions has led to manifest tensions within the institution. The most obvious tension is the one between research and graduate education on the one hand and vocationally oriented undergraduate training on the other. In the *Minerva* article referred to above I have tried to spell out why university professors tend to be discipline-oriented and why they feel a stronger loyalty towards their university and do not care much about the relevance of the knowledge they produce. They conceive their role to be that of extending the frontiers of knowledge and of contributing to the construction of an adequate "knowledge base" which defines (for instance) a university department. The broadening of access and the increased vocationalization of programs mean that an increasing number undergraduates are less discipline-oriented than their counterparts in the European universities two decades previously. The outcome has been a mounting tension between the research system and the training system in the mass university. What Parsons and Platt refer to as the "academic core system" has tended to become more isolated not only because of the difficulties of bringing the senior researchers into classroom contact with the undergraduates but also because of differences in academic orientation and ethos. In some instances the preparation and execution of undergraduate programs and courses demands so much time that matters pertaining to research and supervision of graduate students tend to get swamped.

The development towards a "multiversity" with widely different functions of teaching, service, and research has indeed given new facets to the problem of access. Evidently, since the research function is more elitist and requires hard scrutiny and selection, access to graduate institutions has to be more restricted than to vocationally oriented *ad hoc* courses at the undergraduate level. But since graduate students would have to be recruited from the undergraduates, access to certain institutions and certain undergraduate programs might have to be designed so as to serve the academic core system.

What Should be Meant by Equality of Access?

My own position as regards the concept of equality in education is rather close to that of Mary Warnock as spelled out in an article in the *Oxford Review of Education* 1975. In the first place, it means equal benefits, rights or treatment according to some kind of principle or rule that has been laid down. It does not mean that everybody should be the same as everybody else. It does not mean, for instance, that everybody should feel obliged to go on to higher education. Somebody might simply not want such an alternative. This is one reason why it would be absurd to define equality in education between sexes, social classes and races as equal *representation*, (as the direction of affirmative action policies in the United States would sometimes seem to convey). Everyone "has an equal right to as much education as may enable him to have more if he wants it: and when he has been educated so far, he thereafter has a right to equality of *opportunity* for more. Whether he actually gets more will depend upon his inclinations, upon the amount of the commodity available, and the kind of competition involved in getting it."

The crucial thing is the amount of the "commodity" available, because, irrespective of how selection for further education is carried out, it tends to favor those of favored background. This is a lesson learned in all types of societies, even in those where some kind of positive discrimination has been tried.

Now in the mid-1970s we are both conceptually and empirically in a position to deal much more fruitfully with problems pertaining to equality of access than we were some twenty to twenty-five years ago. In the first place, we now have a more sophisticated conception of equality. Equality was formerly regarded primarily as equality of opportunity: everyone should formally "start from scratch" in the race for success in life. Furthermore, it was taken for granted that education was the main determinant of social mobility and life chances. The core idea behind the old liberal conception of equality was that the important thing was equality of starting point in the formal educational system. Thus the American school reformer Horace Mann referred to education as the "Great Equalizer." Everybody should by means of education be given the opportunity to achieve the social status to which he was entitled by his God-given inherited capacity. The main policy instruments for achieving this objective have been the removal of economic and geographical barriers to further education and provision for increased participation. Nevertheless in spite of recent explosive increases in participation, imbalances between social strata tended to remain. Research conducted during the last decade – ranging from macro-statistical surveys, such as the ones on participation and social background for the OECD Policy Conference in 1970, to micro-level studies of parent-child inter-action – has contributed to a more sophisticated conception of equality. We have as a consequence begun to realize what I have called certain "equalization incompatibilities", such as that between equality and economic efficiency, not forgetting the main theme for the present conference, that is to say, equality versus excellence.

A striking feature of the conception of the value of education during the last ten years has been the change from the optimism about what education might achieve to scepticism, not to say deep pessimism, about its potential. The mood has swung from the almost euphoric conception of education as the Great Equalizer to that of education as the Great Sieve that sorts and certifies people for their slots in society. This change is, for instance, reflected in a comparison between the reports from the OECD Conferences on Educational Policy for Economic Growth in 1961 and 1970 respectively. In the Summary report from the 1970 conference it was pointed out that policy makers a decade earlier, in envisaging a considerable expansion of education, assumed that "by making more facilities available, and distributing them properly in the right neighborhoods and areas, there would be a marked change in the social composition of the student bodies, and in the flow of people from the less favored classes into the secondary schools and the higher educational institutions. This has not happened to the degree expected." The problem, it was pointed out, "is more difficult than had been usually supposed, and needs, in fact, to be posed in new terms."

Thus, the problem was not the simple one of providing free access to further education and making provision for more education so as to increase participation. Educators have always been notorious in conceiving of their institutions as if they lived an entirely independent life in a socio-economic vacuum. During the last decade there has been a growing realization of the close relationship between the educational system and society at large. In the first place, it is not just formal education that matters when it comes to equality. By the early 1960s research had brought into focus the importance of the pre-school years. Furthermore, surveys were conducted which indicated the differences in scholastic achievement were to an astonishingly large extent accounted for by social background. The unquestioned value of formal schooling in enhancing individual life chances came under criticism. Thus it was realized that the educational system cannot serve as a substitute for social and economic reforms. One cannot have more equality in education than exists in society at large.

Will Increased Access Lower Standards?

What effects will increased access have on the intellectual level of the enrolled students?

It has been maintained by genuine conservatives that when opportunities are broadened "more means worse." That is to say, by admitting an increasing proportion of the age group one of necessity also lowers standards – in the first instance the initial cognitive competence of those who enter universities. Such a prediction can logically be expected to be valid only on the assumption that, in an elitist system, access to higher education is granted only or mainly on the basis of proven competence, and that social background plays an almost negligible role. There is, however, as I shall spell out later, abundant evidence to prove that such an assumption is false. On the contrary, empirical studies show that in highly selective systems a considerable loss of talent takes place.

All policy actions aimed at equalizing access to higher education contribute to the broadening of opportunities in terms of promoting talent (however defined) and the minimizing of the influence of social background. As we have seen, the classical liberal conception (still predominant) of how this works is that talent in all social strata is thus given the same formal chance to become developed. Also, according to this conception, talent is chiefly genetically determined and therefore constitutes a strictly limited capital: once we have taken all possible steps to detect and develop talent above a certain IQ level, further broadening of opportunities would mean lowering of standards. Thus, "talent hunting" has its own law of diminishing return.

We have for quite some time become used to the idea that intellectual competence is distributed by some kind of metaphysical necessity according to the bell-shaped probability curve, with the majority of individuals around the mean and increasingly fewer individuals the closer we move to the extremes of the curve. About one-sixth of an unsorted population is scoring one standard deviation or more above the mean. This is, by the way, the limit that Trow sets between elite and mass higher education. By enrolling more than 15 per cent of an age group we have entered the stage of the mass education university.

Before examining the proposition that an increase of enrollment beyond, say, 5 – 10 per cent of the relevant age cohort will lead to a lowering of the average intellectual level of the intake, it would be appropriate to remind ourselves that to a large extent scholastic aptitude also comprises non-cognitive attributes. Extensive empirical research tells us that at most half of the individual differences in educational attainments are attributable to purely intellectual factors. The rest may be attributed to motivation, interest, perseverance, health and, of course, home background.

The bell-shaped distribution of the IQ, as it appears when intelligence tests are administered to unsorted populations, is by no means given in the nature of things or divinely ordained. It is simply a statistical artifact of the norm-referenced procedure by means of which the tests are constructed. As can be seen in any textbook on psychological or educational measurement, items are chosen so as to cover symmetrically the entire scale of difficulty. This procedure in itself make the distribution of total scores esthetically attractive by it being symmetrical and bell-shaped. The level of intercorrelations between the items determines how slim or how flat the curve will appear. Criterion-referenced procedures of test construction come up with a quite different distribution of scores.

With these technical reservations in mind, let us now examine the empirical evidence available on the effects on intellectual standard of broadening of opportunities as part of a programme of equalization. We shall focus on three types of investigations: (1) surveys of the "reserve of talent" or "pool of ability" (2) studies of the effect on distribution of intellectual competencies when access to upper secondary and university education is expanded, and

(3) studies of the standards of the elite in comprehensive and selective systems of secondary education.

(1) Surveys on the "reserve of ability" *(Begabungsreserve)* have been conducted in countries such as Sweden, the Federal Republic of Germany, Austria, France, and the United States with the primary aim of assessing what proportion of an age cohort possesses the ability to profit from further formal education, (in most cases upper secondary education preparatory to attendance at university) and what proportion has not had the opportunity or has not taken advantage of it in spite of scoring above a certain level. I have reviewed this research in some detail in an OECD-sponsored monograph from 1975. Suffice it to underline here that the very expression "reserve of ability" is scientifically misleading, since it suggests that there is a genetically fixed pool which has to be detected in order to be developed. The rapporteur of the OECD conference in 1961 on *Ability and Educational Opportunity*, Professor A. H. Halsey, pointed out that the metaphor is scientifically misleading, because it suggests a fixed pool of talent in the population. But there are sources of evidence in social science research which indicate that the pool of talent is to some extent (and I repeat, *to some extent*) expandable. Follow-up studies conducted by myself and my co-workers show that IQ can be considerably "improved" by additional formal education. Cross-sectional studies of successive age cohorts, such as those conducted by the Scottish Council for Educational Research, show improved standards of performance noticeable over a period of some ten to fifteen years.

Back in the 1940s, when I published the first surveys in Sweden on the "reserve of ability," employing a rather crude methodology, I arrived at the in my own view conservative estimate that some 15 per cent of an age cohort was capable of passing the matriculation examination which was the prerequisite for university entry. Since at that time only some 5 per cent of an age group actually took the examination, it appeared ridiculous to maintain that almost twice as many belonged to the "reserve." I even dared in a subsequent article to maintain that the intellectual capital of a nation is not a fixed asset but is subject to influences by the social and economic policies adopted, by means of which it can be expanded and better utilized to the benefit both of the individual and of society. I noted in 1968 when the matriculation examination was abolished in Sweden that some 20 per cent of the age group had actually passed the examination that year. The overwhelming majority among them went to the university. Thus, the "reserve" by far exceeded the size that some twenty years earlier had been regarded as ridiculous.

(2) During the period 1918 to 1943 the enrollment in high school in the United States more than doubled from some 12 to 25 per cent. Finch collected information on the distribution of intelligence test scores for high school students during the entire period. In addition, he compared two high-school populations from the same area of the state of Illinois, the first having been

tested at the beginning of the 1920s and the second more than twenty years later. The mean scores for all the former investigations were plotted against the time axis. The ensuing curve showed an upward trend. The area study also came out with an increased mean. Thus, in spite of the strongly increased enrollment, there was over the twenty-five year period a slight improvement in the average mental ability of high-school students. Berdie and his associates found the same trend in the state of Minnesota from 1928 to 1960.

Taubman and Wales collated information on intellectual level in terms of IQ over the period 1920 to 1965 in a study conducted for the Carnegie Commission on Higher Education. During the period covered by the investigation the average level of ability among college entrants has risen from the 53rd to somewhere between the 60th and 65th percentile among an unsorted population of high-school leavers. The differences between entrants and non-entrants during the same period *increased* considerably: from 5 to some 25 to 30 percentile points. These findings indicate that intellectual capacity as measured by scholastic aptitude or IQ tests plays a more important role now than some forty to fifty years ago in determining entry to higher education, at least in the United States. There are indications that the same applies to recent European developments in university enrollment. The "loss of talent" which I once referred to in a paper on selectivity and dropout in secondary education seems to have diminished in recent times – most likely, and in spite of remaining social imbalances, as a result of the broadening of opportunities both in terms of places available and the removal of geographical and economic barriers to further education. In fact, as far as the United States is concerned, the increase in the number of high-school graduates entering college has been particularly marked in the upper quartile of the aptitude distribution.

(3) One hypothesis pertaining to the structure of secondary education which was tested in a series of surveys evaluating national systems of education (the so-called IEA-project), was stated in popular language: more means worse. Put less succinctly, will the level of achievement of the elite – say, the top 5 – 10 per cent of the students – be lower in systems with a higher enrollment ratio than in those with a low enrollment ratio? The comparison between upper-secondary school leavers from some 20 countries, conducted in subjects such as mathematics and science, showed, as one might expect, that the average performance of *all* students was much lower in countries with an almost universal secondary education than in those where the system was still an academically-oriented one catering to an elite. Thus, high-school seniors in the United States were far below their agemates in the French *lycée*, the German *gymnasium* and the sixth form of the English grammar school. But if comparisons were made between the average level of achievement of the *same percentage* of the relevant age group (such comparisons being made under the assumption that those who had not reached the end of secondary school or even entered it would not show up in the top if tested)

countries with a high enrollment rate at the end of secondary school had the same standard of their top students as those with a lower enrollment rate. For instance, the top 5 per cent of the 18-year-olds in the United States scored at the same level as their agemates in France, Germany or England.

Thus, we can to a considerable extent stretch the cognitive capital. But, evidently, a certain level of enrollment constitutes a point of diminishing return in terms of pure intellectual assets, even if they are promoted by the most progressive social and economic policy. We should, again, not forget that academic pursuits also depend to a large extent upon motivation, interest, and perseverance. This applies not least to the high-level academic pursuits that we call research.

Stategies of Admission to Higher Education

In a clarifying analysis of the role of individual differences Härnqvist distinguishes between three models of admission to higher education: (a) competitive selection, (b) non-competitive admission, and (c) adaptation through placement. Since the third of these must still be regarded as a purely academic exercise, I shall confine my comments to the first two models.

Competitive selection has two basic characteristics: the number of places is fewer than the number of applicants and the instruments of selection (such as marks, examinations, achievement and/or scholastic aptitude tests) are derived from within the educational sphere. Criteria of outcomes or of competence achieved are almost never derived from the vocational sphere. Thus, both selection instruments and criteria of proficiency are taken from the educational domain. Educators want good and docile students. The most secure way of guaranteeing that the selection works according to their intentions is to apply their own criteria of assessment. The narrowness of criteria has certain consequences. In the first place, docility and scholastic receptivity is overemphasized at the cost of other talents such as practical and social intelligence or creativity. Secondly, the system can easily assume a strong built-in social bias and can work against efforts to equalize admission. Traits that constitute docility are correlated with social background and are part of the parental heritage in homes from which students entering higher education have traditionally been recruited.

Non-competitive admission simply means that attempts are made to accommodate all applicants who meet certain minimum basic requirements which will make them profit from higher education. This strategy has been brought to the fore by the tremendously increased diversification of secondary-school leavers during the last two decades. The traditional school-leaving examination, be it *Abitur, baccalauréat* or *A-level,* cannot in a pluralistic system of higher education any longer serve as a uniform entrance ticket to a higher education that in its turn has also become increasingly diversified and special-ized. This was the main reason why, for instance, the matriculation examina-tion was abolished in Sweden. In addition to secondary-school leavers, an increasing number of adults with work experience is entering the university, mostly for short-term "packages" of training. These students have widely different backgrounds not only in terms of formal education but particularly in work and other types of experience which can be brought to bear on their studies.

The admission problem then is to determine the prerequisites which the students must meet in order to profit from higher education in general and specific programs or courses in particular.

Specific Problems of Access to the "Multiversity"

Given the changes in the systems of higher education that were briefly sketched above, the problem of equality of access cannot be solved by advancing a simple formula. It is, indeed, as multifaceted as the institutions of higher education themselves.

My analysis of entrance requirements to what I prefer to call postsecondary or tertiary education is based upon the following assumptions. In the first place, I assume a system of mass higher education moving towards a system of universal education. Secondly, I envisage a political commitment on the part of society to support such a system. Thirdly, I envisage a system of basic courses, either single or "packaged" in programs or lines of study, with the aim of providing marketable competencies. Under such assumptions the admission policy would have to be rather liberal and flexible. Depending upon the degree of discipline-orientation of the studies and the level of abstraction of the subject matter, certain basic requirements would have to be established, including:

(1) Communication skills, consisting of reading comprehension and the ability to express oneself orally and in writing in one's mother tongue. For students in countries outside the areas where the world languages are spoken, good reading comprehension in one of these languages would be a require-ment;

(2) Study skills, which to some extent are by-products of previous studies. Applicants with very limited formal schooling but with promise would have to take an introductory compensatory course in this field.

(3) Study interests and some motivation are obviously necessary prerequi-sites.

As pointed out above, in countries with a uniform state system of higher education more attention would have to be paid to the recruitment of undergraduates who could be expected to possess the potential for post-graduate studies and research training. In the United States this problem has been resolved primarily through the existence of a private sector which has traditionally played a leading role not least in research and has therefore developed centers of excellence with a national recruitment of top-level undergraduates, a high proportion of whom proceeds to graduate studies. But differentiation also exists within the state systems, the most outstanding example being the University of California.

The required competencies for higher education in Sweden have been considered by two Royal Commisions since the mid-1960s. The first commission based its considerations on the reform of the *gymnasium*, which traditionally had been the preparatory form of education for university entrance. The enrollment and the programs of the *gymnasium* had been considerably broadened (provisions were made for some 90 per cent of the age cohort which completed the comprehensive school) which evidently had certain consequences in terms of requirements for entry into higher education. The commission made a fruitful distinction between general and special competencies. The former consisted of the competencies and skills needed for studies in higher education in general. The latter referred to the special field of study the applicant wanted to enter. Legislation based on the work of the first commission was passed in 1972: the two year course in the *gymnasium* (instead of, as earlier, the three year course) was made the general qualification for entrance to higher education, provided that a certain standard has been achieved in the mother tongue and English. In the meantime, a pilot program had been launched in which adults who had reached the age of 25 and had at least five years of work experience could be admitted *ad hoc* irrespective of formal schooling.

The second commission was appointed in order to consider the consequences for admission to higher education implied in the terms of reference and later the recommendations advanced by the U68 Commission (appointed in 1968) that drew up a completely new blueprint for the system of higher education in Sweden. U68 started its work in a period when higher education was expanding by leaps and bounds, and its terms of reference reflected the impact of the explosion in enrollments. At the same time that the new system of higher education was conceived as an instrument of equalization – not least in providing opportunities for adults, who earlier had "missed out" to go back to education within the framework of a strategy or recurrent education – it was made explicit by the Government that the financial resources available would not make it possible to universalize higher education. Some kind of selection would therefore have to take place, with two main quota, secondary-school leavers and adults with work experience. These quotas had to be accommodated within a total annual intake decided upon by the government. This is the meaning of the so-called "total dimensioneering" of the system.

The 1972 commission on qualifications for higher education submitted its report in 1974 in time for consideration in conjunction with the preparation of legislation ensuing from the recommendations of the U68 Commission. In considering various methods of selection the Commission decided to propose that in addition to school marks from the *gymnasium* (which had been used for a long time as selection instrument for "closed" subjects such as medicine or engineering) one would qualify on the basis of age, work experience and scholastic aptitude test scores. All involved agreed that a good system of guidance would have to be created in order to cater particularly for adults with widely varying background in terms of formal schooling and work experience. The technical problem, as Härnqvist points out, involves establishing appropriate "cutting scores" with regard to aptitude. It was eventually decided that applicants could, if they wished, refer to their aptitude test scores, but the scores could not be used to their disadvantage. The new legislation passed in connection with the U68 recommendations makes provisions for a nation-wide testing program, which is something quite new to Sweden.

There is no doubt in my mind that a system which takes into account non-educational criteria, such as work experience, will better serve a system of mass education at the postsecondary level, where the majority of students, be they secondary-school leavers or adults with job experience, have rather structured career plans. They want to obtain marketable skills and knowledge. An open, non-competitive admission strategy as far as it is financially feasible, is the natural one in such a system.

The recruitment of prospective researchers and scholars is another matter. Evidently, many of those who proceed to more advanced studies have to be recruited among undergraduates who at the outset did not plan to go on to advanced studies. Here the competitive selection strategy applies. It could even be considered to recruit at a few institutions undergraduates who show particular promise for advanced studies.

Concluding Observations

An overarching problem, that some who are interested in higher education today are trying to come to grips with, is whether a mass postsecondary or tertiary education can be accommodated within the shell of the traditional university, where scholarly functions, such as basic research and graduate training, are by definition pursuits for which a few are selected. Nobody would seriously advocate an open admission to graduate institutions or departments. Since the latter are the institutionalized organs in our society responsible for the extension of the frontiers of knowledge and for training in the various academic disciplines, they indeed deserve the label suggested by Parsons and Platt, namely the "academic core system." As I have mentioned earlier and discussed in more detail in a separate publication, the scholarly core functions which are germane to the university easily come in conflict with a cafeteria-type system of vocationally oriented courses. Modes of teaching, administration and governance tend to differ between the two domains. The discipline-oriented academics are in the first place loyal to their disciplines, departments, and to the international community of scholars in their particular field. An elaborate cafeteria system calls for an elaborate machinery of coordination and administration with a big staff responsible for registration, counselling, accounting, evaluation and many other functions. Decision-making by necessity has to take place according to the "vertical" or hierarchical principle. Traditional university governance in scholarly affairs has been collegial or "horizontal." Decision-making prerogatives have been based on successively assessed academic competence. This assessment is traditionally the only hierarchical element in academia.

What kind of solutions would have to be contemplated that will overcome the tension between the mass tertiary education functions on the one hand and the so-called core functions on the other? Several students of the "multiversity," for instance James Coleman, have asked themselves whether the solution would be to differentiate between the two main functions, that is to say, to separate radically one way or another research and graduate training on the one hand and the system of basic and/or undergraduate courses on the other in the sense of assigning them to different decision-making and administrative machineries. Whether there should be a complete institutional divorce or a loose association between the two would seem to be a matter of convenience depending, among other things, upon historic circumstances. It should be pointed out to those who think that research and teaching have always been united in a harmonious marriage and that university teaching without close contact with active research is impossible, that the "marriage" in those countries where it took place was relatively recent. It first occurred in Germany during the nineteenth century and the alliance was copied in, other countries, not least in the United States. In France the major portion of research goes on outside the universities in the Centres de Recherche Scientifique. In the Soviet Union research takes place mainly under the aegis of the academies, as it did in the rest of Europe before the middle of the last century.

Irrespective of whether the marriage between undergraduate teaching and research is dissolved, or whether the partners remain in some kind of loose relationship with each other, the present situation calls for different models of admission to higher education. We can, by and large, distinguish two types of students who enroll at research-oriented institutions at the tertiary level. One category comprises those who are more or less oriented towards a certain vocational sector, or even a specific occupation, and who want to acquire competence for that sector or that occupation as readily and efficiently as possible. The second category, being in a minority, is primarily intellectually oriented. Their major concern is not to prepare for a particular occupational slot but to broaden their perspective. They want the university to help them to open up new vistas. The latter group has, of course, in recent years also become increasingly preoccupied with finding a livelihood after completing their studies, which, however, are not primarily regarded as a means of achieving that goal.

Research-based university teaching in almost every country which has experienced the enrollment explosion, has to be limited, for reasons of financial stringency, to a few institutions. These institutions would have to consider appropriate methods of enrolling undergraduates who showed particular promise as potential scholars and researchers.

I pointed out at the beginning of my presentation that the problem of achieving equality in higher education is a complex one, simply because higher education itself is so complex. The present-day university, to use the expression coined by Parsons and Platt, consists of a whole "bundle" of the most diverse functions and activities. When policy makers talk of bringing about equality of access and opening the universities and taking care of those adults who "missed out," they have in mind the increasing majority of people who want the institutions of higher education to give them competencies that will enhance their subsequent career economically or rather in terms of *opening up new options* and creating more flexible occupational careers.

The professors are at least as interested in those students whose interests are primarily academic and who are willing to devote their life to scholarly pursuits.

Implications for Educational Policy of Individual Differences in Learning Ability: A Comparative Perspective*

Introductory Observations

The way individual differences are perceived and taken into account in organizing formal education in various national systems is, indeed, worthy of study from a comparative point of view. The way individual differences are perceived with regard to origin and size as well as the practices that ensue from these perceptions reflect differences between political ideologies closely related to social and economic orders that vary from country to country.

Problems related to individual differences and their policy implications surfaced when society began to change from an ascriptive one, where everybody had to remain in the class or caste into which he was born, to a society of mobile social status where status attainment increasingly depended on educational achievements. Problems of differentiation and uniformity of school provisions are products of the era of the liberal philosophy of equality of educational opportunity. Large-scale surveys by means of intelligence tests first emerged in England and were children of the eugenics movement initiated by Francis Galton. He was interested in mapping the differences between social classes in terms of intelligence with the purpose of eliminating "inferior" genes that were threats to the British race. In the United States, Lewis Terman's genetic studies of genius were partly conducted in the British tradition. Intelligence tests were also to be used as instruments in discovering the scarce gold of talent among the mass of young people. On the other hand, there was among American liberals with affiliations in social psychology and the melting pot ideas the concept of intellectual ability as being mainly influenced by environmental factors.

It would, indeed, be tempting to try to review comprehensively the nature-nurture controversy with regard to its educational implications, particularly since over many years I have devoted a considerable part of my own research to studies of how social factors influence cognitive performance. But since I

* Reprinted from "Policy Implications of Individual Differences in Learning Ability: A Comparative Perspective," by T. Husén from the *Scandinavian Journal of Educational Research*, Vol. 22:4, 1978, 173–191, by permission of Universitetsforlaget, Oslo.

shall concentrate on how various national systems have responded to individual differences by the degree of differentiation of educational provisions, I shall here limit myself to a few summary observations.

The nature-nurture controversy was for a long time regarded mainly as an aloof, academic issue with no particular relevance for the general public. But by the early 1970s a strong polarization occurred that could hardly have been predicted a decade earlier. The 1960s had added new political dimensions of applicability to a field of research that earlier had been regarded as "pure" and ivory-tower academic. Studies of the relative importance of heredity and environment were expected to provide answers to problems such as "Is compensatory education worthwhile?" or "How should one differentiate between the more gifted and the rest of the pupils and at what age?". An overriding problem in many countries was to what extent the educational system was able to rectify social handicaps in lower class children and racial minorities.

Certain basic circumstances have seldom been considered in the nature-nurture debate. In the first place, the type of behavior assessed by so-called intelligence tests is not monogenic. Secondly, nobody has been able to link genetic material, once identified, with this kind of cognitive behavior. Thirdly, the concept of "heritability" which has played a key role in the Jensen debate does not apply to individuals but is, as pointed out by Dobzhansky, a characteristic of a population, not of a particular individual. Estimates of heritability, in case they are valid, which in itself is a doubtful proposition, are applicable only to the particular population studied by particular instruments at a particular point in time. This is a special case of the general principle that heredity is not a status but a *process*. Furthermore, in the method employed by Burt, Jensen and others, who contend that the larger portion of individual differences is attributable to genetic factors, the research findings are valid only for those *individual* differences which are studied by means of identical twins, whereas policymakers are primarily interested in *group* differences which are more readily manipulated by policy measures.

The task of the educator is to bring about worthwhile changes in the behavior of individuals. Such changes are achieved by environmental and not by genetic means and are accessible to direct observation. Since no links between specific genes and concrete cognitive behavior have been identified the burden of proof as to how genetic factors act as restraints to educative efforts rests with the hereditarians and not with the environmentalists. Environmental influences on mental development are the only ones that can be directly observed and measured with increasingly refined techniques developed within the behavioral sciences. What remains unexplained after the environmental influences have been assigned their "share" could conditionally be referred to as genetic factors, after reasonable consideration has been given to measurement error and to theoretically important but unmeasured environmental factors.

The need to clarify conceptually the heredity-environment issue is of utmost importance since otherwise quite wrong policy implications might be drawn. It cannot be emphasized strongly enough that heredity is not a status, a kind of fixed point, but a process. The hereditary component of a personality trait, say scholastic ability, can only be inferred from a process of development that is *not directly accessible to observation and/or measurement.*

Before attempting to review how the diversity-uniformity problem has been dealt with in various national systems of education, which operate under different social and economic orders and with different historical background, I shall deal briefly with the equality problem which has taken such a prominent place in recent educational policy and rhetoric.

The Quest for Equality

Considerations about diversity and unity in education have a long history in Western Europe and North America that go back to Helvetius and to Rousseau's famous *"Discours sur l'Inégalité parmi les Hommes"* of 1755. Since all human beings have the same political rights as reflected in their right to vote in general elections, they also have the same right to basic education. The issue over the last decades has been to what extent this provision should be common or not, that is to say how far up in the system children from all walks of life should be accommodated under the same roof and if and when separate provisions for an intellectual and/or social élite should be allowed.

Apart from giving everybody his chance to go ahead in society, the quest for equality has another aspect: In order to work, democracy in the modern, complex technological society requires a citizenry not only with a high level of education, but also with a common frame of reference – that is, common in terms of basic skills, notions, and basic values as well. This idea played an important part in the deliberations of the School Commission of 1957 in Sweden which gave the final shape to the comprehensive school on the basis of pilot programs.

A main argument behind the establishment of comprehensive secondary schools in the United States was of a similar kind: the melting-pot philosophy. The children of the immigrants should via the school system be brought into the "mainstream." The school gave them either by indoctrination or by implication new civic values. They learned to master a new language which was the basic prerequisite for obtaining a new frame of reference common with those who were already in the mainstream.

In Western and Northern Europe labor in large quantities has in recent years been imported from the Mediterranean area, that is to say, from areas with often poor school provisions. Millions of *Gastarbeiter* or guestworkers have poured into France, the Federal Republic of Germany and Scandinavia, either temporarily or for good. In Sweden they can now after a certain time vote in local elections without holding Swedish citizenship. Ten per cent of the school children come from homes where Swedish is not usually spoken. This has led to massive attempts to assist these children in taking advantage of what is offered in the public school system but in a somewhat different way than under a melting-pot philosophy. Thus, efforts are made to avoid that the immigrant children become crippled in their mastery of both their mother tongue and the language of their new country. In urban areas where the great majority of the immigrant workers have settled, teachers, mostly from the home country, on an individual basis give at least weekly lessons in their mother tongue and assist the Swedish teachers in taking care of immigrant children in other subjects. Thus, one wants to avoid the alienation between not only the children and their parents that easily occurs when they find that the new language is the only valued means of communication, but also the downgrading of their background and national heritage that easily follows.

How the Diversity-unity Problem has been dealt with in Different National Systems of Education

It is, indeed trivial to note that educational policy is closely related to the general policy of a national system which in its turn reflects the prevailing social and economic order in the particular country as well as its historical traditions. When comparing various national systems with regard to how they try to come to grips with problems of individual and group differences in devising policies of admission, school structure, promotion and examinations, such policies have self-evidently to be viewed and analyzed in a wider societal framework.

An overriding issue in education in the highly industrialized countries with their increased geographical and social mobility enhanced by education has been how to establish greater formal equality of opportunity. In most social systems, even in those that are relatively ascriptive and show little social mobility, ardent lip service is paid to the principle of equality, particularly with regard to access to education beyond mandatory schooling. The catchphrase used to characterize the efforts to implement policies to this effect has been to "democratize education."

The liberal version of this policy under the heading of equality of educational *opportunity*, whereas the more radical, but not necessarily marxist version carries the banner of equality of *results* or equality of life chances. The liberals put more emphasis on self-development or self-realization, whereas the radicals stress the development of capacities that will serve human collectivity. I shall in what follows try to illustrate how these philosophies have materialized in educational policies in various national systems.

The two main forces between recent expansion at the secondary and tertiary level have in the first place been the social demand spurred by the increased standard of living resulting from economic growth boosted by the mobilization of highly skilled technical manpower for rapid industrialization. The expansion at the secondary level put the following problem in focus: How much parallelism should be allowed in a system that allegedly is designed to provide equality of opportunity? More specifically, at what age should the students considered to be academically talented be separated from their non-academic classmates? Furthermore should they transfer to another program in a separate school, to another program in the same school, or simply to separate classes within the same program in the same school? The heading for this set of problems has in the Swedish school debate been "differentiation." The starting point of all debates on differentiation is the commonplace observation that pupils differ greatly with regard to abilities and interests. The way such differences have to be taken care of has until recently overtly been conceived almost entirely in pedagogical terms, that is to say, in classroom practices pertaining to grouping and methods of instruction. The debate has purportedly dealt with the effects of various practices in terms of student competence: What could be considered most "efficient" – restricted ability ranges at the secondary level or more or less unrestricted ranges of ability? But behind this has loomed the growing awareness that basically this is a problem of career opportunities.

Three types of models

There are essentially three typical solutions to the problem of how individual and group differences are taken into account in designing educational systems so as to make provisions for individual differences.
These are:

(1) The *American* model with the primary and then the comprehensive high school which accommodates all or most of the students from a given catchment area under the same roof but with differentiation by means of programs and ability grouping or homogeneous grouping within programs. Between-school and between-region diversification is built into the system by provisions for local autonomy and by the existence of parochial schools.

(2) The *Western European* model with a transfer of a selected elite from primary to secondary academic school before the end of mandatory schooling. Such a transfer has until recently typically taken place after four or five years of primary school but has gradually been postponed by means of the introduction of "orientation cycles" and other practices. In some countries provisions for the entire mandatory school attendance is under one roof, at least in one type of school.

(3) The *Eastern European* model of a unitary school (*Einheitsschule, école unique*) that integrates all types of schools covering compulsory school age, be they academic or vocational.

By no means all national systems of education can be fitted into this procrustian scheme. But at least most of the systems in the industrialized countries can. Japan, however, could be regarded as a special case due to particular historical and cultural circumstances. It offers the paradox of providing opportunities for further schooling for a much higher portion of the young people than most European countries but is at the same time characterized by an internal differentiation and a tough competition for entry into the prestige institutions which goes far beyond the most selective systems in Western Europe. In his book *Das Dilemma der modernen Bildungsgesellschaft* (Stuttgart 1976). (The Dilemma of the Modern Educative Society) Ulrich Teichler has described the "educative meritocracy" of Japan and its status-distributive function.

The American model. The common public school which provided basic formal education to all children in a given area epitomizes the classical American conception which is represented by Horace Mann of the school spearheading democracy and progress against conservative forces.

The American comprehensive high school was in a way a materialization of the American Dream of equal opportunity. By being exposed to a uniform pedagogic milieu with equal resources and by being mixed with age mates from all social strata and ethnic groups equality of life chances would in a mysterious way be achieved. But the conception of equality of educational opportunity that emerged from the era of social Darwinism was beset with a basic dilemma. The massive surveys that were conducted in the 1960s, such as the Coleman report in the United States, the Plowden report in England, and the IEA 20-country study, revealed that social background accounted for more between-student and even between-school differences in student achievement than did school resources. One began to realize that the school cannot at the same time serve as an equalizer and as an instrument that establishes, reinforces and legitimizes distinctions. There is to a varying degree inherent in the educational system an incompatibility between selectivity and equality. A young radical American educational sociologist, Jerome Karabel has stated the problem in the following somewhat provocative way:

> The ideology of academic standards brilliantly reconciles two conflicting American values: equality and equality of opportunity. Through the system of public education everyone is exposed to academic standards, yet only those who succeed in meeting them advance in our competitive system. Everyone enters the educational contest, and the rules are usually applied without conscious bias. But since the affluent tend to be most successful, the net result of the game is to perpetuate intergenerational inequality. Thus academic standards help make acceptable something which runs against the American grain: the inheritance of status.

Benjamin Bloom has been questioning the entire concept of individual differences in achievement which has served as an axiomatic foundation of school practices over the last century when primary schooling has become universal in the industrialized world. Student performances are judged against uniform, linear standards (bright, average, slow learner, or whatever labels we want to use). In such a system some are destined to fail and some to succeed, irrespective of their absolute achievements. A student who belongs to the bottom group in a school with high standards perceives himself as a failure, even if his attainments by national norms are far above average. Conversely a student with the same absolute level of performance perceives himself as a success in a school with low standards. Such perceptions are strongly affecting student motivation which in its turn contributes to widen differences in attainments.

Instead of serving as an equalizer of life chances, as envisioned by nineteenth century liberals, the common school in modern society tends to contribute to social differentiation.

The Western European model. The Western European model has for a long time been characterized by parallelism between the upper grades of the elementary school and the selective junior secondary school. This structure has recently gradually become modified by reduction of the number of parallel grades and increased comprehensivization. In addition, selectivity at both primary and secondary level has operated by means of repetition and dropout. I shall illustrate the model and how it has become modified with four countries: the Federal Republic of Germany, France, England, and Sweden.

Well into the 1960s the decisive juncture in the educational (and life) careers of young people in *Germany* was at the age of 10 when transfer on a selective basis took place to the nine year *Gymnasium*, which prepared for the university. Some 20–25 per cent were selected for the *Gymnasium* or the middle school. Of these only one-third or one-fourth graduated with an *Abitur*, which served as a uniform entrance ticket to the university.

As pointed out, structural parallelism was combined with repetition to the extent that it was referred to in the German debate as the *Sitzénbleiberelend* (repetition misery). Repetition was even more frequent among the select group of *Gymnasium* students than among those in the *Volksschule* (primary school).

The pronounced selective features of the German system contributed to the crystallization of the tremendous imbalances between social strata in terms of participation in secondary and higher education. In the early 1960s Ralf Dahrendorf showed that 50 per cent of the university students came from homes of civil servants and professionals, who represented some 1 per cent of the work force, whereas 1 per cent came from working class homes who made up 50 per cent of the work force. The IEA surveys showed that the Federal Republic of Germany had the most pronounced social bias in the social composition of upper secondary school enrollment among all the participating countries.

The reform movement, finally epitomized in the *Strukturplan* of the German Educational Commission (Deutscher *Bildungsrat* 1970) and in the ensuing policy document, the *Bildungsbericht '70*, issued by the Brandt government in 1970, contributed to modifications of the parallelism and to lessening of the selectivity. The changes were, however, considerably more modest than envisaged by the proponents of the reform that in the 1970s got stalled in financial and other difficulties. A development towards less parallelism was furthered by the extension of schooling up through the junior secondary stage so as to make it universal. In several German states experiments began to be carried out with a "promotion stage" (*Förderstufe*). Its aim was similar to that of the "observation cycle" in France namely to postpone a definitive allocation to a particular academic or non-academic program from the age of 10 or 11 to some years later. In, for instance the Land of Hesse a pilot program with a nine year comprehensive school (*Gesamtschule*) was launched.

The *Bildungsbericht* envisaged every young person attending school until 16. The soaring enrollment at the German universities led in the early 1970s to a *numerus clausus* which elicited an enraged debate about fairness and justice in selection and to concerns about the repercussions on the lower stages in terms of performance pressure and competition (*Leistungsdruck*). Thus, paradoxically, the widening of opportunities has in its wake increased competition at the primary and secondary stages and in selection for university entrance, which was something new in Germany.

The famous 1959 decree in *France* which followed upon a long stalemate of structural reform, modified the selective and differentiating features at the junior secondary level, i.e. the age range 11 through 15. Compulsory schooling was extended from 14 to 16. Provisions were made for an "observation cycle" (*cycle d'observation*) before the pupils were definitively allocated to different types of secondary schools. The rapid expansion of the *collèges d'enseignement général* led to making them part of a common system of basic education.

A striking feature of the French school system in differentiating students has been the frequent practice of grade repetition. Thus, as late as in the 1960s some 30 per cent of the pupils in the first grade of primary school repeated the grade. At the end of grade 5 of primary the average student had 1.6 repetitions. This affected students of low socio-economic status several times more often than those from high socio-economic status. In connection with an OECD review 1969 on French educational policy and planning I visited the headquarters of the primary school teachers' union. I asked the union leaders whether they were concerned about the statistics on repeating. The answer was "no:" they regarded it as a quite natural practice that was to the benefit of all categories of students. This incident has been added to the storage of experiences I have on how blind we are to the dysfunctions of our own system that we even regard them as reflections of a natural order of things!

The 1944 Education Act in *England* made provision for universal secondary education up to 15. At 11 allocation or rather selection for grammar school education on the basis of academic criteria had to take place. The Act that allegedly was a "breakthrough" of democratization of further education, where places for "scholarship boys" from working-class homes were no longer reserved proved not to level out the imbalances between social classes in institutions of post-compulsory education. On the contrary: as Jean Floud and her co-workers showed, imbalances grew worse, since the middle-class 11 year-olds were more successful in competing for grammar school places than were working-class ones. Thus, among British radicals the 1944 reform was not looked upon as an instrument of equalizing opportunity as did its liberal proponents. The Labour Party policy has been to comprehensivize secondary education and in government it has intermittently tried to push the LEAs to "go comprehensive" and to abolish the sorting of students at the age of 11. The 11+ examination is gradually vanishing.

The comprehensivization policy, particularly attempts to abolish the 11+ examinations and the practice of "streaming " at the primary level, have been two prime targets of the "Black Papers," authored by a group of conservatives. It was maintained that recent changes have brought about a marked decline in standards. The "ideology of egalitarianism" was accused of doing away with the "essential toughness" on which quality depends. A case was made for the élitist system on the basis of research on individual differences conducted among others by Sir Cyril Burt, himself a contributor to the "Black Papers." Burt contended that scholastic aptitude was largely inherited and sided with the conservatives in defending the élitest grammar school.

The case of Sweden. In order to resolve the controversy over parallelism versus comprehensivization, that is to say, how much differentiation and how much unity in school structure is appropriate, policy makers in *Sweden* have since the 1940s turned to behavioral scientists, in the first place to educational psychologists. The case seemed *prima facie* to be a clear-cut one. Once psychologists had mapped out how individual differences developed, proper conclusions for educational policy could easily be drawn. If differences in scholastic aptitude were due mainly to genetic factors and if schooling could achieve modest modifications only, differentiated provisions had to be made in order to avoid "fighting against nature." The school had to be structured – according to the principle: to everybody according to his inborn capacity. On the other hand, if the margin of influence on scholastic aptitude open to environmental factors was large, then schooling could take place in a more unified structure.

Let me use the following case as an illustration. The Swedish School Commission, that in its main report of 1948 drew up the blueprint for a comprehensive nine-year school, sponsored a massive research project on "practical" and "theoretical" aptitudes and how they developed in school children. Successive age groups from 7 through 16 were tested with extensive test batteries that were then factor-analyzed in order to reveal the "ability structure and factorial maturity." The purpose of this research endeavor was to get an answer to the question as to when the two types of abilities were sufficiently differentiated to allow diagnosis and allocation to academic and vocational tracks respectively. The investigations indicated, or seemed to indicate, that theoretical or general intelligence was much easier to identify than practical intelligence. It was more simple and unitary, practical aptitude was more complex and matured later. Academic aptitude could be identified already at the age of 11 but the problem was a substantial positive correlation between the two types of aptitude. About half the unsorted population of 11-year olds were found to be not decidedly practical or theoretical, whereas about one quarter was predominantly theoretical and one quarter predominantly practical.

Having been given the "facts", however imperfect, one would have expected the Commission to recommend differentiated provisions for the group that could be diagnosed as theoretical. But the snag was, of course, the correlation between the two types of aptitudes. An early differentiation could result in premature decisions taken for many who, for instance, had both a practical and theoretical bent. In addition to consideration to the correlation between the two aptitudes and the later maturation of practical abilities, the Commission advanced a potent political argument in favor of postponed differentiation. If scholastic aptitude were to be the determining factor in allocating students to different tracks at an early age (say 11), the theoretical track would then receive not only pupils with high scholastic and low practical ability but also the élite who were high on both. This would mean that most of the gifted students would be channeled to professions and that the "manual occupations would be deprived of people with high general ability. This would result in successively lowering their prestige and in creating a gap between social classes and thereby bring democracy into jeopardy." If the final decision about what "side" in terms of amount of academic schooling a pupil was to obtain was postponed until the end of junior secondary school, when the special abilities and interests that constitute practical aptitude have matured, a proper balance between various types of education would be established and all walks of life would get "their share" of talent.

One could at this juncture venture some generalizations about recent developments in the Western European countries.

(1) The trend after the Second World War has been towards comprehensivization of mandatory schooling and gradual abolition of parallel institutions or tracks for an intellectual and/or social élite. This has been achieved by extending the common school, the *tronc commun*, and by postponing selection for academic élite schools and programs. Certain reforms have gone half way to establishing more flexibility by means of an "orientation cycle" after the primary stage and before the definitive separation between academic and non-academic takes place.

(2) Comprehensivization has been spurred on by the enrollment explosion at the secondary level, at which, a few decades ago, selective schools catered for 20–25 per cent of the age group or less. The enrollment explosion at the junior secondary level has caused that type of school, as a former Swedish Minister of Education put it, to be "blown up from within." Universalization of secondary education has contributed to comprehensivization also in terms of widening the range of programs and curricula. Vocational and semi-vocational programs and schools have been integrated with academic ones in the same institutions and under the same roof.

(3) Widened access to upper secondary education has led to increased competition for entry into higher education, where limited access in most countries is the case. This has had repercussions on the lower stages of the system of a paradoxical nature. In spite of widened opportunity competition at all stages has increased which has led to "performance pressure" (*Leistungsdruck*) and to enraged debates on selection procedures and about marks, examinations, and standardized tests.

The Eastern European model. The *Eastern European* model, or since it was first instituted in the USSR, the Soviet model, based on the notion that differences in scholastic attainments reflect inequalities inherent in the social order of the capitalist class society or are vestiges of such a society. The ruling élite in the capitalist countries has usurped the privilege of having access to high level and high quality education which prepares for leading positions. Thus, in order to give young people from the working class a fair chance to enter the intelligentsia and to become specialists, they should be provided with genuine equality of opportunity within the framework of a unitary basic school common to all children of mandatory school age. The establishment of an *Einheitsschule*, a unitary school has therefore been a prime educational goal of the communist parties. Such a school can serve as a major instrument in achieving a classless society. It should, however, be pointed out that early Soviet educators were intrigued by Western liberal progressive thinkers, such as John Dewey. Progressive educational thinking in America among other things focused on individualized pedagogy which was closely related to the testing movement. On both sides of the Atlantic – more so, however, in England than in the melting pot America – intelligence test scores were assumed to reflect inherited more than acquired cognitive competencies. In the Soviet Union testing was for some time used but was denounced together with other "pedological" practices by decrees in the early 1930s.

It was indeed a tremendous achievement in a country whose adult population to a large extent was illiterate at the time of the Revolution to make not only primary but also some secondary education available over a relatively short time. The rapid change, politically, socially, and not least economically over a few decades makes the role played by education in social stratification in the socialist countries a fascinating study.

When Chairman Khrushchev in 1958 introduced the new Education Act to the Supreme Soviet, he revealed that only some 30–40 per cent of the students at Moscow's institutions of higher education came from the working class and peasantry, whereas the majority came from the intelligentsia and the functionaries who were a minority in the work force. He expressed concern about this and suggested that steps should be taken in alleviating these glaring imbalances. His mentioning of group disparities was quite sensational, because according to the officially sanctioned philosophy education in socialist systems is much more open to advancement of talent irrespective of family and/or class background than in capitalist societies.

Surveys on educational aspirations of Soviet youth and on admissions, attainments and achievements as related to family background began to be published in the 1960s. Such studies consistently showed a rather strong influence of parental education and parental occupational status on educational aspirations and attainments. No wonder, then, that young people from the intelligentsia were over-represented among applicants for admission to institutions of higher education, particularly the high prestige ones. The surveys further showed that the system of higher education itself was differentiated according to prestige and social recruitment. Some institutions tended to admit a particularly high percentage of young people from homes of the leading stratum.

Since the educational system in socialist countries according to the official philosophy is more open and more conducive to the promotion of talent, irrespective of home background, than in capitalist societies, one could expect the Soviet system to be more meritocratic. Available information on intergenerational social mobility seems to confirm this. The mobility from manual to non-manual strata is much higher than in Western Europe and the United States. However, there are convincing indications that the outflow from manual to non-manual occupations is not higher than in the Western countries. This seeming contradiction is an artifact of the rapid expansion of the intelligentsia and the specialist strata in the Soviet Union.

Conclusions

The tendency of Soviet children from more educated and socially advantaged background to move ahead further in the educational system is to some extent similar to the one we obtain from systems with earlier differentiation. We find cutting across the systems a marked tendency of children from educated backgrounds and from socially, but not necessarily materially, privileged backgrounds to be heavily overrepresented among both applicants and admitted students to institutions of advanced learning. They are furthermore, once admitted, more successful on all counts: have better marks, lower repetition and dropout rates, and higher success rates in selective examinations. They are particularly successful in getting into prestigious institutions and programs which prepare for attractive positions in working life.

It should, however, be pointed out that there are differences in degree between the two systems, the one with early and the one with late school differentiation. The imbalances in the educational system and the ensuing degree of mobility between strata are correlated with the structure of the basic school system up through the junior secondary years. On the basis of the evidence gained from the IEA 20-country survey two broad generalizations could be ventured.

(1) The earlier the selection takes place for separate academic schools and programs which run parallel to schools and programs for the remainder of students of mandatory school age, the stronger the association between family background and school attainments. Thus, the longer the period of common schooling for all children, the less pronounced the imbalances between social strata.

(2) The more centralization in terms of uniformity of structure and financial resources, the lower the between-school variability in outcomes. In the IEA survey it was found that the between-school variance as related to between-student variance in student achievement among 14-year olds was 80 per cent in India, 20–25 per cent in England and the United States, and only 8 per cent in Sweden.

I think that we should not overemphasize the impact of differences in material resources between social strata on differences in educational outcomes in societies where a certain material minimum has been achieved. When I reviewed the available research on social background and participation in higher education in an inauguration lecture in 1953, I noted a more rapid increase of private automobiles than university students in Swedish working class families. Not least Soviet sociologists, in trying to explain differences of the kind cited above, point out that differences in value-orientation and aspirations account for a considerable part of the differences in representation of manual and non-manual strata at institutions of higher learning. In a system where material wealth cannot be passed on to the next generation, it becomes more important to encourage one's children and to assist them in all respects in their educational careers. As long as we do not sever the ties between children and their parents altogether, that is to say, do away with the family and bring up the children in collective institutions, we can hardly avoid that those who are better educated, socially more successful and more ambitious about the future of their offspring, will bring up children who are more successful in school and subsequently in life.

There is as pointed out above an inherent element of meritocracy in modern industrial society. Increased industrialization with concomitant technology means a movement towards greater rationality. The dominant figure in the industrial, and particularly in the post-industrial society, is in a broad a sense the engineer of the new technology. The technocrats, also taken in a wide sense, those who exercise authority by virtue of theoretical and technical competence acquired by advanced education and specialized training are becoming increasingly influential. There seems to be a convergence between highly different economic systems in terms of how social stratification is shaped by education, the division of labor, the distribution of rewards and the criteria for promotion.

IV. Impact of Education on Career

Lifelong Learning in the "Educative Society" (1964, 1969)[1]
Talent, Opportunity and Career (1968)[2]
Employment of the Highly Educated in the Society of Today and Tomorrow (1978)[3]

Introduction

As has been spelled out in the previous section: in modern society a person's life chances are increasingly dependent upon the amount and quality of formal education. The employment system screens according to it. But education is not just a "filter." As can be seen from the longitudinal study, in which the author has been participating since 1938, formal education "boosts" intelligence as measured by so-called IQ tests. It also affects adult earnings as does, of course, formal schooling as such.

A dominant feature of education in modern society is that it is "life-long" and "recurrent." In several industrial countries there are more adults than young people enrolled in regular courses in formal education or in training or re-training programs. Schooling taken at an early age cannot in a rapidly changing society provide the entire fare for the rest of life. The ongoing changes in production and society at large require repeated upgrading and retraining and a widening of the basis for all this, that is general education and the skills that go with it.

"Talent, Opportunity and Career," which was originally given as a guest lecture at the University of Chicago, sums up the longitudinal study until the mid-1960s. The follow-up has been going on since then. It comprises 1500 10-year-olds of 1938 who are now (1986) 58-years-old. Their social, occupational and medical status has continuously been followed.

The so-called enrollment explosion, first at the secondary and then at the tertiary level, has given rise to concerns about young people being "over-educated" and of the imminent risk of getting an army of "educated unem-ployed." However, employment statistics in all industrial countries are consistent: unemployment is high among those with the mandatory minimum of education and low among those with some university education. The former group, which at least until the age of 20, to a large extent appears to be "superfluous," constitutes a "new underclass" referred to in Section VI.

A monograph reporting on the so-called Malmoe study with the same title as the paper included here was published in 1969 by T. Husén, Ingemar Emanuelsson, Ingemar Fägerlind and Robert Liljefors (Stockholm: Almqvist & Wiksell International). Ingemar Fägerlind has studied how adult earnings are related to formal education in *Formal Education and Adult Earnings* (Stockholm: Almqvist & Wiksell International, 1975). OECD published a report by a task force chaired by Clark Kerr under the title *Education and Working Life in Modern Society* (Paris: OECD, 1975). The author was a member of the task force.

Notes

1. Originally (in 1964) given as a lecture to a group of Swedish industrialists. Translated and later published in the *International Review of Applied Psychology*, Vol. 17:2, 1969, 87-99. A somewhat abbreviated version appeared in *Convergence* (Ontario Institute for Studies in Education), Vol. 1:4, 1968, 12-21.
2. Published in *The School Review* (University of Chicago), Vol. 76:2, 1968, 190-209. A slightly different version of the same paper also appeared in *Educational Research* (National Foundation for Educational Research, London) Vol. 10:3, 1968.
3. Prepared in 1978 for an international seminar.

Lifelong Learning in the "Educative Society"*

IN THE following, theoretical considerations will be given to the subject of continuing education in the modern industrialized and rapidly changing society. My thesis is that educational planning in modern society must take lifelong learning as a basic assumption.

Before I proceed to develop this thesis and analyze its consequences for the school system and for in-plant training programs, I shall outline the conventional view of formal education and its relation to the vocational career. This view, at least as it has prevailed in Europe, may be described in schematic terms as follows: From their childhood and up to their teens, young people are supposed to receive the general education and vocational training they need to qualify them for two roles – as citizens of their community and as participants in the labor force. The relatively few of them who stay at school to the age of 20 provide recruits for an even smaller élite group who will spend several more years at university, where they are trained for the professions and positions of high status in the job world. By the time most people are about to conclude their schooling they are supposed either to have made their vocational choice or to have been helped to make this choice. Whether young people enter the job world before they are 20 or several years afterwards, the majority of them are assumed to remain faithful to the occupation or at least to the occupational area in which they started, in spite of actual changes of employment.

Selective Migration and Occupational Mobility

This picture is based on the experience of a static society, where geographic mobility was relatively slight, and social and occupational mobility even slighter. It certainly does not apply to today's dynamic society. Assuming that present tendencies hold, only a small minority of young people will be in the same occupations after 20 as in the first few years after leaving school. This observation is corroborated by several studies; one of these studies, by Neymark, *Selective Mobility* (Stockholm 1961), will be cited.

The industrialization of society originated mostly in urban areas and in turn gave rise to more urban areas. A main driving force for this expansion

* Published in the *International Review of Applied Psychology*, Vol. 17:2, 1969, 87–99. Reproduced by permission of the International Association of Applied Psychology.

of the economy was the influx of manpower from rural areas to the cities and towns. The "flight" from the countryside was chiefly a flight from the farms, whose share of the gainfully employed population has accordingly dwindled in all countries with expanding economies. In the United States some 5 per cent of the labor force is now sufficient to produce more than enough food for the rest of the country. The corresponding proportion in France is over 15 per cent, and in Sweden somewhere in between.

This massive depopulation of the countryside in the past century is a universally known fact. Most of the people who now live in cities had ancestors who tilled the soil only a couple of generations ago. But how are we to interpret the rural-to-urban migration in purely qualitative terms? Has it had the same impact on all levels of qualification, whether these are of a personal or educational nature? Or is some form of selective migration at work? As far as Sweden is concerned we still have very little information to go on. All the investigations made by economists or ethnographers have applied to limited regions. The dynamics of an industrial society are generated not only by people when they move from one place to another, but also when they embark upon new occupations, take new employment, and change their social status. Only in exceptional cases do young people nowadays choose their parent's occupations. Technological advance continually creates new occupations and phases out others. In the "educative society," climbing up the social ladder depends very much on the opportunity and ability to climb up the educational ladder.

Our knowledge of how these different types of mobility operate in Sweden has been greatly increased by, for instance, Neymark. In 1948 he selected a national random sample of male youths and followed their careers for a period of eight years. He also retrospectively mapped up their careers from 1942. The principal aim of the study was to elucidate the mechanisms of the vocational-selection process. This process is evidently linked with large-scale migration, and at the same time the education, ability, and social origin of the young people may be expected to govern both migratory and vocation-searching tendencies in various ways.

From the records filed at the Central Conscript Bureau of the Swedish Armed Forces a 10 per cent sample numbering 4,500 young men was drawn who were born in 1928 and were called up for induction to military service in 1948. The files included particulars on education, school, test scores, and medical condition. This information was supplemented by the responses of two questionnaires, the one sent out when the young men were twenty-one years of age and the other when they were twenty-eight, in which they were asked to state their communities of legal residence in specified years, as well as their general vocational training, elementary school grades, and employment status.

The place of residence was ascertained for 1942, 1949, and 1956 and, according to the responses given Neymark could divide his sample into different categories of "stay-at-home" and "migrants," depending on the types of community and the distances involved in the migrations over the fourteen years under investigation. After calculating net migration losses and gains for different regions, agglomeration levels, and other quantitative measures, Neymark then tackled the central problem: How much "selective migration" is there? In other words, to what extent are the quantitative changes linked to qualitative changes? He demonstrated that rural-to-urban migration is positively correlated with education, ability (as assessed by school marks and test scores), and social class. The highest order of correlation appeared to be with general education. The higher a young man's educational attainments, the more likely he is to move to the cities and towns. The longer his formal schooling, the more usual it will be for him to move further from home, in this case from a rural area into one of the cities. No less than 75 per cent of the rural youths who had taken some form of pre-university education left home for the cities, as compared with only 25 per cent of those who did not go beyond elementary school. In terms of ability, too, the rural migration losses were greatest at the highest levels. Thus 57 per cent of those with the highest scores in the intelligence test left home as compared with only 14 per cent having the lowest scores. Special attention was given to the group which, according to test scores and psychiatric examination were mentally retarded. Within this category only 17 per cent moved to the cities and towns as against 38 per cent of rural youths of normal intelligence. The gifted sons of farmers are more inclined to move to the towns than the gifted sons from rural working-class homes in non-farm occupations. Thus, the migration tendency among farmers' sons was two-and-a-half times greater for the most able than for the least able 25 per cent in this group; the corresponding ratio in the rural non-farm group was 1.6 to 1. On the other hand, sons of working-class fathers in the countryside showed a stronger *general* tendency to migrate than farmers' sons – 40 per cent as compared with 25 per cent.

A question that Neymark touched on only incidentally, but which is more relevant for our present purposes, is this: Does the process of emigration he surveys represent a more primary "brain drain" on rural resources? In other words: To what extent is a loss of inherited ability also involved? If the measures of ability are taken to reflect mainly hereditary differences between individuals, it would take no more than two generations for the countryside to lose virtually all its superior talent. But we know that although rural-to-urban migration in Sweden, as in the other industrialized European countries, has been intensively going on for generations, the institutions of higher education are in spite of this rapidly increasing the proportion of students from the countryside. Further, the correlation between social background and formal education is very high for rural areas. By way of example, 90 per cent of the sons of salaried employees have completed at least lower secondary academic schooling (up to grade 10 or 11) as compared with only 5 per cent of the farmers' sons and between 6 and 18 per cent of the rural working-class sons. This suggests that quite a lot of the selectivity operative in migration from country to town is on the social and educational plane. The migrants are made up not only of those having higher educational attainment and high test scores, but also of young people who come from homes with greater education and career ambitions.

Social mobility

In their book, *Social Mobility in Industrial Society*, (1959) Lipset and Bendix demonstrated that social mobility increases with growing urbanization. The more urbanized the environment in which a person grows up, the greater the probability of his reaching a higher occupational status than his parents. But urbanization is an integral part of industrialization. Accordingly, we can expect a much higher degree of social mobility – and occupational mobility as well – in the cities than in the towns, which in turn are higher on both counts than the villages. In the second part of his book Neymark subjects both occupational and social mobility to exhaustive analysis. He found that no less than 42 per cent of the young men in his sample changed occupations between the ages of 20 and 28. Only one-third had remained in their starting occupations (at age 20). In the intervening period the rural non-farm trades had lost one-third of their practitioners, while agriculture lost an even greater share. The differences in occupational shifts between the "stay-at-homes" and the rural-to-urban migrants were not as large as could be expected, considering that such shifts often entail a geographic move.

The element of social mobility in occupational choice was considerable both in town and country. Only 6 per cent of the urban youths and 11 per cent of the rural youths in the sample pursued the same occupations as their fathers. When these proportions were adjusted to make allowance for changes to similar or allied occupations, Neymark estimated that one-sixth of the urban youths and one-tenth of the rural youths ended up in their fathers' occupations. This means that only a very small minority received any kind of vocational training or guidance in the home.

Even though the 1950s was a boom period which gave rise to "excessive mobility," especially among young people of the generation considered in Neymark's study, it illustrates that occupational mobility and the relative independence of social origin for vocational choice are rather typical of the industrialized, educative society. An expanding economy, with its ever-increasing and insatiable demand for well-trained manpower, will further accelerate not only geographic but also social mobility. We must also in this connection consider what I should like to call "adustment mobility" – in other words, the need to adapt flexibly to new requirements after one's teenage years are far behind. This means that the educational system cannot afford to make too early commitments to specific occupations. By the time many school-leavers reach middle age, they will be performing jobs which simply do not exist at the present time. It will become normal in the future for the gainfull employed to take retraining not only once, but several times, during the course of their working careers. Obviously, the need to retrain will become most urgent for those whose current usefulness to the labor market derives from fairly specific skills. As for personnel with a broad background of general education, augmented by skills of the kind that can cover a wider gamut of working situations, the problem of retraining largely boils down to provision for further education.

Consequences of the "Knowledge Explosion"

The dynamics of this process, whose consequences for the job world have been briefly sketched, are certainly no less dramatic when we consider what is regarded as the primary investment factor in an educative society: knowledge and skills. An important condition for the swift rise in productivity and living standards during the postwar years has been the advent of new technologies based on increased knowledge, which in turn ultimately derives from research and development. In many fields, especially in the physical and social sciences, the increment of new knowledge has been so great that we can rightly speak of a "knowledge explosion." An attempt to measure the force of this explosion in chemistry was made a couple of years ago by a chemist, who based his estimate on the number of scientific publications appearing since the time of the Swedish chemist, Jöns Jakob Berzelius (who died in 1848). If I remember correctly, he arrived at a "fission period" of seven years for the number of scientific publications in chemistry. This means that the volume of research in this field will have multiplied about thirty times since 1945 alone.

The consequences of the knowledge explosion hardly need further elaboration. It should suffice to point out that much of what we learned when we went to school is becoming obsolete. The ravages are wreaked not only by time alone, but also by the head-long surge of science and technology as it affects our everyday lives. I shall consider the consequences of this development below.

Skill Versus Content Subjects

In a collection of essays, entitled *The School in a Changing Society (Skolan i ett föränderligt samhälle)* published in Swedish in 1961 I sought to explain the impact of change on school curricula. The impact may be expressed in terms of two practical theses. First, today's school must put far greater emphasis on the skills or "instruments," that is, subjects which are necessary in order to study other subjects successfully, as opposed to the content subjects, where the acquistion of a fixed quantum of information is the chief aim. For instance, the ability to communicate with other people in one's own or in a foreign language is increasingly essential in an internationalized world. Fewer and fewer people will be working in jobs consisting mostly of routine duties; instead, a growing number will move into the service occupations, which put a premium on ability to deal with other people. The ability to find the information one needs and to learn on one's own will gain in importance as previously acquired knowledge of specific subject matter rapidly becomes obsolete. Today's school must instil in its pupils a vivid awareness that the intellectual fare they receive will not last them for the rest of their mortal days; in short, they must be made to feel that education is a lifelong process. Further, it is necessary to impart – at least to a broad élite of pupils – a zeal for learning, so that they will have an incentive to explore at closer range the terrains of knowledge which the school has only adumbrated. This attitude towards knowledge should be accompanied by a flexibility of mind: the readiness to accept change and appreciation of the need to learn more – above all, to relearn much of what has already been learnt.

The Importance of a General Education

My second thesis is that prolonged time for schooling must be used chiefly to enlarge the basis of *general education*, and not to impart specialized vocational proficiency to the young. When we in Sweden were still debating the structure of the compulsory nine-year basic school, there were some who argued that the ninth year – or even the eighth year – should be largely devoted to preparatory vocational training and, in certain cases, training for specific occupations. It is easy to sympathize with the reasons for this view. Local supplies of manpower may fall short of meeting urgent demands. Young people themselves are eager to earn money, and may find it easy to get jobs which require little in the way of previous skill – though it should be added that the demand for unskilled manpower is consistently declining. As for their parents, who grew up in a society of limited educational opportunity (indeed, the job world asked little of them in this regard), many of them would still like to see their offspring earning their livelihood as soon as possible. Understandably, too, these inclinations may be encouraged by the teachers, who certainly have no easy time maintaining discipline in their "book-weary" pupils who – it should be added – are often deprived of the instructional program and methods adapted to their needs.

A solid background in the skill subjects equips a person with instruments that can be applied to a broad spectrum of situations, many of them unforeseen, both in the job world and outside it. The person who speaks and writes his native tongue and one or more foreign language fluently, who has learnt how to learn and is able to continue studying on his own, who commands the fundamentals of mathematics, and who has learnt to think in the categories which characterize the content subjects – that person will possess extremely useful tools which will enable him to cope with changing conditions and requirements. We know that the greatest difficulties in retraining for new and more highly-skilled occupations are encountered by those with the poorest formal education. The United States constitutes an example of this. In that country we have a remarkable paradox: on the one hand, the release of several million employees rendered redundant by mechanization and automation; and on the other hand, a shortage of skilled workers, who can also be counted in the millions.

The process of change is also constantly at work in our leisure-time lives, making flexibility no less imperative in this sector. The mass media, not least television, have expanded our horizons in a way which was unthinkable fifty years ago, when most of us did not see beyond our own parishes or communities. Nor is it only the complications of the international scene that have been admitted to our living rooms. These media incessantly convey information which didn't even exist when we went to school. This means that a great deal more needs to done in the way of interpretation.

The Structure of Qualifications in the Job World

Let me now try to adduce the consequences of a rapidly changing society for the pursuit of our working careers. I shall do so in relation to two figures which, though highly schematic, will, I hope, illustrate the points essential to my argument.

Figure 1 shows what I should like to call the conventional qualifications pyramid. In terms of qualifications the job world has been generally assumed, and for the most part rightly so, to consist of a pyramidal structure, within which different strata or levels may be discerned in regard both to requirements and status. The "pyramid" presupposes a system of education which caters for each stratum separately, which until recently has been the case in Europe. In the late 1950s the *Deutscher Ausschuss für das Erziehungs-und Bildungswesen* contended, in their report on the school structure in the Federal Republic of Germany, that the *Volksschule* catered for the needs of all the people, whereas the *Gymnasium* was preparing for the professions and the *Mittelschule* for lower-middle-class occupations. Relatively slight mobility between the different strata of the pyramid is assumed. All the same, there may be considerable mobility *within* each stratum. The classical model for, say, a large industrial firm would then look something like this. At the bottom of the pyramid we have a big stratum of relatively un-skilled workers, with no formal education beyond elementary school. At the next level we have a much smaller stratum of "white-collar workers," with at least a lower secondary academic education and perhaps some pre-university education as well. At the top we have a very small stratum of people from the universities. When we study the educational debate that was waged in Sweden from around 1880 up to the 1940s, we find that most of the people who gave thought to the matter conceived of such a pyramid both for the educational

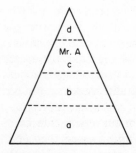

FIGURE 1. THE CONVENTIONAL "QUALIFICATIONS PYRAMID"

a. Unskilled workers
b. Skilled workers (mainly manual)
c. Office, supervisory and technical
   personnel without university education
   (middle school and senior secondary school)
d. Executive and technical personnel
   with university education

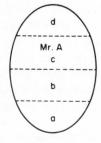

FIGURE 2. THE "QUALIFICATIONS HIERARCHY" AS IT WILL
LOOK BEFORE LONG (somewhat exaggerated by the author)

system and the economic sphere. As late as 1944 a Royal Commission of inquiry was saying that it was wrong in principle to enable all intellectually qualified pupils to continue into secondary academic education as a charge on public funds. According to the Commission, such support would not only starve the manual trades of gifted manpower, but would also create an intellectual proletariat. Both this inquiry and its predecessors were imprisoned by static approaches to the problem of school and society.

Figure 2 is not directly meant to be the proverbial Egg of Columbus, though the resemblance is admittedly deliberate. The structure of qualifications in regard to both general education and vocational training tends to change from a pyramid and to take the shape of an egg, with the narrowest end at the bottom. Down there we find a rapidly diminishing group of job openings for which little or no vocational training is required. On top of that we have a broad stratum of workers, who will not only be required to have much more formal education behind them but who will also have to take further education and undergo retraining to a great extent during the course of their careers. The stratum above – which, incidentally, will be increasingly difficult to separate from the manual workers (indeed, it might be more apt to call them technicians) – contains a group which we have been accustomed to calling white-collar workers or salaried employees. At this level, too, there will be a much greater need for further education and retraining. Consider for a moment the impact that electronic data processing and other examples of office automation have already had on salaried employees in many industries! At the top we have two strata, the one representing people who have completed education of pre-university standing, while the other consists of the university graduates. The membership of both these strata is rapidly expanding. I need only point out that today's 55 – 60-year-olds in Sweden belong to a generation in which no more than one in every 20 qualified for university entrance, while more than one in every five of today's 20-year-olds possess the same qualification. By 1980 the proportion of young people entering the job world with a pre-university education or its equivalent was more than half.

Demands for Further Education in a Static Economy

As indicated above, this way of illustrating the qualification hierarchy is grossly schematic. This caveat applies with even greater force to my outline of particular details regarding the hierarchy. The essential fact is that we are in the midst of an "educational explosion," which does not take place in a vacuum but in response to the demands of a rapidly changing economy. Given our background for discussion, we should now ask: What do these changes entail for the working adults who left school a long time ago, irrespective of the level at which they finished?

Let us follow the career of a hypothetical character whom I shall call "Mr. A." In the pyramid-shaped system, Mr. A could expect to retain the same status throughout his working life, provided he did not advance from one level to another, that is, was promoted so as to enter the next higher stratum. The longer the time that has elapsed since he finished his education, the more he is likely to have "forgotten" what he learned at school. A large part of this loss has presumably been offset by the experience gained on the job. A German economist, C. C. von Weizsäcker, has advanced a theoretical model purporting to show how the knowledge of, for instance, a chemist with a university degree deteriorates and what this means in terms of the necessity to keep up to date. On the basis of certain assumptions, von Weizsäcker arrived at an annual deterioration rate of 3 per cent.

As was stated earlier, the pyramidal qualification structure presumes a relatively static economy – at least static in the sense that the changes are not of today's dramatic magnitude but where, say after twenty years or so, roughly the same structure in regard to production techniques and occupational requirements prevails. Given these conditions, our Mr. A may find it necessary (to an extent which obviously will vary a good deal from one occupation to another) to keep refreshing his previously acquired store of knowledge and skills. However, he need make no particular effort to keep in touch with new developments in his own field of competence since, on the applied side at any rate, there are likely to be only a few innovations.

Demands for Further Education in a Dynamic Economy

Within the egg-shaped system, or, more accurately, within the structure which during the course of one generation is in the process of being transformed from a pyramid into an egg, conditions will be different for Mr. A. Let us assume he was recruited to start with into stratum "b," where he has been assigned to perform fairly specialized office work. During his term of service more and more employees have entered the stratum above his. When these persons first joined the company twenty years ago, they may have comprised between 2 and 3 per cent of its work force. Mr. A knew many of them. Since he started with the company their numbers have increased to between 8 and 10 per cent of the total. By the time he is pensioned twenty years hence, their proportion will probably exceed 20 per cent. Thus in the forty years of his working life Mr. A has experienced a considerable *relative* loss of status. More and more people have been placed above him in the hierarchy. The majority of these newcomers were young when they started, and many of them took only a few years to reach their present higher-level positions after completing their education.

If Mr. A is to be able to function at the level for which he was originally trained, he will have to add to his store of knowledge from time to time, notwithstanding the experience he has gained on the job. If his duties are essentially altered, he may have to submit to retraining. But even if nothing more drastic happens to change his work situation, he will still have to pursue some form of further education in order to grasp the techniques which are gradually being introduced, and in order to get the background needed to perform satisfactory work. Thus he will not only have to "brush up" old knowledge and skills, but also acquire new knowledge and skills. Assume further that Mr. A doesn't want to lose relative status: in other words, he is bent on climbing the ranks so as to keep pace with the structural changes taking place in the qualifications hierarchy. He must then return to the school bench from time to time for a more sustained and systematic effort to assimilate not only knowledge of a general nature, but also the specific vocational know-how that will enable him to keep up with the transformation itself. However, this is not a question of advancement in relative terms, since structural transformation within a company serves to advance the qualifications of most employees.

The Unfolding of Careers

Given the conditions herein outlined, what shape will careers take in the future, especially for those who belong to the upper stratum in the "egg?" Research in this field is still rather meager. Neymark's study of a representative group of Swedish working males has already been discussed. I myself have been in charge of a project in which we are following the careers of about 1,500 people in the city of Malmö born in 1928. We have been accumulating educational and vocational data as well as test data for this group since 1938 (see Husén *et al.*, *Talent, Opportunity and Career*, Stockholm: 1968). In the United States an exceptionally interesting study has been made by Professor Donald Super of Columbia University, who closely followed the progress of a group of young people from the age of 14 to 25. The main purpose of this study is to determine whether the degree of vocational maturity at the age of 14 can be made to predict progress in the 25th year of life. The vocational preference of present-day youth must be seen in the light of changing times. The more capable youngsters in particular are strongly oriented towards the future. They sense more vividly than previous generations that certain occupations are fading out, while others are emerging. During the course of a few decades, the proportion of unskilled workers in the New York area fell off from 33 to 8 per cent of the gainfully employed. Indeed, the vocational preferences of today's young people must be viewed in relation to long-range projections.

In tomorrow's job world placement at a high level will require a longer period of formal education. An ever-increasing number of those at the top will have pursued their education until they are at least twenty-five years of age. For this group the ensuing period could be characterized as "establishment" (to use Super's terminology). For potential executives in administration and production, the trying-out period will be of quite a different character than for the youngsters who enter the job world already in their teens.

Development of Proficiency in a Dynamic Economy

The development of competence will obviously vary greatly according to the industry, job, and hierarchical level under consideration. It can be assumed that the person who more or less as a matter of routine has to apply definite basic knowledge will be required in one way or another to "hone up" in order to counteract the loss that accumulates with remoteness in time from his schooling. However, this problem is of a lesser order for the person who does the work of planning, commanding, and coordinating that devolves upon an executive. On the other hand, the person whose work primarily depends on sheer technical know-how will be compelled to keep constantly abreast of developments in this field. Let us assume that half the basic knowledge in his field is revised by scientific and technological advance over a period of ten years. This means that he must renew his fund of knowledge at the rate of 5 per cent a year. It would be asking too much for the person to do this on his own; instead, he must submit to a form of systematic further education at regular intervals. If his particular speciality has undergone large-scale transformation, he may even have to be trained again from the beginning.

The conclusion is inescapable: at all levels of qualification today's job world imposes demands which yesterday's static society recognized to a much lesser degree, if at all. Those who have a lower level of qualifications must reckon that they will have to be retrained once or more during their working lives as technicians, with end results that may not bear the slightest resemblance to the kind of work they did when they first started. Those at a higher level, especially in engineering positions, will find themselves in a situation where a broad background in economics, social science, physical science and technology will equip them with certain fundamental concepts and principles, enabling them to add new knowledge to their fund without too much difficulty. Once an engineer has learnt to think in basic physical categories, he will not be as susceptible to the whims of technological change as the one who has chiefly engaged in the applied aspects without really understanding the theoretical background. The researchers in education concerned with theories of curriculum-building attach great importance to having pupils learn a subject like physics as a "discipline," as one distinct branch of learning. The pupils are then better able to keep up with the shifts or more ephemeral applications.

The Requirement to Readjust

At the higher levels of qualifications the premium will be put on flexibility and readjustment, on the ability to be prepared for change and to accept it. Or the matter could be put this way: it will be necessary, during the course of both formal education and in-plant training, to create a relativistic attitude. The man who recognizes that sweeping changes may occur is thereby much better equipped to meet them when they do occur. Such an attitude also makes for greater receptivity to new viewpoints and impulses, for a readiness to unlearn habitual ways of thinking. The top-ranking men entrusted with sophisticated management and engineering tasks will have to be more flexible and more creative than other categories of personnel. They must not bog down in mechanical routines or thought patterns, for to do so would set them back far more than it would others. The company would then have no choice but to let most of the creativeness come from "young lions" recruited from outside.

The in-plant or industry-wide training that must be provided to permit keeping up with developments in personnel administration, and a great deal more besides, must include help and guidance to permit gradual adaptation to new "roles." It will not be enough here to learn new technical methods or to understand their rational background. An executive will have to meet and discuss with colleagues and "idea men" from the outside if he is to adapt to the new roles related both to his vocational and general social duties within and outside the company.

Talent, Opportunity and Career*

I THINK that every researcher, irrespective of his discipline, but particularly in the social sciences, at closer inspection tends to have certain permanent lodestars for his scientific endeavors.

If ever I tried to ransack my own career as a researcher, the result would seem evident: my lodestar has been the study of the relationship between school achievement and socioeconomic background. I have over the years carried out several studies of the so-called reserve or pool of ability and of how this reserve is located in various socioeconomic strata. I have zealously studied the relationship between social class and selectivity, or retentivity, of school systems. Most of this research has been policy oriented and closely related to school reforms in my own country.

As a young graduate student of educational psychology at the University of Lund in 1938, I became involved in a survey of all the students in the third grade of the elementary schools in Malmö, which had at that time about 150,000 inhabitants, being third in size in Sweden after Stockholm and Gothenburg. The purpose of the survey was to study the relationship between intellectual performances as defined by group intelligence tests, school marks, and teacher ratings, on the one hand, and social background as defined by parental education, occupational status, income, and social-relief record, on the other. At that time education at most universities in Europe had very remote ties with the behavioral sciences, a state of affairs that still prevails in some countries. It happened, however, that Swedish universities until the end of the forties had combined chairs in education and psychology. Thus several young people who, like myself, were fed up with the continental European *Tiefsinnigkeiten* and confused verbalisms were challenged by the opportunities that empirical studies of crucial educational problems opened up. Problems which in the United States had long been regarded as trivial, and which in Europe today might be similarly regarded – namely, to what extent differences in so-called intelligence might reflect socioeconomic and cultural differences – obsessed the young graduate student for many years to come.

But the mere lapse of time made new problems emerge. The 1,500 ten-year-olds who were tested in 1938, and whose social background and school achievements were so carefully mapped out, grew older. Four years later

* Presentation given on the occasion of receiving an honorary doctorate at the University of Chicago 1967. Originally published in *The School Review*, Vol. 76:2, 1968, 190–209. Reproduced by permission of the University of Chicago Press.

additional data relating to the school record of those who had transferred to the secondary academic school were collected. Dr Siver Hallgren, now deceased, who was one of my fellow students in the graduate seminar and who had carried the responsibility for the 1938 survey, conducted the first follow-up, which was confined to the predictive value of the 1938 assessments for success in the junior secondary school. Ten years after the first survey, when our subjects had reached the age of twenty, the boys eligible for military service had to appear before a Conscription Board, where they were tested and interviewed. Since I happened at that time to be in charge of the research section of the personnel selection service in the Swedish Armed Forces, I took advantage of the opportunity to use the data which automatically were available for the majority of the young men from Malmö. Thus two major problems could be elucidated: first, the influence of formal schooling upon intelligence test scores and, second, the relationship between family background and further schooling, in particular academic schooling, beyond the age of fourteen, when mandatory school attendance expired. The outcomes of the 1948 follow-up were published in 1950 in Swedish (*Testresultatens prognosvärde*, The Predictive Value of Test Scores, Stockholm: Almqvist & Wiksell).

As more years elapsed and all the ten-year-olds had embarked upon their vocational careers, we thought that it would certainly be worthwhile to look at these careers in the perspective of the starting points, such as family background, formal schooling, and I.Q. My research partner, Hallgren, was able to collect from the school records information on marks, grade-repeating, and graduation before he died in 1961. I was then solely responsible for the project with the assistance of two of my graduate students, Ingemar Fägerlind and Ingemar Emanuelsson.

Thus in 1962 we started to locate *all* the 1938 subjects, of whom only the males had been dealt with in the meantime. The unique feature of this enterprise seems to me to be that we managed to find practically all individuals from the original population, apart from those who had emigrated. This is due to the uncannily effective public registration system in Sweden, which in its turn is due to the fiscal zeal which sees to it that everybody is kept track of! Therefore we could obtain actuarial information for practically the entire original population, data related to school career, occupation, taxed income, criminal record, social relief, etc.

We also tried to secure information from the subjects themselves by means of a comprehensive questionnaire. After having tried all kinds of approaches we got complete information on occupational, educational, and family career for about 73 per cent of the original group.

Let me briefly spell out the special assets and limitations of the data bank we thereby obtained. In our particular case the original group has in certain respects been followed up almost 100 per cent. In other respects, the loss has been moderate. Thus we have followed a population comprising both intellectually and socially the whole range. We have been lucky in avoiding the sample distortions due to loss of cases, distortions which gradually have made many previous follow-up studies less interesting with the increasing age of the subjects.

Furthermore, since fairly accurate information exists about the social starting point in life and school records of our subjects, we are able to establish long-range predictions, which are much more difficult in case the original sample was strongly selected and/or distorted by loss of subjects. I am thinking particularly of the possibilities of shedding some light on the problem of the role of formal education in shaping the occupational career in relation to social class and I.Q. as assessed at the beginning of formal schooling.

There has been a special set of problems which I think are particularly brought into focus in Sweden. The societal changes between 1938 and today have in some respects been rather dramatic. This is the period when the social-welfare state was born and the social-class differences began to be leveled out. It is also a period of structural change in the Swedish economy. The city population we have been following up has been strongly affected by the shift of the center of gravity of the economy from industrial to service occupations. Of great interest in this connection is the problem of how far basic formal education and continuing education have served to facilitate the transfer from one occupational family to another.

Far be it from me to bother you with an enumeration of the variables included in the study. But in order to provide you with enough background for the glimpses I shall give of what happened to the ten-year-olds of 1938, it would seem appropriate to mention the following.

1. The 1938 survey comprised school records, teachers' ratings, and family-background information.

2. The 1942 follow-up dealt exclusively with the school careers of those who had transferred to the junior secondary school. The remainder were still in the elementary school.

3. The 1948 follow-up comprised, as mentioned earlier, only the male part of the original group and included intelligence scores, school records, and occupational data.

4. The 1964 follow-up, finally, comprised actuarial data such as occupational title, taxed income, criminal record, and social-welfare record. furthermore, by means of the questionnaire, which had been tried out on a random sample drawn from the Malmö records of those born in 1929, detailed information was secured about vocational and educational career, present family, continuing education, present economic situation, leisure activities, etc.

The 1938 population consisted of 1,545 third graders. In 1948 data were secured for 722 boys at the age of twenty, who constituted 86 per cent of the original group. In 1964 all the original individuals had been located. For 70 per cent or more, actuarial data were available. Questionnaire data were obtained for 1116 cases, or 73 per cent, of the 1938 population.

Obviously, to report within the scope of a single lecture the findings of a study that has been going on for more than twenty-six years presents a considerable *embarras de richesse*. I shall therefore, naturally enough, confine myself to the predictive aspects, particularly the predictive value of the 1938 data. The criteria will then be the educational and occupational career as well as the social career at large as indicated by such matters as expressed satisfaction with life, entry into criminal record and so on.

Before starting to deal with the substance of my presentation I should like to give you some background about the school structure. When our subjects went to school, Sweden had the school organization which until recently has prevailed in most western European countries. After grade 4 of the mandatory seven-year elementary school, about 10 per cent transferred to the academic junior secondary school. After grade 6 another 20 per cent transferred to a less prestigious type of secondary school that had been established in the twenties. Finally, at the end of grade 7 another 5 per cent transferred. Thus 38 per cent of the group had the opportunity to enter secondary education, which in this case meant academic, pre-university education.

Which factors defining the life situation of the ten-year-olds were most important in shaping their respective life careers up to middle age? What is the relative importance of these factors? There are three types of predictors, each defined by several measures: namely, ability, social background, and education. The first two factors were measured mainly at the age of ten, except for I.Q., which for the male part of the population was measured both at ten and at twenty. Education is defined by the type and amount of schooling received, including the university level.

In the following I shall deal in turn with ability, social background, and education.

Ability as a Career Predictor

Ability for the 1938 group was defined by a conventional intelligence group test taken by the third graders, by teachers' ratings of intelligence on a five-point scale, and by class standing on a three-point scale, indicating the top 15 per cent, the intermediate range, and the bottom 15 per cent.

How, then, should we define "career?" There are plenty of criteria, both within and outside the occupational sphere. Let me mention some which by consensus would be regarded as important measures of life success: occupational status, taxed income, civil status, participation in community affairs, occurrence in the Criminal Register, and expressed satisfaction with what has been accomplished so far in life.

Let me start with the criteria of success which are closest in time, that is, those derived from the educational records of our subjects, and then success-ively move to those which are chronologically more remote. To what extent does I.Q., as assessed by a simple group intelligence test at age ten, predict educational career? The test scores as well as the teachers' ratings are in the following presentation given on a five-point scale.

The first criterion, which is between one and a half up to three and a half years removed from the time of testing, is transfer to academic secondary education, in most cases transfer to the lower section of the university-preparing school. The number of students in per cent who transferred from the various test-score categories were:

Test score level	1 (low)	2	3	4	5 (high)
Transfers (per cent)	6	13	30	53	64

When teachers' ability ratings are used we get on the whole the same picture:

Ability rating	1 (low)	2	3	4	5 (high)
Transfers (per cent)	5	9	30	55	72

Since at that time school achievement to some extent constituted the entrance requirements, teachers' ratings could be expected to be more predictive than I.Q.

About one-third transferred from the elementary school to the academic secondary school. Somewhat more than half of these students either graduated from junior secondary school and/or entered senior secondary school (*gymnasium*). About 5 per cent passed the *studentexamen*, which was the qualifying examination for university entrance. This examination was taken about ten years after the group test had been administered. The percentages of those who passed *studentexamen* at the various ability levels were as follows:

Test-score level, 1938	1 (low)	2	3	4	5 (high)
Percentage passing *studentexamen* about 1948	1	0	2	8	16

Thus the probability that a student of average I.Q. will climb so high on the educational ladder as to qualify for university entrance was only one-eighth that of a student with an I.Q. of 115 or higher.

Teachers' ratings in the third school year were only weakly related to the grade-point average obtained in the *studentexamen*. Only one student, who in 1938 was assigned the two lowest ratings, passed the examination, and none entered the university. About two-thirds of the students who passed the university entrance examination had the highest rating, that is, belonged to the top 15 per cent.

To what extent was the grade-point average at age ten predictive of the one at twenty when the *studentexamen* was taken? The correlation is rather low but is of course affected by the extreme restriction of range that had taken place in the meantime in terms of school marks. Those who belonged to the top 15 per cent in 1938 had a grade-point average ten years later about one-third of standard deviation above that of students with an average test score in 1938.

We have complete records for fifty-four individuals who entered the university. Of these, ten left the university without taking a degree, thirty-three took a basic degree either in the faculty of philosophy or in one of the professional schools, and eleven completed doctoral degrees. Except one student, all who completed degrees were of average or above-average test-score standing. Forty-seven out of fifty-four were of above-average standing, and thirty-one belonged to the top 15 per cent in 1938.

So far, we have dealt exclusively with the educational career. But to what extent is "intelligence" as assessed as early as age ten predictive of adult education activities and of the educational aspirations held by the subjects on behalf of their children?

We asked the thirty-six-year-old subjects whether they would be interested in enrolling in the university-preparing (*gymnasium*) courses, which a couple of years later were made available to all adults who want to climb the educational ladder. Almost half of the men and between one-fourth and one-third of the women said "yes." The majority of those who replied in the affirmative indicated that they would be willing to take partial or total leave of absence from their jobs in order to complete studies. The willingness to enter the university-preparing program varied considerably with I.Q. as assessed twenty-six years earlier. Thus 15 per cent of the men and 18 per cent of the women in the bottom group so aspired, as compared to 34 and 36, respectively, in the top group. One should remember also that those who previously qualified for university entrance had come mainly from the top group.

Interestingly enough, the more than twenty years that had elapsed did not seem to have extinguished the effects of the school experiences, as mediated by teachers' ratings. The subjects were asked what level of formal education they wanted their own children to reach. Only about one-fourth were content with the basic nine-year school plus vocational training. About one-third wanted their children to complete the senior secondary school preparing for university entrance, and another third aspired to have them enter the university. The level of aspiration that parents in Sweden hold nowadays has dramatically changed. It is a combined effect of the social-welfare program embarked upon in the thirties and the school reforms after 1950, which have tremendously widened the opportunities. Only 23 per cent in the bottom group as defined by teachers' ratings aspired to see their children enter the university as compared to 77 per cent in the top group. In the former group one-third would have been content to see their children enter the secondary vocational program as compared to none in the top group.

Family Background as a Predictor

We asked our subjects how they thought that they had on the whole succeeded in life. The overwhelming majority replied that they had succeeded "above expectation" or "pretty well." Only 5 per cent said they had either "partly failed" or "completely failed." There was no relationship at all between expressed satisfaction and I.Q. as measured in 1938. The same applied to satisfaction with present occupation.

Civil status at age thirty-six was related to I.Q. as measured in 1938. Twice as many in the bottom group, according to the test, had never been married as in the top group. To hold a driver's license had in Sweden not reached the same level of universality as in the United States. More than eighty-five of the men held licenses as compared to only about half as many among the women of the same age. Whereas the relationship to I.Q. was only slight among men, it was much closer among the women. In the top group twice as many as in the bottom group held licenses.

All persons convicted of having violated the criminal law on account of certain offenses (including more serious traffic violations) are entered into the Criminal Record, which provides information about the type of offense and sentence each time the defendant has been convicted. The government can grant researchers access to the record for scientific purposes. Of our 1,500 subjects 6.7 per cent were found in the Criminal Record (10.4 per cent of the men and 2.4 per cent of the women). Class standing as indicated by the three-point scale at age ten showed a clear relationship among men but not among women. Among the bottom 15 per cent, 21 per cent of the men and 3 per cent of the women were found in the record as compared to 5 and 2 per cent among the top 15 per cent. The same picture on the whole appears if ability is defined by I.Q. and teachers' rating of intelligence on a five-point scale. Eighteen per cent of the men in the bottom group as compared to 6–7 per cent in the top group were entered into the record.

Finally, when dealing with ability as a predictor of career we should not forget what is perhaps the most important criterion of success, occupational status. We have year-by-year information of type of occupation or those 1,116 subjects who responded to the questionnaire. If we relate I.Q. in 1938 to occupational status in 1964 according to the six-point scale, the differences in average occupational status between the I.Q. levels are statistically significant: 54 per cent of those in the top group had occupations belonging to the upper part of a six-point status scale in 1964, as compared to 27 per cent in the bottom group.

So far we have examined the extent to which subsequent career is related to ability as assessed by tests and teachers in 1938. Since we have been able to trace practically all the original subjects, it is of great interest to analyze the long-range relationship between family background and subsequent career. The predictors available in 1938 were occupational status based on occupational title, parents' combined taxed income, number of children at home, and information in the Social Relief Record. On the basis of these factors the children were in 1938 classified in four social groups: (1) professional and managerial, (2) subprofessional occupations requiring some higher education (including the bulk of white-collar jobs), (3) skilled workers (mostly manual), and (4) unskilled workers. In the following I shall use this classification as an index of social background and label it "social class."

Social class tends to have a cumulative effect on a person's life career. If he happens to be born and brought up in a home with educated parents who hold an elevated occupational status, he tends to be provided with good secondary education, which in its turn provides him with access to higher education, which in turn fits him for entry into high-level occupations, etc. This process can be studied in more detail by following our subjects from the third grade in the elementary school up to their present occupation.

At the time when our subjects went to elementary school there was quite a lot of non-promotion and grade-repeating. These were related to social class of the students. Thus only 1 per cent of the students from social class 1 repeated a grade as compared to 8 per cent in social classes 2 and 3 and 14 per cent in social class 4. The transfer to junior secondary school differed considerably between social classes. Thus 45 per cent of the males in social class 1 transferred as compared to 13 per cent of those in social class 4. The corresponding frequencies for the girls were 64 and 19, respectively. The higher transfer rate among girls was due to the fact that certain semivocational programs of higher prestige than those of the ordinary vocational schools (preparing for office and sales jobs) were open to girls. Consequently, when giving figures for the drop-out rate from the junior secondary school, I have confined the comparison between the social classes to boys of those who entered junior secondary school, 24 per cent in social class 1, 47 in classes 2 and 3, and 57 per cent in social class 4 dropped out, as a rule because of non-promotion. Of those who entered secondary academic education, 59 per cent of the boys from social class 1 after eight or more school years passed the final examination, which qualified for university entrance, as compared to 10 per cent in the other three groups, which differ only slightly in this respect. The corresponding figures for the girls were 28 in the upper class, 8 per cent on the next level, and 3 per cent in the two lowest classes.

The number of years of formal schooling is also related to social class. At that time seven years of elementary schooling were mandatory in most parts of Sweden, including the city of Malmö. Whereas about one-half to two-thirds of the children in the lower brackets left school after having completed their mandatory years, this was a rare exception in the upper class. There 70 per cent or more had eleven years or more of schooling, which in most cases meant university-preparatory education and university entrance.

The aspirations that the thirty-six-year-olds held for their own childrens' education were to a strikingly high extent connected with their social class at the age of ten. The percentages who wanted university education for their offspring were:

	Social Class							
	1		2		3		4	
	M	F	M	F	M	F	M	F
Want their childrent to get university education (per cent)	80	76	49	43	37	34	34	30

During the quarter of a century that has elapsed since the subjects left elementary school, the structure of Swedish society had changed considerably. The leveling out has affected not only the economic standard but attitudes toward education as well. It is, however, interesting to note that still fewer than half as many parents of working-class background (of whom now about more than one-third have risen to middle-class standing) aspire to a university education for their children in comparison with those of professional and managerial background, of whom by now about half hold occupations below the 1938 level among their parents.

The occupational status at age thirty-six as related to the social class of parents in 1938 reflects the leveling out which was mentioned above. Almost one out of five from the upper-class homes in the mid-1960s held a job in the semiskilled or skilled bracket. Fewer than one-third of those whose parents in 1938 belonged to the unskilled group held semiskilled or unskilled jobs. Three per cent had risen to the professional or managerial level, and about one-third held jobs which are classified between the top level and the skilled level. These data reflect the structural change that has taken place in the economy since 1938. Fewer and fewer unskilled or semiskilled jobs remain. The same process is mirrored in the follow-up data about the subjects' fathers, whose occupational status in 1948 and 1958, respectively, were asked for.

One could expect satisfaction with career achieved at middle age to be related to social background, since level of aspiration as to education and career is connected with social class. The predicted relationship appears, but it is rather weak. In the upper class 86 per cent of the males declared that they thought that they had succeeded "above expectation" or "pretty well," as compared to about 70 per cent in the two middle classes and 60 in the lower class. It should also be pointed out that men in the top group were much more definite about themselves being successes or failures than those in social class 4.

Education and Income

Economists in the early 1960s have attempted to assess the economic contribution of education. One of the major approaches has been labeled the "direct-returns-to-education approach" or the "rate-of-return approach." The lifetime earnings of persons with more education have been compared with the lifetime earnings of people with less education. The difference can then be related to the costs involved in obtaining the education. The procedure is as simple as it is deceptive and has often led to premature conclusions and policy suggestions. Figures giving the average income of adults with elementary school only, as compared to those with academic secondary school and university degrees, were published a year ago by an economist on the staff of the Central Board of the Swedish Labor Unions. The wide income differential between various levels of formal education was thereby brought into focus, and its justification was seriously questioned on the grounds of both an egalitarian philosophy in general and the fact that all education in Sweden is tuition free and (on the secondary and higher level) based on state allowances and loans to support the young people. Nobody would conclude that the average difference in income between members of, for example, Rotary and people in general would be due to the membership in that particular association, but people naïvely step into the pitfall implied in the propaganda that a university degree will add so and so much to a person's life income. It is, of course, quite reasonable that factors associated with education, such as family background, I.Q., and motivation, are associated with higher income.

The follow-up data provide us with a unique opportunity to analyze to what extent factors other than just formal education (in interaction with continuing education) contribute to raise a person's income. Previous studies suggest that ability plays a role in determining the rate of return of a person's education. So far, I have seen no more comprehensive study of the problem of whether and to what extent family background is related to income level in adult years. In our particular case we have access to information about social class and assessment of ability during the early school career. Furthermore, the Internal Revenue data, being publicly available in Sweden, gave us information about the taxed income of our subjects at age thirty-five. By drawing upon the school archives and the questionnaire we were able to keep a fairly detailed record of the school career of our population.

In the following I shall carry out the exercise of "holding other things constant" when estimating the differentiating "effect" of education upon income.

The results of my simple analysis are presented in a set of tables which relate income at age thirty-five to amount of schooling, family background, and ability as measured by the test administered at age ten. I have throughout divided the population into four subgroups by educational level: fewer than eight years of schooling, eight through ten years, eleven through fourteen years, and more than fourteen years. This division approximately corresponds to elementary school, junior secondary school, senior secondary school (including the first one or two years of university study), and university (irrespective of whether a degree was taken or not).

TABLE 1. *Taxed Income (in Swedish Crowns) at age thirty-five as related to level of formal schooling*

Formal Schooling	N	M	S.D.
		Males	
<8 years (elementary school only)	273	15,751	6,026
8–10 years (junior secondary school)	170	18,571	7,566
11–14 years (senior secondary school)	94	25,181	22,669
>14 years (university)	40	40,400	17,830
		Females	
<8 years	196	3,694	4,344
8–10 years..	208	3,958	5,038
11–14 years	58	5,362	6,152
>14 years	24	7,792	7,342

The figures in Table 1 convey a familiar picture. The more education, the higher the average income level. Particularly striking is the difference between those with higher and those with elementary or lower secondary education. As can be seen from the standard deviations, the spread increases strongly with increased level of education. The income range at the upper secondary and the higher education level is very large. This leads us to hypothesize that besides education there must be other factors, such as family background, which contribute to the income differentiation.

The figures have been reported separately for the two sexes, because about half the women were housewives and about a fourth had part-time jobs, factors which could be expected to obscure the picture. But, as can be seen, the figures for the women show the same trends as those for the men. Average income level increases by level of formal schooling, and so does successively the range at the four levels.

TABLE 2. *Taxed Income at age thirty-five as related to Social Class at age ten (males)*

Parental Occupational Status	M	S.D.	N
Status group 1 (professional, managerial)	34,622	27,306	74
Status group 2 (subprofessional middle class)	18,383	10,496	133
Status group 3 (skilled workers)	17,529	8,384	225
Status group 4 (unskilled workers)	15,303	6,984	231

Table 2 shows the income level at age thirty-five by family background in 1938. Those of professional and managerial background tended on the average to have double the income of those coming from the other three status groups. In addition, it is extremely interesting to note that in 1938 the taxed income of the parents in the three latter groups was 4,150, 3,050, and 1,880 crowns, respectively. In 1964 their children, who were then almost their parents' age in 1938, had on the average 18,400, 17,500, and 15,300 crowns, respectively. Thus the range between the social classes had shrunk tremendously.

If we relate education to income, holding family background under control, the range of average income at a given level of education is small or nonexistent at the elementary and junior secondary level, but it is quite large at the senior secondary and university level. Persons with a working-class background and at least eleven years of schooling made 20,000–25,000 crowns a year. They made 40,000 crowns with the same amount of education if they were born in professional and/or managerial homes. The range within the upper-status group varies much more with education than is the case within the low-status group. Thus, if we partial out family background, quite a lot of what is regarded as the contribution made by "pure" education disappears.

TABLE 3. *Taxed Income at age thirty-five as related to I.Q. and Social Class in 1938*

I.Q. in 1938	Social Class in 1938											
	1			2			3			4		
	M	S.D.	N	M	S.D.	N	M	S.D.	N	M	S.D.	N
115+	45,593	39,131	27	23,481	9,579	27	22,750	9,377	40	19,318	7,035	22
108–114	43,667	20,853	12	19,038	6,798	26	17,926	9,486	27	17,107	8,662	28
93–107	22,708	10,680	24	17,564	7,985	55	16,667	7,202	78	15,069	5,889	87
86–92	22,750	7,758	4	15,083	6,764	12	20,192	9,795	26	15,121	8,109	33
85–	24,429	10,458	7	13,000	8,311	13	13,426	4,478	54	13,459	6,048	61

What about ability? As can be seen from Table 3, the average income in 1964 increases at each level by I.Q. as assessed in 1938. At the elementary school level the increase from the group with an I.Q. of 85 or lower to the one with 115 or above is more than one-half of the standard deviation. At the junior secondary level it is more than 1 S.D. At the senior secondary and university level the difference is even larger. Another feature should also be indicated, namely, the increasing variability within the ability levels. The higher the I.Q., the larger the spread in income. This means, then, that more education gives more in terms of "rate-of-return" to those with high than those with low ability. Since children from the upper class are given more ample opportunity to enter secondary school and university, they tended as adults to show a wider range of income by I.Q., as do those who originate from working-class homes. But since a minimal opportunity is offered to these children, we can estimate what I.Q. means to those from the more humble background. Its "effect" could be estimated to be at least about one-half of 1 S.D.

It would be tempting to discuss the findings so far presented against the background of previous longitudinal research, in particular, to relate them to the propositions advanced by Benjamin S. Bloom in his book *Stability and*

Change in Human Characteristics (1964). It would also be tempting to subject them to more subtle analyses, not least statistical ones, such as multiple-regression analysis. My ambition in this context, however, has been merely to give you some glimpses which hopefully convey to you a picture of the interaction between education, social background, or opportunity, and ability in shaping the career up to age thirty-six. The 1,500 third graders in 1938 who have been followed up until 1964 completed their educational careers in a dual-track school system, which was strongly biased against those with an uneducated family background. They started their occupational careers in a social-welfare state with strong leveling-out mechanisms. But these mechanisms were not strong enough to level out the differences between those of upper-class and middle-class background and the remainder, because the opportunity provided by their homes made them come out more successful than the rest. Thus for the generation followed up for more than a quarter of a century by the graduate student who became interested in studying the effect of family background, the social starting point has turned out to be more highly predictive of success in later life than ability.

But their children, who now average ten years of age, are educated in a system which retains the majority in school until eighteen or nineteen. A follow-up of them in 1993, after another twenty-six years, will probably find that ability cultivated by universal education has a much stronger impact than any other factor. He who lives and is interested in carrying on the present study will be able to confirm or refute the meritocratic hypothesis implied in what has just been said.[1]

---

[1] Postscript 1986: The follow-up has continuously been going on. In 1975 Ingemar Fägerlind published a study *Formal Education and Adult Earnings* (Stockholm: Almqvist and Wiksell International). In 1985 Margareta Furu published a study *Life Patterns and Health: A Longitudinal Study of Men from Childhood to Middle Age* (Lund: Liber)

Employment of the Highly Educated in the Society of Today and Tomorrow[*]

OVER the last decade increasing unemployment among college and university graduates has emerged on both sides of the Atlantic (see e.g. R. Freeman: *The Over-Educated American*. New York: Academic Press, 1976). This has been a shocking experience for young university students, because for a long time higher education has been considered to be the best insurance policy against unemployment that one could hold; and for an equally long time, graduates have just been able to pick the most attractive jobs among those available. The present surplus is only partly due to the international economic setback or recession. The "enrollment explosion" has further aggravated the situation, in the sense that the educational system itself has become satiated with staff. Therefore, more graduates are on the market outside the universities and schools at a time when demographic changes sharply reduce the need for teaching staff. Concomitant with the turnaround of the need for university-educated manpower, the salaries in real terms of degree-holders have declined somewhat since 1969, after a decade of substantial increase.

An *ad hoc* committee of experts set up by the Organisation for Economic Co-operation and Development (OECD) has taken a look at problems of education and working life in the highly industrialised countries and has come up with policy recommendations submitted to the governments of the OECD member countries (*Education and Working Life in Modern Society*. Paris: OECD, 1975). I shall, however, not present a summary of its major findings and recommendations but confine myself mainly to some personal observations on the problems dealt with in the report.

First, I shall present some basic facts about what has happened in higher education since 1945. Secondly, I shall point out some changes that have taken place on the labor market, partly under the impact of the enhanced level of formal education among workers. Thirdly, I shall discuss some of the disjunctions or incompatibilities between education and working life and how they possibly could be overcome.

The famous enrollment explosion during the last two decades, when the number of students at institutions of higher learning increased exponentially, has been even more forceful in Europe than in the United States. By 1950, almost 20 per cent of all students of relevant age in America were in college

---

[*] Prepared for a seminar held by the International Council for Educational Development in Barcelona (1978).

and university in comparison with less than 5 per cent in most European countries. Whereas the U.S. enrollment in relative terms doubled until the end of the 1960s, it grew three- to five-fold in many European countries. Just to give one striking illustration from Sweden: The number of first years enrolled in institutions of higher education grew from some 2,000 in 1940-1 to 26,000 in 1970-1. During the same period, the number of full-time students at these institutions increased from some 15,000 to 125,000. The enrollment explosion has in fact hit the European university systems harder than in the United States. The growth ache has been more difficult to overcome in European universities because of certain institutional features, such as "professorial feudalism" and discipline-orientated programs.

The enrollment explosion has elicited a cost explosion which has been even more dramatic, since the unit costs (per student and year) have considerably increased in constant prices. Whereas some 3-4 per cent of the Gross National Product was spent on education in the mid-1950s, the cost increase, until the end of the 1960s, put this figure up to some 10 per cent in the more affluent industrialized countries. The expenditures on education in general, but even more so on higher education, were until the end of the 1960s allowed to grow two or three times as rapidly as the Gross National Product. If the trend of the 1960s is extrapolated, one can anticipate that by 1985 the expenditures on formal education will be far beyond 10-12 per cent of the Gross National Product in the more advanced industrialized countries. Considering a steady state of the entire economy, it is not very likely that increased expenditure will be financed with resources from other sectors. No doubt, the constraints on financial resources that began to be felt by the end of the 1960s, after a period of uninhibited expansion, is likely to lead to a reassessment of the priorities of educational programs at large. This could eventually result in a reshaping of the educational system within the conceptual framework of "life-long" or "permanent" education, something I shall come back to later.

An increase of 15 per cent or more per year was justified on the grounds that in the 1960s education, and particularly higher education, began to be conceived not only as a consumer commodity but also as an investment with a high rate of return to both the individual and the society. Even though the simplistic idea of education as boosting the national economy has been seriously questioned in recent years, the feeling that trained intelligence commands high prices on the market and is allocated to influential and rewarding positions, has prevailed both in capitalist and socialist economies. The so-called human capital approach in assessing the value of education had its heyday at the beginning of the 1960s, when several economists began to regard "human resources as the wealth of nations", to quote the title of a book by one leading American economist Frederick Harbison (*Human Resources as the Wealth of Nations*. London: Oxford University Press, 1973). The almost euphoric appreciation of the value of education, how much, for instance, a college degree adds to one's life earnings, has left room for a more cautious, not to say pessimistic, view on what education can do in bettering an individual's economic life chances. A more sophisticated and critical look at the facts has also been helpful in tempering overenthusiasm.

My favorite example of how the reasoning went is this: Life incomes of university graduates were compared with those whose formal education was limited to a secondary school diploma. The difference of income was explained by the difference in education. This reminds me very much of comparing incomes of members of Rotary with those of non-members and ascribing the difference to Rotary membership!

Until about 1965, the economic position on the labor market of new graduates from colleges and universities on both sides of the Atlantic improved more rapidly than that of secondary school graduates. This situation has been reversed since the end of the 1960s.

Our society has been characterized as the one of "permanent" or "life-long" learning. The formal education system no longer possesses a monopoly in imparting the kinds of knowledge and skills which fifty years or more ago, were the only ones on offer. Today this monopoly has to compete with the mass media and with the learning and training activities going on under the auspices of the voluntary associations and the public and private enterprises. Therefore, education cannot any longer have distinctly defined entering or "cut-off" points, such as examinations and the awarding of degrees. Nor can it in the future be defined by full-time attendance at institutions covering the age range, say, from 6 to 22. Education has become a continuing process with regard both to its extension over the life-span of an individual and its embodiment in other functions of life, particularly in work and leisure. Above all, education can no longer be regarded as identical with schooling. But concomitantly with the increased enrollment and the lengthening of school attendance, formal schooling has become more distinctly institutionalized. It demands more time in the day, it covers more years. Over the last two decades the average level of formal education in the work force in Europe has been raised by four to five years. The institutions themselves have, with manifold increased enrollment, become bigger, with more teaching staff, more varied programs, reduced personal contacts and more formal and bureaucratic lines of communication. The administrative staffs at the universities, at least in Europe, have over the last couple of decades proportionately increased more than the teaching staffs.

Some insightful people have, in recent years, begun to question the worthwhileness of the type of system we have today of keeping all young people in full-time schooling until the end of their teens and even of keeping what might soon be the majority well beyond the age of 20. Their concern has not stemmed from some kind of cost-benefit-analyses, which in my view are difficult, if not impossible, to conduct in education where so many intangible values have to be assessed. The main concern is not the rising costs but the problem of low motivation determined at least in part by the "action poor" approach that teaching takes in secondary school and in tertiary institutions. The additional benefits in terms of competence that accrue to the individual for staying in school some extra years are, in many cases, doubtful if not non-existent. The solution to the problem I have hinted at does not necessarily lie in "de-schooling," but in considering alternatives which would mean that the schools become "de-institutionalized" and brought into closer contact with society at large, including other competence-producing agents. This is what the terms of reference for the OECD committee I referred to above was about. I shall return to this after some observations on what has happened, and what by reasonable forecasts could happen in working life during the next decade or so.

The tremendously expanded cohorts of graduates were in a remarkable way absorbed by the labor market until the early 1970s, when, under the impact of the recession, it seemed to have been satisfied and prospects began to look gloomy. This change in absorbtive capacity was due to several different circumstances. A rapidly increased number of openings for highly qualified manpower has been the result of some important changes in the economy. Thus, the transition from a manufacturing to a service economy has meant an increase of openings in teaching, administration and health care. In the manufacturing industry, the demand for young people who are capable of conducting research and development has meant new opportunities for graduates. The demographic increases that took place after the Second World War created an exceptional demand for teachers. In the United States they increased by more than 160 per cent over twenty years. The public sector has expanded in all countries, irrespective of the type of economy. In Sweden, the number of employed in that sector during the 1960s grew by 100 per cent. It is estimated that the relative number of highly qualified workers in Europe in 1980 will be some 6-7 per cent, a lower percentage than the United States but twice that of 1965. The conditions conducive to a high demand for university-trained manpower have been slackening or not operating at all. A surprising decrease in birthrates, which dramatically affect the need for teachers, has occurred in countries such as the Federal Republic of Germany and the United States, both countries with an impressive machinery of teacher-training institutions built up in order to meet effectively a shortage projected for the next decade. Institutions of higher learning have by now satisfied their own needs for teaching staff and very few graduates are required to replace the newly recruited young staff members. There has been a cutback in R & D spending.

It is difficult, not to say impossible, to make cross-national comparisons of employment statistics. But national time series can be used to illustrate the dramatic shift that occurred at the end of the 1960s. At the end of 1965 only 1.5 per cent of the graduates from English universities of that year were still seeking employment, a figure that grew to 7.8 per cent in 1971. The truth is that the industrial countries at present are not able to provide the number of jobs with the traditional kind of qualifications and status that go with them to accommodate the fast growing number of graduates from the universities.

What, then, are the consequences for the working careers of the rapid increase of young people who enter the labor market with a higher level of formal education than previous generations? Until recently, the world of work could be represented by a "qualification pyramid" with different levels of formal educational requirements and correlated status levels as described earlier (pp. 141 – 146). Until the 1940s, the three strata of the pyramid at least in Europe, were represented in the total work force by the proportions 60-65, 35-40 and 2-5 per cent respectively.

The enhanced level of formal education for young people during the last twenty years will not affect the oldest age bracket of the work force until the 1990s. There will therefore be a considerable generation gap in formal education. For example, in Sweden it is projected that by as late as the year 2000 about 20 per cent of the adult population will have only six to seven years of education, whereas the generation that is just about to enter the labor market will, on the average, have twelve to thirteen years.

The result is that the structure of qualifications will change from a pyramid to what might be represented by an egg standing on its top end (see pp. 141 – 142). At the bottom level we have a group with a minimum of formal education and little or no vocational training. These people will have to take the least attractive jobs in the factories and in the service industries. Such a group can easily become neglected in a highly competitive and efficiency-oriented economy. They will hold the least secure jobs and will be very vulnerable to conjectural swings in the economy.

Even worse, as a result of the "overproduction" of highly educated persons, education becomes a means for the individual to defend his place in the line of job-seekers. The employer tends to prefer applicants with a higher level of education to those with a low but adequate level for the job, because this is an easy way of solving the selection problem. A surplus of highly educated co-exists with strong credentialism. In the middle of the pyramid we could expect the great majority of the work force, which constitutes a large "middle class" with a fairly good level of formal education that offers adequate coping power in a complex society. The top stratum of managers, experts and administrators can optimistically be projected to grow from some 3-5 per cent in 1970, to some 15 per cent in the 1990s.

On the basis of present tendencies and prevailing values, one can anticipate a decrease in social background and inherited wealth as determinants of life chances. Status will increasingly be conferred on the basis of educated ability, which will become the democratic substitute for inherited social prerogatives. The technician, the expert and the scientist will become powerful persons, not only because of the inherent value of their know-how and expertise, but also because politicians tend to waive their authority because of difficulties in translating expert advice into policy action. If increased premium is placed on educated expertise, the society of tomorrow will become more meritocratic in the sense that the highly educated talent will matter more in achieving status.

I have already touched on the problem which could easily cause quite a lot of headaches, not to mention social unrest, in the years to come, namely the increasing discrepancy between the number of traditional openings for graduates and the size of the classes coming on to the labor market. For reasons I have already expressed, we cannot expect these traditional job opportunities to increase considerably over the next ten to twenty years but we know for sure that over the next few years the number of applicants will grow considerably. This means then that many young people are running the risk of having to take dull and unchallenging jobs which do not give them personal fulfillment, simply because employers will tend to raise the formal requirements for the jobs since they can draw upon a larger pool of highly educated people. The conflict between job aspirations and actual status will afflict an increasing number of those entering the job market. University graduates may have to consider non-traditional jobs, such as in banking, insurance and retailing. They may also have to consider first-line supervision and work management in manufacturing industries, and become service and sales representatives, or insurance and estate agents.

We should, however, not take the existing structure of the jobs or the job market as a whole for granted. We know, by ample statistics, that the entire market, from manufacturing to service, is changing. We are, though, perhaps not aware of what could happen at the micro-level to the particular job, when the incumbent becomes more educated. There is evidently an interaction betweeen the job structure and the competence of the job holder, so that the job could be restructured in order to fit more closely the qualities and capabilities of the graduate who takes it. For example, the increasing complexity of life for the consumer and the citizen suggests a need for new personal service jobs which would allow graduates to provide counselling services to consumers and clients.

Thus, it is by no means divinely ordained that education should provide the basis for employment. The world of work may have to be adapted to the capabilities, needs and aspirations of people. This interaction between education and work is strengthened by the fact that exit points from education do not necessarily correspond to entry points into employment, nor to careers that embrace the remaining active life. There are strong indications that in the decades to come, even if the process is slow, there will be a move away from the system of continuous youth education *en bloc*, from which the graduate is slotted into a career track which he pursues until he retires. Under the auspices of a strategy of "recurrent education," with possibilities to re-enter the system and to obtain study leave, the individual will have more freedom to alternate between work, leisure and education. This will enhance his personal fulfillment, not only as a human being but within his work as well.

An increased level of education among the work force will affect the aspirations of the workers and inspire demand for a more participatory work organization and improved work environment. The young people who today enter the labor market have received a more advanced education than their age mates some twenty to thirty years ago and they hold higher aspirations than their elders. They will demand more influence on the way in which their work is organized and they will tend to be less docile than previous generations. Therefore, the time has come for a more active manpower policy, with attempts to enrich jobs, to provide more flexibility of work and careers, to allow greater participation in decision-making and to ensure that opportunities for both jobs and training are provided on a more equitable basis. The essence of such a policy is to provide greater flexibility of individual options, which cannot be entirely left to the free play of market forces.

I am a product of the European university of the late 1930s when I completed my Bachelor's and Master's degrees. This was still a time when a university was conceived as a small place where professors and students in frequent personal contacts tried to come to grips with the eternal problems, a place where one acquired not only an education, be it general or vocational, but also a *Weltanschauung*. I still believe that this should be a major goal of a university, at least in its efforts to take care of students who are possessed of, if not really obsessed by, intellectual interests.

We must not forget that university studies in the 1930s were undertaken during the period of worldwide depression. Tenured employment among graduates was rare, and the unemployment rate was high. In spite of the few who actually gained access into the university, the Swedish government appointed a Commission of inquiry with a mandate to submit recommendations on how entry to the universities could be further restricted so as to avoid creating an intellectual proletariat! At the end of the 1940s, the shortage in most categories of university trained manpower became acute. As I mentioned at the beginning, for more than a quarter of a century young people grew used to a situation whereby further education was a secure entrance ticket into a well-paid and attractive job. Hence, the deep shock that many have experienced in recent years as a result of the turnaround of employment opportunities.

The years of golden opportunities gave rise to the euphoric conception of education as the chief purveyor of good life chances. I remember an international conference held in the early 1960s on ability and educational opportunity. The chairman, with an amused expression on his face, quoted someone as saying that "in our days everybody should have as much education as he could possibly stand!" The belief in education as an investment in human capital justified educational costs being allowed to rise much faster than expenditure in many other public sectors. However, as we have seen, the optimism has given way to distrust and deep pessimism, with a pendulum swing to the other extreme. This pessimism has been inspired not least by the attempts of recent research to assess in a more realistic way what education can and cannot do.

It is easy, at a time of imbalance between jobs and applicants, to conceive of the university primarily as a job/career-building institution and forget the educational values which are not necessarily tied to such careers. Those who advocate more strict career-oriented programs for the basic university degrees have a strong hand when traditional jobs for college graduates are scarce and when those who can offer marketable skills find slots easier than others. I shall, however, not go deeper into this issue here but confine myself to making two points which seem to me to be fundamental. First, apart from certain occupations, such as nursing, teaching and engineering, where on-the-job training has been incorporated into the college or university program, the large majority of jobs which are occupied by university graduates are such that the job-specific competencies are provided by the employer, be he public or private. What is required for these jobs is high-level trainability, which is made up not only of the ability to learn complicated and abstract technical procedures but also of decision making skills, initiative and the ability to deal with complex organisations inside and outside the job world. Such skills which can be applied on a wide – and, in our rapidly changing society, unforeseen – repertoire of situations and tasks, constitute the coping power that is required of highly qualified manpower in our society. Second, and this follows from my first point, the liberal program of undergraduate education in the literal meaning of the word, provides liberty in terms of widening the options not only of today but, and more important, those of tomorrow as well. It would be, in the long run, a great disadvantage to both the individual and society if the university programs were to be narrowed down to fit a temporary employment situation. It would be to the detriment of the individual seeking self-fulfillment to have a limited range of career options during the remainder of his active life. What I am driving at is simply a plea for educational values which constitute the coping power needed in our complex and changing society.

V. International and Comparative Dimensions

The World Community of Academics: Its Nature and Responsibilities (1977)[1]
Internationalizing Education: The Case of Sweden (1978)[2]
The International Context of Educational Research (1983)[3]
An International Research Venture in Retrospect: The IEA Surveys (1979)[4]
Appraising the Quality of Secondary Education: Cross-national Assessments of Achievements (1984)[5]

Introduction

Comparative studies in education with a strict empirical approach have a short history. In 1958-59 researchers from 12 countries, sponsored by the UNESCO Institute for Education in Hamburg, decided to launch an exploratory study measuring achievements of 13-year-olds cross-nationally. The purpose at this stage was to find out whether it was feasible to develop achievement tests with reasonable international validity, instruments that could be uniformly administered and scored across countries and yield data that could be uniformly processed and analyzed. The participating research institutions in 1961 organized themselves as the International Association for the Evaluation of Educational Achievement (IEA). The author was chairman of the association from 1962 until 1978.

The feasibility study encouraged more extensive ventures, first an international mathematics survey in the mid-1960s, still with 12 countries, which was followed by the so-called Six-Subject Survey 1966 through 1973 with 21 countries, the most extensive international research project in education until now. In the late 1970s and early 1980s second surveys were conducted (with 25 countries) in both mathematics and science. This made comparisons possible both over time as well as across countries. In the so-called Six-Subject Survey, by replicating the same study across a large number of countries, IEA hoped to be able to identify social, economic and pedagogical factors that accounted for between-country, between-school and between-student differences.

IEA have produced an enormous research literature of both international and national monographs, technical reports and special papers. In 1979,

T. N. Postlethwaite and A. Lewy published an *Annotated Bibliography* comprising some 300 items.

The first IEA study was launched during the "post-Sputnik" era with its heightened interest in the relative quality of education in various countries, particularly in science and technology. This was a reflection of international tensions and competition in the military and trade fields. The early 1980s saw a revival of such an interest, again inspired by international competition for the world market, for instance in high-technology, between the United States and Japan.

Further reports of IEA research can be read in T. Husén: *International Study of Mathematics I-II* (New York: Wiley, 1967) and D. Walker: *The IEA Six-Subject Survey* (New York: Wiley, 1976). The *Annotated Bibliography* compiled by T. H. Postlethwaite and A. Lewy (Stockholm: Institute of International Education) lists all printed IEA publications up to and including 1978.

Notes

1. Given as a lecture in Washington, D.C. in 1976 at the Annual Convention of the American Council on Education. Published in Stephen K. Bailey (ed.) *Higher Education in the World Community*. Washington, D.C.: American Council on Education, 1977, 197-206.
2. Paper, given at a seminar at the Aspen Institute for Humanistic Studies, Summer 1978.
3. Published in *Oxford Review of Education*, Vol. 9:1, 1983, 21-29.
4. Published in *Comparative Education Review*, Vol. 23:3, 1979, 371-85.
5. Presentation at the Spring Meeting 1984 of the U.S. National Academy of Education in Stockholm.

The World Community of Academics:
Its Nature and Responsibilities*

In my personal library I am fortunate enough to have a copy of a 1662 edition of Amos Comenius's *Janua Linguarum Reserata*, a language textbook with parallel texts throughout the book in Latin, German, and French. On the inside of the sheepskin cover the contemporary owner of the book has written "Simon Segerdahl – légitime possesseur de ce livre, Paris le 21 Avrile l'an 1675." Segerdahl was one of the Swedish students who spent a few years at the University of Paris, a continental center of excellence to which Scandinavian students, among others, were attracted. In the *gymnasium* of his home province and most likely during a stay as an undergraduate at the University of Uppsala, he had become quite proficient in Latin, the *lingua franca* of the international community of scholars of that time. Thus he had most likely bought Comenius's book in order to learn French which, like other modern languages, such as German and English, was not taught in the European pre-university schools until well into the first decades of the nineteenth century. Comenius himself was a true international and pan-European scholar, who was born and grew up in Moravia but was expelled during the wave of religious persecutions that swept central Europe. He then spent most of his active life in such countries as the Netherlands, Sweden, and Poland, incessantly working for international understanding on the basis of his pansophical ideas about the improvement of the spiritual and material conditions of mankind.

The decreasing use of Latin as a means of communication between scholars and professionals meant, at least for some time, an increased provincialism in intellectual affairs. A language is, however, not simply an instrument of communication. It also provides a common frame of reference for historical traditions, cultural referents, and ideas – something which also to a large extent was lost when Latin disappeared from the secondary school curriculum.

Whether English is to become the new *lingua franca* among intellectuals and contribute to cementing international cohesiveness among them is, I assume, still an open question. I am quite confident that my French friends for example would not endorse this proposition. English as an instrument of

* Presentation given in Washington, D.C. at the 1976 Convention of the American Council on Education. Originally published in Stephen K. Bailey (ed.) 1977, *Higher Education in the World Community*. Washington, D.C.: American Council on Education. Reproduced by permission of the American Council on Education.

communication plays an overwhelming role in southeast Asia. French however, has a strong position in Africa because in some countries, such as Senegal and Zaire it is the only language that is understood by everybody with some basic education, and in a way it defines a "nationality" among a cluster of tribes that by colonial coincidence were brought together into a geographical entity. In Africa one gets a strong impression of the role played by the two dominant European languages in articulating the intellectual profiles of the new elites.

When in the following, I refer to "intellectuals," I shall have in mind primarily the "achieved" academics – teachers and researchers at the universities. But the mounting influence of intellectuals in the modern society evidently also operates from extramural bases, such as the mass media and growing government bureaucracy which largely depend for staff on products from the universities.

Academic Ethos Implies Universalism

The very idea of the university is linked to the crossing of national boundaries in order to achieve understanding of the national and cultural patterns of other lands. At the core of the academic ethos lies the hope of achieving the universalism and objectivity which is fundamental to scientific research. Nationalism and political bias are inimical to such endeavors. It is for this reason that academic freedom violated in one country is fervently defended by scholars and students in most other countries. James A. Perkins in 1966 eloquently expressed the thrust toward internationalism: "To join this community [of intellectuals] is to become part of a world that knows no boundaries, whose arena is the total knowledge acquired by all mankind, whose curiosity is never satisfied, whose standards and values are set not by tradition or belief but by the intractable nature of truth." There is, indeed something that Perkins refers to as an international creed among the university-based intellectuals which determines scholarly behavior, such as the unceasing, unbiased search for truth; the scrutiny of subject matter that seemingly has been settled; the rejection of prejudice; and the willingness to contribute to the international body of knowledge.

The international intellectual community is not invested with political power. Its influence derives entirely from society's dependence on it to provide trained manpower, research, and services. Indeed, the community is a frail network of communication and cooperation that is in few respects institutionalized. Its cohesiveness depends on the strength of the academic ethos, which has itself in recent years suffered quite a few shocks.

There is a corollary to the above. In as much as the institutional base for the community of intellectuals is a university in the home country of the individual scholar, radical changes in the university system in a country affect not only its intellectuals but also their role and contributions to the international community. This corollary applies with special force if the changes are entirely initiated and enforced by political bodies. Bonds that have taken generations of scholars to develop can thereby easily be destroyed.

International Solidarity and Academic Freedom

An important aspect of the international solidarity among scholars, and an indispensable part of the academic ethos, is the mutual support that intellectuals are ready to give when freedom of teaching and inquiry is attacked from outside or from within the university. Such attacks are usually thought of as resulting from state political oppression. But infringements of academic freedom can also come from within the university, when organized disruptions of teaching take place or facilities are occupied by students. Obvious outcomes of such upheavals are illustrated by the damage suffered by many European universities during the late 1960s. Germany for instance has been seeing a phenomenon that some twenty years ago would have been unthinkable: an exodus of professors from the universities to independent research institutions. This, by the way, also reflects the loss of prestige that the European professor has suffered as a result of events of recent years.

During periods of acute political crises, academic freedom can suffer setbacks even in countries that like to think of themselves as being unsinkable democracies. I only need mention McCarthyism in the United States during the peak of the cold war and the loyalty oath controversy at the University of California during the hot days of the cold war. In the wake of the political crisis in France in connection with the de Gaulle take-over, some radical professors of the University of Paris were suspended. I submit that in present-day Europe the differences in intellectual freedom and in academic autonomy between countries with a parliamentary democracy and those ruled by governmental decrees are a matter of degree. There is a growing accumulation of power in all central governments that have at their disposal an ever-growing bureaucracy. And the growing power makes life incessantly more difficult for the universities, which are institutions where "success associated with intellectual achievement is actually linked to a propensity for social criticism." Universities have become the only agents of independent criticism and are – to their mounting dismay – regarded as sanctuaries for "irresponsible" critics.

Thus the international solidarity among scholars plays an important role in alerting public opinion to encroachments on freedom of thought and expression. This role applies particularly to the intellectuals who have universities as their institutional base of operation. The international community in this respect works both ways. It promotes a supranational allegiance to ideals of truth seeking and of free exchange of ideas and outcomes of research endeavors. It also operates as a network of guardians of freedom. Not least during the last ten years when universities all over the world have been attacked both from outside and within, the international mutual support has been of immense value in protecting basic rights.

Effects of the Mounting Nationalism

During the last couple of decades there has been an observable mounting nationalism in higher education. In newly established or emerging countries there is a natural striving for national identity. Because the university represents the pinnacle of cultural and intellectual endeavors in a country, the establishment of a national university becomes an important symbol of identity. This patriotic role implies emphasis on supportive symbols, such as the national language (if any pervasive one exists), national history, and traditions. As long as proximity to a particular culture and to national tradition is a prerequisite for the transmission of particular competencies and for conducting research pertaining to problems in the national domain, such an orientation is no doubt beneficial to both major functions of higher education. But a proper balance has to be struck between parochialism and professional universalism.

In an increasingly interdependent world, internationalism is an inherent feature of the intellectual sphere. At the root of scholarly pursuits lies the endeavor to establish universally valid principles and facts. There is no particular British, Swedish, Iranian, or Chilean mathematics or science. In the humanities the situation is less clear-cut. The social sciences are taking an intermediate position.

In most areas of scholarly pursuit, one could easily identify centers of excellence, places or institutions where – often after a long period of development, including personnel resources – the contributions to knowledge have been remarkable. These centers attract not only outstanding professors but also promising apprentices from other lands who join the ongoing pioneering intellectual ventures and then return home with new insights that will enrich their fields of higher education there. For instance, in the latter nineteenth century, young American graduate students went to German universities and returned from Berlin, Leipzig, and other places ready to pioneer advanced programs of study back home. A similar relationship has maintained between the universities of Oxford, Cambridge, and London and the former British colonies. Since the Second World War the United States has been at the forefront in many fields of research and scholarship. No wonder, then, that students from all over the world – in recent years, more than a hundred thousand, many of them graduate students – have flocked to centers of excellence such as Chicago, Harvard, Columbia, Berkeley, and Stanford.

Some years ago I had the pleasure, as chairman of the Governing Board of the International Institute for Educational Planning, to work with a Soviet colleague who was also on the board. His professional field was aeronautics, in which during the 1930s he had taken a doctorate at the Massachusetts

Institute of Technology. During the war he was an important link between the United States and the U.S.S.R in operating the lend-lease program. On our board, he was not simply a highly competent technician. His education and experiences from two large countries had given him a perspective, not least on problems of higher education, which was of great value in an international organization. I remember well the fervor with which he defended the professional autonomy of the institute against attempts by the international bureaucracy for the sake of political expediency to infringe upon its freedom of research.

Communication Network among Intellectuals

During recent decades, communication among intellectuals and scholars worldwide has increased tremendously, and international congresses and conferences have proliferated. Many meetings are now so heavily attended that they become almost unmanageable and counter-productive to their purposes of promoting exchange of ideas, research findings and professional experiences through paper presentations and small-group discussions. However, regardless of size of attendance the most important yield is usually the interaction achieved by informal contacts and discourses with colleagues.

The international exchange of students and scholars has also increased enormously since 1945. By 1970, universities in Europe and the United States had enrolled more than a quarter million foreign students, to a large extent from the Third World. Although recessions have slowed the increase, by 1980 the figure had approached a million students. A similar increase has occurred in the exchange of university-based intellectuals, professors, and researchers. Worthy of mention is the Fulbright exchange program which has been of immense value in promoting intellectual contacts and scholarly exchange between the United States and Europe.

Contributing to the network of communication among intellectuals are publications of various kinds. Books and learned monographs aside, there are three types of which the first two mainly serve the intellectual generalist and the third caters to the specialist. In the languages that serve as *linguae francae* in the world today, some newspapers are more or less indispensable for the intellectual who wants to know what is happening on the international scene in domains such as literature, science and technology, education, and the arts. Illustrations are the London *Times* and its supplements, the *New York Times*, *Le Monde*, and *Frankfurter Allgemeine Zeitung*. Second, some magazines provide comprehensive coverage of cultural and intellectual events; among them are the *Economist*, the *Saturday Review*, *Le Figaro Litéraire* and *die Zeit*. Such publications reflect the world intellectual culture and provide their readers with notions of the direction in which *der Zeitgeist* is moving.

The third category, the scholarly journals, present the outcomes of research endeavors in increasing specialized disciplines.

International and Regional Cooperation

During the last quarter century various international bodies have been created to promote exchange of information in various fields of culture, research, and education. The best known is, of course, UNESCO. In addition there are other specialized U.N. agencies that provide networks for professionals in particular fields.

The extranational networks of communication, exchange, and cooperation among scholars and intellectuals are to a large extent regional. Such cooperative endeavors are often based on shared political and economic interests of a group of countries. The Council of Europe and the Organization of American States are regional cooperatives that are promoting far-reaching cooperation in matters related to education and culture. Another example is offered by the Scandinavian countries. I have long been involved in the educational activities of the Nordic Cultural Commission, an organ of the Nordic Council, the political agency appointed by the parliaments. The close cooperation in intellectual matters between the four Nordic countries has, of course been facilitated by the high degree of affinity among the languages of the Scandinavian countries, the existence of a common labor market, and a tradition of cooperation. The European Economic Community has recently entered upon cooperative programs that pertain to education and research.

It is beyond the scope of this paper to spell out the role of intergovernmental organizations in promoting an international community of intellectuals. I shall only point out that the very fact that an organization is intergovernmental can create problems of academic freedom and professional integrity. For example, one such agency has attemped to influence the content and the mode of publication of research reports which certain member countries had perceived to be unfavorable to them and therefore tried to use political leverage to stop publication of certain findings. Needless to say, if reports from cooperative endeavours have to be cleared by national governments before they can be published, international research runs the risk of becoming invalid and thus meaningless. Such working conditions can easily make it impossible to attract scholars to research institutes that operate under the aegis of intergovernmental organizations.

Over the past fifteen years I have gained some experience in building up and operating the International Association for the Evaluation of Educational Achievement (IEA), a cooperative machinery for multinational research in education. An incorporated private organization, originally created under the auspices of UNESCO it is an association of competent educational research institutes in some twenty countries. Thus far, it has conducted surveys in seven subject areas for the purpose of identifying social, economic, and pedagogical factors that account for differences in scholastic achievements between countries, schools, and students. Some of the study outcomes have had important implications for education policy in the participating countries.

This type of multinational research illustrates that even in education, a field molded by national patterns, it is possible to agree on a uniform research design and to carry it through with the same methodology and timetable in countries with widely different socioeconomic structures, such as the United States, Hungary, Australia, Chile and India. Despite varying styles in adhering to timetables and responding to letters (and with some fifteen languages involved), it proved possible to bring such an ambitious research endeavor to a successful conclusion.

The Need for Generalists

Explosive specialization has affected intellectual life inside and outside the universities. The fragmentation of scholarly pursuits has increasingly impeded pursuit of general education goals within the university. The ideal of the educated man that still prevailed at the beginning of this century has succumbed. The common frame of reference that in earlier days pervaded the thinking and the values of the educated élite is gone.

Within the university, it has become almost impossible for the scholar who has an ambition to preserve an overview of a broad field of inquiry or who takes interdisciplinary approaches to keep up with the torrent of publications. In many disciplines, during the last few decades the number of reports published in scholarly journals has doubled every six to eight years, and in some scientific fields the number has increased by some 3000 per cent since 1945. In addition, most departments in graduate institutions distribute interim report series in order to speed up communication with their sister institutions.

The proliferation of literature has a consequence. The university intellectual generalist, who needs and has the capacity for synopsis, tends to be replaced by the specialist in a narrow field who has achieved, through what somebody has termed "a short-sighted scrutiny of documents," something that technically qualifies him for a professorship. Generalists, particularly in the social sciences are needed in a society of increasing interdependence that calls for "systems solutions" to its problems. The specialized, fragmented approach to problems has been one reason why so much of our social and educational policy has failed.

What I have in mind here is not the polyhistor found in the seventeenth and eighteenth-century European universities, the scholar who had so to speak, read most of the books in many disciplines and had himself produced books in several of them. Rather, I am thinking of the philospher of that era who, not too many decades ago, could still be found at our universities, a man who in the original sense of the word was an adorer of wisdom and knowledge that cut across all intellectual areas. Déscartes was an outstanding example of the all-embracing approach with a unity of knowledge about both nature and human affairs and no gap between the "two cultures."

Such remarks about the generalist-philosopher may appear nostalgic and out of place. But they have a particular relevance in an international context. It was no coincidence that universalistic minds represented by Erasmus, Comenius, and Déscartes, were primarily internationally orientated. Their home countries – if they were allowed to reside in them – were regarded as anchoring places, and Europe was their field of operation. Their all-embracing intellectual curiosity was hindered neither by disciplinary boundaries nor by national borders. The universal approach in intellectual matters is, indeed incompatible with a provincial or narrowly nationalistic orientation.

Too little attention has been paid to disciplinary fragmentation and the collapse of general education as major causes for the inner tension, fragmentation, and disintegration in the university today. A community of scholars with broad orientation makes sense, but a community of specialists is a *contradictio in adjecto*. To restore the cohesiveness and to countervail the institutional anarchy that characterizes the university of today, it will be essential to reconsider the goal of general education so as to reestablish a common frame of reference among senior and junior members of academia.

The world is a place of increasing interdependence to the extent that international cooperation and mutual assistance have become matters of life and death for individuals as well as for nations. Intellectuals face the particular tasks of being in the forefront in building a spirit of cooperation and of mobilizing the massive technical competence needed to manage the concrete problems of interdependence – the global problems of production and distribution of food, fair distribution and utilization of natural resources and energy, the limitation of population growth, and the attainment of universal literacy.

A large work force of technicians trained to deal piecemeal with these problems within a nation will not suffice to cope with them on an international scale. For instance, the technicians' contribution to technical assistance is easily crippled unless they have acquired a mind set to see their work in a wider context. The world needs what I (for lack of a better expression) call an international peace corps of intellectuals who, apart from their technical competence, see their overriding task as representing the world's conscience and who are ready to devote their first loyalty to humanity.

Internationalizing Education: The Case of Sweden*

Some General Observations

One recent catchphrase which entered intellectual discourse in the 1970s was "global interdependence." It articulated a fact that has become increasingly obvious to the insightful, namely that we now live in an indivisible world. Modern trade, technology, means of communication, and – not least – modern warfare, have brought humanity into a common fate. The limited resources, and uninhibited exploitation of these by the haves to the detriment of the have-nots, the effects of this on the ecosystem, exacerbated by the population explosion, are other parts of the same syndrome of concerns.

"Internationalizing education" had two major objectives, one more idealistic and elusive and one more tangible and pragmatic. In the first place, by certain programs and studies in the formal system we want to achieve a heightened awareness among young people of global interdependence by, among other things, presenting them with certain basic facts. We could regard it as a sensitivity training in international thinking. The other overriding objective is to impart certain competences that will enable young people to function in an international setting, such as mastery of foreign languages, knowledge and insights into foreign cultures, and the history and geography of other nationals.

When governments take actions which aim at extending the international dimension of formal education, the more pragmatic aspect is considered in the first place, among other things because it can more easily become operational by programs and monies. By making young people in one's own country proficient in at least one of the world languages and more knowledgeable about countries who are prominent trade partners certain immediate and obvious advantages can be achieved.

The fact that my presentation of the steps taken in Sweden to internationalize education almost entirely deals with the second aspect does not imply that I perceive the first objective as less important. Again, the pragmatic approach lends itself more easily to tangible policy measures and actions. You can quite objectively assess proficiency achieved in a foreign language,

* Presentation given at an international seminar on higher education at the Aspen Institute of Humanistic Studies (1978).

which we did in the IEA survey of the teaching of English and French as Foreign Languages in some ten countries. But how do you measure the degree of awareness of global interdependence and the moral commitment that ensues from it?

Some Background to Swedish Attempts to Internationalize Education

Recent attempts in Sweden to internationalize its educational system at all levels, not least the post-secondary one, should be viewed in connection with certain historical and social conditions that have been instrumental in shaping modern Swedish society.

1. It is a country with a small population of about $8\frac{1}{2}$ million people who have so far enjoyed great ethnic and racial homogeneity, which recently however has partly changed by the immigration of labor from Finland and the Mediterranean region. It has had a 170 year history of peace, which explains the fervor and consensus with which a policy of neutrality in military (but not in ideological) conflicts, is embraced by all parties.

2. A growing awareness of global interdependence and solidarity, not least with the Third World, expressed in a strong commitment to development aid. The shaping of this mentality can be accounted for by the following: (a) The Labor Movement, both its trade union and its political arm, early committed itself to internationalism. This has had a strong impact in the country, since we had a Social Democratic government for forty-four years from 1932 to 1976. The Swedish Labor Movement has closely cooperated with sister parties and unions in other countries. (b) Sweden was the first of the affluent countries to achieve the 1 per cent goal of the GNP in contributions to international assistance.

3. Half the economy depends on export (iron ore, paper and pulp, motor cars, appliances, ballbearings, etc.). Therefore, international recessions become Swedish recessions. A considerable number of young people who go into business and industry in Sweden must possess certain competences, not least the mastery of foreign languages, in order to conduct their jobs properly.

4. The immigration policy has on the whole been rather liberal. There was an influx of refugees in the 1930s and 1940s. From the early 1960s Sweden has had a big influx of what Germans refer to as "guest-workers," but who, since most of them remain in Sweden, more accurately should be called immigrants. The policy of the Swedish Government has been to assist them in their adaptation to Swedish society. They immediately after employment become members of unions and are paid according to the rate settled in union contracts. The employers are obliged to release them during paid working hours to attend classes in Swedish for foreigners. However, strong emphasis is put on a policy to promote cultural and linguistic identity of the immigrants, and particularly in their children, who otherwise easily become alienated

from their parents by the fact of going to school with children of Swedish origin. New legislation (depending upon how many they are in a given school) provides instruction in their mother tongue for a certain number of periods per week. Teachers from their home country are often employed to be in charge of this instruction. These foreign teachers also assist the Swedish teachers by serving as bridges between the mother tongue and Swedish.

5. There has in Sweden for quite some time been a strong belief in social intervention and planned change. An American, who in 1965 wrote about educational change in Europe for the *Saturday Review*, gave the article on Sweden the title "Paradise for Planners," which had a certain ironic overtone. Planned social intervention at the national level and with the purpose of having nation-wide effects has been prevalent in Swedish labor market policy and accounts for the fact that full or close to full employment has been maintained throughout all business cycle fluctuations.

The belief in planned and rationally prepared change is epitomized in the practice of appointing what previously was called Royal Commissions, but now simply Government Commissions. Such Commissions have traditionally been charged to inquire into and by their recommendations draw up blueprints for social, economic, and educational reforms and sometimes initiate them. I shall not go into detail about how these commissions operate but simply point out a few important features. They are, of course, appointed by the Government. Their terms of reference have in advance been discussed with the interested parties and pressure groups who are also represented on the Commission.

Thus, the various interest groups would have to settle their differences within the framework of the Commission. Representatives of the various political parties, central federation of trade unions, and professional groups often serve on these commissions. They work often for several years, but then come up with rather elaborate blueprints for change and reform in a particular field. They are thereby also important instruments not only in setting new goals and devising new means of achieving them but also in building new public institutions. I mention this because the system of commissions operates in what, so far, has been an atmosphere of the politics of consensus which is possible in a rather small, and homogeneous country.

When it comes to institutionalize efforts in the field of international education, Sweden did not appoint a Government Commission but one that formally worked within the framework of the National Board of the Swedish Universities and Colleges which, however, did not make much difference. By and large it conducted its business as a regular Government Commission. Its reports were submitted for review to various bodies inside and outside the world of education in order to assess their views before legislation on the basis of the report was drafted.

Goals of Internationalization in Swedish Schools

The Commission on Internationalization of Higher Education in its main report stated a series of goals. It was pointed out that internationalization should be part of general education at all levels of the educational system and is not particular for higher education. The Commission therefore inquired into what could be done all the way from kindergarten through the university.

The general goals should be:

1. Awareness of global interdependence and the building up of international understanding.
2. The building up of international solidarity as expressed in the efforts and resources devoted to financial and other assistance to developing countries.
3. Acceptance of the Western pluralistic value-orientation and tolerance towards ambiguity.

The more specific, and at the same time more pragmatic, goals should be:

1. Employability on the international labor market, including international, inter-governmental organizations.
2. Orientation towards the future.
3. Specific skills and knowledge necessary in order to function in an international context, such as language skills, knowledge about other cultures, etc.

Implementation

Most school subjects have what could be called an international dimension, which is, of course, most evident in the study of foreign languages. In order to study them fruitfully it does not suffice to acquire an abstract instrument of communication without the historical and cultural referents that go with it. Thus, what in language instruction is referred to as *realia* are to be acquired in history, geography and civics.

As always, pious hopes of achieving changes in the schools are easily thwarted if the teachers are not in favor of them and/or are simply not knowledgeable about them. Thus, the Commission envisaged a massive in-service teacher training program in three major steps. One should begin by training a core group of teachers who could serve as regional experts on internationalization and take leadership in setting up working teams for in-service training at the local level. This aims at changing teacher attitudes.

University research is by definition international, since basic research in order to be of any value aims at arriving at universal principles and scientific laws. In the first place, the methodology of research is international. There are no French, German or American methods in physics, even if there can be different schools applying different strategies in their research. The topics tackled can be international or cross-cultural in nature, for instance, studies conducted in comparative education or comparative law. The organization of research can be internationalized by establishing cooperation over national boundaries between institutions or by exchanging scholars between institutions. Finally, the dissemination of research can be internationalized. To take one simple example, dissertations submitted for the doctorate at Swedish universities *must* have ample summaries in one of the world languages. Funds are available for having them translated in their entirety.

Language Studies

Until the early 1940s, foreign languages in Sweden were taught in academic secondary schools only. This meant that the majority, or some 80 per cent, who left school only with mandatory elementary schooling at the age of 14 had had no foreign language instruction at all. In the junior secondary school, grades 5 through 9 or 7 through 10, two foreign languages, German and English, in that order, were mandatory. Those who wanted to proceed to the upper secondary school, the *gymnasium*, had to study French as well, since good reading knowledge was necessary for university studies. At this stage most textbooks were in the three languages. I had to take an intensive course in French after having completed the *realskola*, the junior secondary school. I happened to hate the teacher who taught French and, without my parent's knowledge, did not take French for two years.

The 1940 School Commission that was the first Commission of three which until 1961 were inquiring into the structure and curriculum of Swedish education up the age of 16, proposed that English should be compulsory in the basic school that covered 8, and later, 9 grades. It was gradually introduced in grade 5 in the late 1940s through the 1950s. The greatest problem was the shortage of competent language teachers. Two steps were taken to cope with that problem. Instead of employing teachers trained at the university in order to become competent to give language instruction in secondary school, a massive in-service training of elementary school teachers with self-contained classroom competence was launched. They were brought to the level of competence to which the universities brought its students after one semester of full-time study devoted entirely to English. Secondly, during the early years the Swedish Radio Corporation provided instruction. In one region *all* the teaching in English was radio instruction under teacher supervision. The 1962 Act on the introduction of the nine-year comprehensive school moved the introduction of English as a mandatory subject down to grade 4. The 1969 revision of the curriculum moved it further down to grade 3. This means that a majority of students of the nine-year basic school are taking seven years of English.

Sweden participated in the evaluation of the teaching of English as a foreign language conducted by the International Association for the Evaluation of Educational Achievement (IEA) in some ten countries. The outcomes were encouraging because Sweden and the Netherlands were the two countries with the highest achievements in reading, listening and understanding, pronunciation, and written production of English. The survey put an end to the criticism that Swedish youngsters, due to the favoring of the so-called direct method, were far behind students in other countries. A thorough analysis of how English was taught showed that very few teachers used an extreme methodological approach. Most of them used what was referred to as a "modified direct method" with considerable teaching of grammar.

Thus, English enjoys a favored position in the Swedish school curriculum to the extent of almost becoming a second language for many young people. But it has also been at the forefront in adult education, particularly in evening classes. The Stockholm University Extension Service in the early 1950s founded the British Center which was instrumental in bringing teachers of English from England to Sweden and placing them all over the country where they were teaching both evening classes and in primary and secondary schools.

The status of the other two languages traditionally taught in Swedish secondary schools has, relatively seen, been lowered. The curriculum of the compulsory nine-year school offers German or French as options. For some time a majority of students in grades 7 through 9 took one of the two. But even if, due to more attractive options that were offered in later curriculum revisions, the number has somewhat diminished, about one or two students at that level take either French or German for three years which both absolutely and relatively is many more than before 1950. But the level of competence achieved after three years of study is rather poor. In recent years misgivings have been aired about the status and teaching of these two languages that, not least for Swedish foreign trade, are of great importance. French has suffered, particularly since it is studied only for two years, which in most countries seems to be almost a waste of time, because of the low level of proficiency that can be achieved within that time.

In the upper secondary school, the *gymnasium*, that also prepares for the university, the 1960 Gymnasium Commission in its curriculum proposal ranked languages in three categories, A-, B- and C-language. The A-language was mandatory English, B-language could be either French or German, and C-language could be either the other B-language or Russian, Italian, and Spanish.

The fact that most students who enter university can only get along with texts in English means that particular attention must be given to language instruction of the skill type at that level. It is in most cases out of the question to assign readings in German or French. We therefore now find university texts in Swedish and English only, whereas when I took my undergraduate studies a considerable portion of my readings was in German and French.

The Commission on internationalization took a special interest in what it refers to as the *fackspråk*, the language for special purposes, for instance English used in physics, sociology, computer science, and economics. Thus, the Commission discussed the possibility of studying the language as part of the subject specialization. The Commission referred to this as the "integrated skills language training," and advanced rather detailed recommendations for how such programs concretely should be implemented. On the whole, it strongly emphasized the "crucial role played by skills in foreign languages for future employment prospects."

International Exchange of Faculty and Students

The Commission on Internationalization of Higher Education identified four kinds of obstacles preventing exchange:
1. Structural, such as design of courses and degree requirements,
2. Formal, laws and regulations, such as work permit regulations,
3. Communicative, limitations caused by language competence, availability of documentation, and
4. Economic, such as travel costs and need for subsistence allowance.

The Commission made recommendations about how these obstacles, particularly the formal and economic ones, should be overcome or removed. It also set forth general guidelines within which the individual institutions could build up broadened exchange.

For various reasons, not least economic, it is hard to envisage that all undergraduates at public expense could be provided with an opportunity for study abroad, the exceptions, of course, being those who are majoring in foreign languages.

The Commission thought that in principle a period of study abroad should be part of the *graduate* program. This has so far on a very modest scale been implemented by means of financing group studies abroad at the graduate level. Thus, students of human geography at the University of Stockholm accompanied by some faculty every year go to Kenya, Africa, for a few weeks of field studies. Graduate students at the Institute of International Education visit the International Institute for Educational Planning for a week.

The Nordic Cultural Commission, which is a body for internordic cooperation in culture and education, has done much in order to bring about reciprocal accreditation of educational attainments. Each university department is left with quite a lot of discretion, when it comes to admitting foreign students. I have in the Institute of International Education at the University of Stockholm over the last ten years had graduate students from more than half a dozen countries and have had the authority to evaluate their previous course work in Swedish equivalents. Needless to say, quite a lot of flexibility has to be exercised in doing so.

The general rules of admission to Swedish higher education that were passed by the Parliament as part of the new Higher Education Act in 1975 sets a ceiling of some 10 per cent foreign students. Presently, about half of the foreign students are in the country as immigrants. They are eligible for financial assistance according to the rules that apply to Swedish students.

Faculty experience abroad is generally acquired either by travel to international meetings of various kinds or by periods of guest professorships in other countries. The Commission recommended that one should make it possible, which can be done at a low cost, for Swedish faculty to switch posts with colleagues in other countries. Furthermore, funds should be made available to employ foreign faculty on a temporary basis.

Of course, guest professorships have existed long since but have been very few in Sweden. As a matter of fact, there has been a striking lack of balance between the number of Swedish professors taking guest professorships abroad and foreigners coming to Sweden, for instance, on Fulbright fellowships. But one should keep in mind that instruction at Swedish universities, with few exceptions, is given in Swedish only. At the University of Stockholm there are only two institutions both with graduate students and with teaching conducted entirely in English, namely the Institute of International Economics and the Institute of International Education.

Institutional Framework

The Commission proposed an International Secretariat in the Office of the Chancellor of the Swedish Universities – he was, after all, the one who initiated the Commission. This was rejected by the various university bodies who were asked to review the commission's report. They insisted that the effort to internationalize research and teaching in the university should be anchored in the various *departments*. It is at that level that the international network of contacts embracing the international community of scholars is established. The departments need central stimulation, not least by means of funds in order to keep these contacts alive by exchange and travel.

Internationalization of Programs

Three different types of program arrangements were contemplated by the Commission:
1. Internationally oriented "theme courses," for instance, the university in the modern world, survival problems in the global society.
2. Thematic continuation courses, which build on specialized knowledge and competence from different disciplines, for instance human ecology.
3. Area studies focussing on new continents. Uppsala University has been the site of the Nordic Africa Institute. The Commission recommends other area studies, such as Latin America and Asia.

Concluding Observations

The task of internationalizing education by necessity varies between small and big nations. The goal of including English as a mandatory school subject in Swedish basic school since the late 1940s has been to make English a second language that can serve as an instrument of communication on the international scene. In addition, those who go on to higher education, or at least those who enter graduate studies, need to acquire at least some reading knowledge in one or two more languages.

In a big country like the United States the mother tongue has increasingly become the prime instrument of international communication in both East and West. Only persons with certain specialized functions, occupationally or otherwise, need to master foreign languages. Even with some 19 million Hispanics the mastering of Spanish is not necessary except in some areas, such as New Mexico. People employed in foreign trade, in the military, and in diplomatic service have quite specific language competency needs. In 1978 I had in my role as an OECD examiner of compensatory education the opportunity to visit Southern California and New Mexico. In the latter state about half the student population came from Spanish-speaking homes. But legislation on bilingual education was rather emphatic in aiming at English as the medium of instruction. The prime goal is to make all these children proficient in English, not primarily to strengthen their cultural and linguistic identity.

How can we get the message across to legislators and other policy makers about the importance of enhancing "global awareness?" This is a formidable task, because we are here dealing with something which does not lend itself to fund authorization as readily as does the promotion of foreign language study. It can only be achieved by a change in attitude and mentality that takes quite some time to occur. A concerted effort by teacher trainers, curriculum developers, and media people is called for.

Again, the problem of internationalizing education takes on a different shape in the less developed countries, most of which until recently were colonies, whereas most of the developed countries gained nationhoods long ago. Nation-building around a common language and a national history covering a longer period has started late in most developing countries. Most of the African countries in the Subsaharan region were colonies, territories, that by accidents of history were brought under colonial rule by major European powers. Latin America relatively early gained independence from Spanish and Portugese rule that had lasted for several hundred years. South and Southeast Asia has been under British, Dutch, and French rule.

Subsaharan Africa provides perhaps the most striking example of difficulties entailed in nation-building. The former colonial languages, recently even in Angola and Mozambique, have become media of instruction from early school years with what that entails of difficulties in maintaining cultural identity. Thus, these countries are faced with the paradoxical problem of *too much* internationalization in crucial aspects. Since these countries have many tribal languages which sometimes causes serious communication difficulties, the former colonial language, which as a rule is mastered by the educated class, becomes a convenient *lingua franca*. There are several troublesome consequences of this. There are problems of establishing a country-wide identity based upon other criteria than past colonial history. The mastery of the language of the former colonial masters is perceived as a symbol of status and power, which means that the educated who master the language easily became alienated from the mass of the people. The educated élite by virtue of mastering a world language and often having acquired university-based professional education in Europe or the United States, is internationally employable and not insensitive to the lure of the material and other benefits accruing from taking positions abroad. The Indian and Pakistani doctors in England are cases in point illustrating how the internationalization of the professional elite in the Third World easily results in brain drain. Those in many Third World countries who have had the benefit of advanced education easily identify themselves with their equals in the affluent countries, that is to say, with the international community of professionals in the same way as did students from Northern Europe who studied in Paris, Salerno, Oxford or Prague, who communicated in Latin.

Having been an active social science researcher for more than forty years I have increasingly become aware of the international character of scholarly endeavours in our time. The tiny fraction of these that are pursued in small countries like my own have, in order to be noted and properly evaluated, to be presented to an international forum of scholars, where lasting and substantial contributions to the discipline are sifted from the ephemeral and irrelevant ones. This means, then, that scholars in these small countries must be able to follow what is published in the world languages. Furthermore, it is imperative that they publish their research in one of these languages in order to make it available to professional fora.

Centers of excellence in the various disciplines are not evenly spread over the world. Exchange of faculty and students must take place in order to provide good research apprenticeship for promising students with opportunities for contacts with creative, established masters in the various disciplines.

The International Context of
Educational Research*

LET me begin with two, briefly described, cases which both relate to the international context of educational research.

Many years ago, in 1952, a workshop on the role of educational research was organized by the American High Commissioner's office and the German Institute for International Educational Research in Frankfurt on the subject of the bearing that educational research could have on current problems in German school education. Some twenty German professors of education from universities or *Hochschulen* for teacher training were invited along with some twenty researchers from the rest of Western Europe and from the United States. The purpose, I assume, was to bring Germans, who for obvious reasons had been rather isolated, into contact with colleagues from abroad, but I suspect that the organizers also regarded the workshop as a refresher course. Some of the professors had a background in history and philosophy of education and tended – to use a favorite term of today – to apply a different "paradigm" from their colleagues from abroad in tackling the problems we decided, after a two-week briefing period, to put on the agenda for the six-week workshop. I still vividly remember a heated discussion on whether the empirical – the word was not yet "neo-positivist" – approach used by educational psychologists with their measuring rods was of any use in educational research. My American colleagues were rather shocked by the allegation that the methods they had learned in courses on tests, measurement and statistics were of little or no use, or even suspect. Others, like myself, had more understanding, since some of us were familiar with the German philosophy providing the backbone to humanistic research, particularly the philosophy of Wilhelm Dilthey, who in a famous paper from the 1890s programatically denied that what John Stuart Mill had referred to as moral philosophy, and others later as behavioral sciences, could employ the methods of the hard sciences. The humanistic approach was the one of *Verstehen*, understanding, whereas the hard sciences tried to *Erklären*, explain. But John Stuart Mill and Auguste Comte had proclaimed that all genuine endeavors had to emulate those established by the hard sciences.

I shall not go further into this but simply mention that since then the pendulum, on both sides of the Atlantic, has begun to swing back. There is

* Originally published in the *Oxford Review of Education*, Vol. 9:1, 1983, 21-29. Reproduced by permission.

a strong counter-movement against the positivist approach, even to the extent that it is denounced as an instrument of the capitalist system of oppression and dehumanization. A group of younger German professors of education has produced an encyclopedia of educational research in which they deliberately try to advance a qualitative, understanding and interpreting or, to use another word from the jargon of today, hermeneutic approach. I cannot help having a feeling of *déjà vu* of my undergraduate days back in the 1930s as well as of our Frankfurt workshop in 1952.

The second example refers to UNESCO. Its education department in the 1950s had to implement a program voted by the General Conference of the organization according to which curricular guidelines of a more or less universal character should be drawn up for school education in member countries. The Secretariat first appointed an international committee for elementary and then one for secondary education. For strange reasons I was assigned the task to chair the second committee. We met for a week during each of three consecutive years and discussed at some length what appeared to be major issues in establishing guidelines which could be met with reasonable consensus. One such issue discussed over more than two days was that of general versus vocational education. The French member of the committee, who was an *Inspecteur Général de l'Instruction Publique*, spelled out in a long introductory statement what was meant by the French *culture générale* and how it was promoted by the study of classics. *Culture générale* constituted in his view general education. The Russian colleague, a vice-president of the Soviet Academy of Pedagogical Sciences, maintained that in his country the problem had been solved by polytechnical education. General and vocational education were sides of the same coin. Our American colleague, a school superintendent in one of the major cities and holder of an EdD in curriculum, suggested that general education was the common core curriculum of the public school. And so, driver education was an important part of general education.

These two sketchy examples illustrate the high degree of provincialism in education which should be carefully watched by comparative educators. Consider for a moment that we in the Northern hemisphere have been exporting our model of formal schooling, which has emerged from our particular social, economic and historical conditions, to the Southern hemisphere with serious, not to say sometimes disastrous consequences.

Differences Between Europe and the United States

When looking at the institutional context of educational research it would be appropriate to begin with the national context, as my two illustrations show. I have been conducting a study of how educational research relates to policy-making in four countries: Britain, the Federal Republic of Germany, the United States and Sweden (Husén and Kogan, [eds.] *Educational Research and Policy: How Do They Relate?* Oxford: Pergamon Press). Well into the late 1950s research on educational problems, which in many cases meant problems pertaining to school reforms, was conducted in England and Germany mainly outside the university setting. Studies requiring the collection of big data sets for statistical analysis were conducted in institutions such as the National Foundation for Educational Research in England or the Max Planck Institute for Educational Research in the Federal Republic of Germany. Large-scale interventionist programs for specific purposes, such as educational planning (which by 1970 by a change in the constitution became a prerogative of the national government in Germany), the National Defense Education Act in 1958 or the Elemenary and Secondary Education Act in 1965 in the United States elicited massive support for research which was related (at least formally) to the programs. Although the initiative was still with the researchers who submitted proposals reflecting academic priorities, the growing number of requests for proposals on the part of the governmental agencies led to an increasing dependence on the grant-giving agencies with regard to the choice of research topics.

There are certain similarities as well as differences in institutional conditions between the four countries as well as between others not included in my study on how research and policymaking are related.

It is striking to note that research in education was indirectly strongly supported by public school teachers in the U.S. as a means of gaining them professional status. In order to get promoted or become an educational specialist one had to do postgraduate research. When I was a postgraduate in the late 1930s and early 1940s, those of us who were not teachers jokingly referred to the elementary teachers who after many years of teaching had conducted their studies part-time, as "those studying for the inspectorate." The striking difference between the United States and most continental European countries has been that that secondary school teachers were almost non-existent in Europe in educational research. The reason why is obvious. They already had a strong professional status through their university training which is almost entirely limited to subject matter preparation in the disciplines they are supposed to teach. A brief course in pedagogy was given by a seasoned school principal or by a professor of education who had a background either in psychology or in the history or philosophy of education. Their supervised teaching practice took place after they had completed their degree, which, by the way, could just as well be regarded as the first step in advanced, post-graduate studies in their field of specialization. In some cases, as in France, special training as well as courses in pedagogy were regarded as completely useless. The person who mastered the discipline he had specialized in could *eo ipso* also teach it successfully. No pedagogy in the world could add anything significant to his competence as a teacher.

Advanced degrees in education are rare birds among chief education officers in the U.K. This is an exception in the sense that for promotion to higher posts in other countries, like my own, an advanced degree was not a formal but a real requirement.

In Europe national governments were not only governing the formal system of education. Depending upon the political constellations they were also trying to reform it. One pivotal issue was to what extent there should be a parallelism between primary, mandatory schooling and academic secondary schooling. Or more specifically: at what age should transfer from primary to secondary school take place? The issue could also be formulated as that of comprehensive versus the selective system of schooling. Educational researchers with a background in psychology and/or survey research became involved in the issue, since they were called upon to elucidate its ramifications. England, Sweden and Germany are typical cases. In England the 11+ issue was a special case of the general problem. One could not avoid the impression that in the 1940s and 1950s the major portion of resources in educational research went to investigating the selection procedures for grammar school: the validity of the tests used, the degree of parity of esteem between the various secondary programs, the social implications of selection, etc. I shall come back to this later.

Breaking Away From Provincialism

It is in the very nature of education as a field of practice to be provincial or national in character. It is after all molded by the cultural and historical tradition of the particular country it serves. By the middle of this century there was in several respects a reversal of this introversion. International competition in trade, weaponry and not least space technology, between the superpowers and, more recently, in electronics and computer technology between the United States and Japan, has inspired comparisons between countries in terms of what the educational systems are able "to produce". Intergovernmental agencies, such as UNESCO and OECD, have been instrumental in promoting exchange of experiences and in launching comparative studies. The willingness of educational planners, a new breed of the mid-twentieth century, to learn from colleagues in other countries goes far beyond what their predecessors (whatever they were called) in the era of *Auslandspädagogik* were ready to take in. Under such auspices comparative education as a new field of academic inquiry was born.

Educational research has also transgressed national confines. Scientific research in general, not least in the natural sciences, has always been international in character, given its ambition to discover principles and facts with universal validity. Research in education, however, for a long time lacked universalistic ambitions, simply because of the unique or particular features of the country and the national system of education where the researchers were based.

Over the last twenty-five years we have witnessed large-scale attempts to conduct cross-national studies in education by means of empirical methodology. Most notable in this connection are research ventures where national systems of education have been evaluated in terms of student achievement and attitudes. Here I have in mind, of course, the international evaluations conducted by the International Association for the Evaluation of Educational Achievement (IEA). What expanded to become a huge multi-national and multi-subject area of study was inspired by the lack of empirical evidence when making comparisons between countries about "standards" achieved, an issue of great importance during the years after launching of Sputnik.

Another phenomenon of great importance with regard to the internationalization of research in education has been the diffusion and actual influence of research focussing on issues at the forefront of public policy in several countries. Over decades the problem of comprehensive versus selective secondary education has been such an issue. Social Democratic parties in several European countries were after the War in favor of a secondary school with all the pupils and all the programs under the same roof. The social divisiveness that beset a system of parallelism, with one type of school for a select social and intellectual élite and another type for the remainder, would thereby be overcome.

The American comprehensive high school, which had been characterized as "the American Dream applied to education," was regarded, in Sweden, for instance, as a model to be emulated. Educational research prior to and after the 1944 Education Act in the U.K. was mainly geared to elucidating the efficiency by means of which the 11+ examination predicted success in grammar school. Studies such as the one by Philip E. Vernon on secondary school selection or the one by Yates and Pidgeon on grammar school selection got quite a lot of attention in other European countries, where the organization of secondary education was a major issue in public policy.

In the 1950s British sociologists, such as Floud and Halsey, began to draw attention to the relationship between selectivity and social background, and so some years later did the Stockholm study where it was found that the earlier selection for élite education took place, the stronger the social bias inherent in the system. Anthony Crosland, for instance in his book *The Future of Socialism* in 1956, was aware of this at an early stage, whereas in Sweden for example the advantages and disadvantages of the two systems of education were still discussed mainly in pedagogical terms.

The 1950 Education Act in Sweden made provisions for a ten-year pilot program with comprehensive education during the entire period of mandatory schooling. The local authorities were invited to establish a comprehensive structure, and besides political convictions state subsidies served as incentives. The Act prescribed a continuous evaluation of the pilot program which implied research on the relative merits of the "old" and the "new" system. It was tacitly assumed that the criterion of merit should be pupil achievement. Several major research projects with bearings on the school structure were launched. One of them, for which I took the initiative, was the so-called Stockholm study. The project acquired quite a lot of international fame, because it was regarded as exemplary of how research could form the basis for policymaking in education. This applied particularly to countries where reorganization of secondary education was under debate or imminently contemplated. This was the case with Britain.

The Stockholm study, indeed, capitalized on a unique situation which came close to what could be regarded as a full-fledged experiment. The City Council in the mid-1950s on a try-out basis decided to introduce comprehensive education in the southern half of the city, while the traditional practice of selection for the academic secondary school at the age of 11 was still kept in the northern half. All the pupils in a given age cohort were followed up from the fourth to the ninth school year. Comparisons between the comprehensive and the selective system were conducted in terms of how the pupils achieved and how attainments were related to ability and social background.

As mentioned above, the study apparently drew quite a lot of attention among educationists and policymakers outside Sweden, not least in Britain. Maurice Kogan, a British political scientist with considerable experience of how policymakers and social science researchers relate, conducted long conversations with two outstanding ministers of education in the 1960s, Edward Boyle, a "reluctant conservative", and Anthony Crosland, a "cautious revolutionary". The conversations plus his analysis have been published in his book *The Politics of Education*. As, formally a Conservative, Boyle was somewhat lukewarm *vis-à-vis* comprehensivization, whereas "going comprehensive", as pointed out by Susan Crosland in her biography of her husband, was at the top of Crosland's political agenda, when he took office as Minister of Education. Both ministers in retrospect make reference to the research that I and my co-workers had been conducting. Boyle deplored the short time span available for a minister with his usually short period of tenure. He refers to Swedish social democratic planning covering "a cycle of twenty years over which a major piece of social engineering was achieved": first five years of planning, then, "five years of research by Husén", etc. Boyle evidently thought that research played a pivotal role in the Swedish school reform and regretted that given the lack of long-range political stability this was not possible in Britain. Crosland, as is clearly evidenced by Kogan's long interview, also held educational research in high esteem, to the extent of inviting me to come to London in August 1965 and meet for a full day with him and his advisers at Curzon Street when he was contemplating his famous circular 10/65 to the Local Educational Authorities on plans for the reorganization of secondary education. But he held a more realistic and in a way more cynical conception of the role of research. In reponse to Kogan's question on why the circular was not preceded by research he said:

"It implied that research can tell you what your objectives ought to be. But it can't. Our belief in comprehensive re-organization was a product of fundamental value judgements about equity and equal opportunity and social division as well as about education. Research can help you to achieve your objectives, and I did in fact set going a large research project, against strong opposition from all kinds of people, to assess and monitor the process of going comprehensive. But research cannot tell you whether you should go comprehensive or not – that's a basic value judgement."

It is interesting to note that, depending upon political affiliation, research findings on school structure in a given country were used both as arguments for and against the comprehensive model in other countries. Swedish findings were interpreted as support for the *Gesamtschule* by German Social Democrats and Liberals, and as confirming that comprehensiveness would lower the standards by the Christian Democrats. The same happened in England. In the mid-1960s I was invited by Anthony Crosland, who was then Minister of Education in the Labour government, to discuss with him the issue of comprehensiveness and report on our studies on the social and pedagogical effects of comprehensive schooling. A few years later, in the so-called Black Papers issued by right-wing conservatives, I was somewhat inconsistently portrayed both as the "demon king" of the Swedish reform and as an extremely naïve person. I can go along with the latter but unfortunately not with the former epithet.

Another area in which researchers began to play a leading part was curriculum development and evaluation. The curriculum was conceived to be too important to be left entirely to educational bureaucrats and classroom teachers. Research was launched to a large extent outside the universities, for instance in the independent Max Planck Institute for Educational Research.

In the United States until the mid-1960s a considerable volume of research (in comparison with Europe), mostly with a background in psychology, was conducted at the universities. A modest federal program of cooperative research with grants from the U.S. Office of Education had been launched in the early 1950s. Under the dubious label, "national defense," additional resources were made available at the end of the decade. Then, suddenly, overnight, under the provisions of the Elementary and Secondary Education Act, enormous resources were poured out. This was a result of a blueprint for federal action in the field of education that a presidential task force of outstanding educators (among them Clark Kerr and Ralph Tyler), chaired by John Gardner, had worked out for the President.

Research In Comparative Education

The early 1960s saw a rapid growth of comparative education. It had been born in the 1950s under the auspicies of, among other things, the Sputnik psychosis in the United States and the rapidly growing involvement of the multilateral and bilateral aid organizations in technical assistance in education in Third World countries. Most of the pioneers in the field had a background in the qualitative disciplines which education draws upon, such as history and philosophy. Those who were more imbued with the empirical-positivist "paradigm" urged that comparisons be made by means of more quantitative methods. Under such paradigmatic auspices the International Association for the Evaluation of Educational Achievement, known under the acronym IEA, was born. It comprised from the outset researchers from a dozen countries, represented by an equal number of research institutes, who decided to conduct a cross-national study of achievements in mathematics and to account for differences between students, schools and nations. This body has grown to comprise more than 30 nations.

It is interesting to note how differently "national centers" were defined in the IEA sample survey research where massive collection of data had to be conducted on a national basis. In some countries the research center was part of or directly under the Ministry of Education, whereas in other countries it was a private and independent research body, like the NFER in England, which, possibly with governmental support, was responsible for the contribution of the country. In other countries it was a leading university department of education or even two departments, as was the case in the United States where Teachers College Columbia and the University of Chicago cooperated, with the so-called principal investigator located at Chicago.

The international impact of educational research has no doubt been considerably enhanced by intergovernmental agencies, such as UNESCO, OECD and the Council of Europe. This impact has been mainly achieved in three different ways. Leading researchers have frequently been brought together for the exchange of ideas and experiences. The international Association for the Evaluation of Educational Achievement grew out of regular meetings hosted by the UNESCO Institute for Education in Hamburg. The Council of Europe has set up committees that have dealt with the role of research and development in education and the institutional conditions for research. OECD has brought senior officals together, and not least by its Center for Research and Innovation (CERI), which has sponsored a series of projects on equality in education, recurrent education and curricula in science and mathematics, has been instrumental in promoting educational reforms in member countries. Finally, documentation, such as the one provided by the International Bureau of Education in Geneva and the Council of Europe (EUDISED), has been strategic in the diffusion of research findings and widening the horizon of educational researchers.

Concluding Remarks

By the mid-1960s we saw on both sides of the Atlantic how national governments were carried by a strong belief in what educational research could achieve in improving education. They were, of course, also carried by the almost euphoric belief in education which in its turn was carried by a substantial and continuing growth of national economies.

The 1970s were a period of disappointment, not to say disenchantment, in the wake of financial contraction and stagnation. The expectations about what educational research could achieve were conceived within a framework of R & D taken over from science and technology. Typically, research was expected to improve the efficiency of teaching in the same way as technological devices in industry had been able to enhance production and save manual labor. It is also typical that educational TV and program learning mediated by teaching machines were launched. The new educational technology would make the pupils more knowledgeable, and, by saving teaching time, at a lower price. Since then, we have seen both the rise and fall of the technologies of the 1960s and we know that the cost per pupil and year in constant prices has gone up by some 50 – 100 per cent since the mid-1960s. The IEA studies seem to show that the pupils have not become more knowledgeable. We should be grateful if they are not less competent now than earlier when it was much cheaper to teach them.

No wonder then that many policymakers and school practitioners are disappointed. Some years ago I happened to be on the same flight as a former German minister of education. His background was that of a mining engineer and he had been a professor at a major technological institute. He was deeply disappointed and aired his misgivings aggressively. From all the money he as a minister had been instrumental in channeling into research, he said "virtually nothing, nothing had come out." There were many in his category who shared his views, although not expressing them so loudly.

What, then, would I conclude, after forty years as an educational researcher, of which the better part has been spent in international cooperative research endeavors?

I have become more and more convinced that major research universities with quality graduate programs should try to confine themselves to the study of fundamental problems which may or may not yield any immediate useful results for the educational enterprise. The temptation to take on big – and I emphasize particularly big – governmental research contracts easily corrupts the purpose of the university. After all, it is the only place where fundamental or so-called pure research is institutionalized, whereas there are plenty of institutions outside Academe where big-scale, commissioned studies can be carried on.

In two respects true academics and policymakers are not on the same wavelength:

(1) Problems which are not on the political agenda do not exist for policymakers, but they might offer intellectual challenges to academics who are paid by society in order to look critically into problems which are seen as "impractical."

(2) The time perspective differs between them. The politician's time horizon is set by the next election or parliamentary session. The only relevant time horizon for the researcher relates to his budget.

I cannot claim to have lived as I am now preaching, but would at least want others to take advantage of my experiences.

An International Research Venture in Retrospect: The IEA Surveys*

THE International Association for the Evaluation of Educational Achievement (IEA) venture which started more than twenty-five years ago is an interesting piece of recent educational research history, representing not only incipient attempts to establish a science of empirical comparative education based on close cooperation between institutions in many countries but also how tied to the prevailing *Zeitgeist* and its paradigms a research endeavor can be. Hindsight gives us somewhat different perspectives on the theoretical framework and the methodology employed.

More important is to put on record some experiences gained in launching the large-scale survey research that IEA embarked on around 1960. The administrative, economic, and methodological difficulties and failures deserve to be put on record for the benefit of future endeavors of this kind. This article is not an attempt to do this comprehensively but is a report of my personal views on selected problems and how I *ex post facto* perceive them.

The IEA Six Subject Survey was originally reported in nine volumes that appeared from 1973 through 1976.† In addition, a host of special studies based on further analysis of data available in the IEA data bank have been published in a monograph series under IEA auspices. Such a venture conducted in an adventurous and pioneering spirit is, of course, begging for criticism. The mathematics survey which was conducted from 1962 through 1965 has been criticized harshly by a professor of mathematics of education who directed his criticism mainly against the mathematics tests, their content, and how they were developed. The reading survey has been criticized by a

* Originally published in the *Comparative Education Review*, Vol. 23:3, 1979, 371–85. Reproduced by permission of the University of Chicago Press.

† The most comprehensive and at the same time "official" reporting of the Six Subject Survey has been available in the series International Studies in Evaluation, published jointly by Almqvist & Wiksell, Stockholm, and Wiley (Halsted Press), New York. The volumes are the following: L. C. Comber and John P. Keeves, *Science Education in Nineteen Countries: An Empirical Study* (1973); Alan C. Purves, *Literature Education in Ten Countries: An Empirical Study* (1973); Robert L. Thorndike, *Reading Comprehension Education in Fifteen Countries* (1973); E. Glyn Lewis and Carolyn E. Massad, *The Teaching of English as a Foreign Language in Ten Countries* (1975); John B. Carroll, *The Teaching of French as a Foreign Language in Eight Countries* (1975); Judith V. Torney, A. N. Oppenheim, and Russell F. Farnen, *Civic Education in Ten Countries: An Empirical Study* (1975); A. Harry Passow et al., *The National Case Study: An Empirical Comparative Study of Twenty-one Educational Systems* (1976); Gilbert F. Peaker, *An Empirical Study of Education in Twenty-one Countries: A Technical Report* (1975); David A. Walker, *The IEA Six Subject Survey: An Empirical Study of Education in Twenty-one Countries* (1976).

specialist in reading, one of whose major points is that the tests have been inadequate for the less developed countries. The most comprehensive, incisive, and informed review of the Six Subject Survey is that by Alex Inkeles, who was commissioned by the U.S. National Academy of Education to take a look at the IEA research in its entirety. Unfortunately his review covers the subject area reports but not the technical report. Most of the Inkeles criticism deals with the methodology of the survey.

This paper, however, does *not* advance any rebuttals to these critiques; that would require another format. My purpose is to spell out what I regard as failings in the conception, administration, and methodology of the IEA surveys. Naturally, these ex post facto views may not necessarily be shared by my colleagues.

There is a perceptual problem involved. The review exercise I am doing covers a period of twenty-five years and is being conducted in a spirit of what the French refer to as *l'ésprit de l'escalier*. This means the indulgence in second, or even third, thoughts on the staircase after leaving the scenes of emotionally loaded encounters. I have had ample opportunity to indulge in that spirit and feel that I have been descending the staircase of a skyscraper!

What we did twenty to twenty-five years ago in planning the surveys should be judged by the standards for the state of the art *at that time*. We were, as all researchers are, prisoners of the then prevailing paradigms – theoretical and methodological orientations – and of the difficulties of breaking with conventions. To do this is easier for an individual than a collective. One cannot employ standards derived from present insights and achieved in the social sciences in general, and in comparative education in particular, to judge research planned and conducted more than a decade ago. For example, the IEA research was initiated before the intensive debate on the theory and methodology of large-scale survey studies took off as a result of the Coleman and Plowden surveys. When the IEA surveys were first planned, comparative education was conceptually very much in its infancy. The attempt to advance theories and develop methodological frameworks by Noah and Eckstein had hardly begun, although Bereday's book on method in comparative education was available and was referred to in the mathematics study. As Inkeles points out in the above-cited review of the Six Subject Survey, IEA had to conduct ground breaking work in developing a methodology for quantitative comparative studies. At that time, no cross-national surveys in education using representative national samples had been undertaken.

Background and Historical Setting

The bold idea of conducting a study of cognitive development in children belonging to different national systems of education was first brought up at a meeting of educational researchers from a dozen countries at the UNESCO Institute for Education in Hamburg in 1958. The year before that institute had hosted an international meeting of educational psychologists – most of them psychometricians – on problems of evaluation. This was a field in Europe to which little thought had been devoted at that time. In the United States, through Ralph Tyler's pioneering research, evaluation had long been an area in which educators took great interest.

At a previous meeting in 1957 it was realized how little empirical evidence was available to substantiate the sweeping judgments that were commonplace about the relative merits and failings of various national systems of education. Concerns about the quality of secondary education in general – science education in particular – had begun to be aired in the United States by Admiral Hyman Rickover and the history professor Arthur Bestor. American schools were under attack, accused of a lack of intellectual rigor and standards. Similar concerns had begun to crop up in other countries, where secondary education was in the process of becoming universal. These concerns reached an almost hysterical level in connection with the launching of Sputnik, the spectacular achievement that was ascribed, in the last analysis, to superior education in the Soviet Union. At research meetings during the late 1950s the lack of *internationally valid standards* for student competence in key subject areas was pointed out. The level of student competence was at the center of concerns about standards.

Given the lack of hard evidence, the question arose: Why not study the experiences gained in some countries from large-scale testing programs – particularly the Anglo-Saxon countries – and the survey techniques that had begun to be employed in the spirit of American positivism? These techniques had already made their way into authoritative handbooks of social science research. Given the state of the art of cross-national social science research, the development of instruments that could be used to measure outcomes of school education in a number of countries was quite an achievement.

It was in Hamburg at the UNESCO Institute in 1958 that the proposal was put forward for a cross-national study of how schools contribute to shaping the cognitive deveopment of children in different countries. The idea of cross-national surveys was further discussed at two meetings in 1959, one at the Hamburg Institute and one at Eltham Palace in England. A feasibility study was launched with the purpose of finding out whether, methodologically and administratively, instruments could be developed that were cross-nationally valid and could be administered uniformly over a range of countries with different school systems. We also wanted to find out whether data could be made accessible in order to make the processing of data and statistical analyses possible at one central place.

For the feasibility study data were collected in a dozen countries, and the outcomes were reported at a meeting in Hamburg in 1961. Since it was taken for granted that participating research institutes in each country would be able to draw representative national samples according to a uniform design, such an exercise was not included. This was proved a wrong assumption.

There being no time for a laborious, time-consuming exercise of test development, those in the group who were experts in test development drew upon items already available, most of them from England and the United States. A 120-item omnibus test measuring competence in reading comprehension, arithmetic, science, and geography was put together. Some "culture-free" items measuring abstract reasoning of a type that the British were using were included in order to assess nonverbal intelligence. The participating national centers made the data available on punched cards to Teachers College, Columbia University, where Professor Robert Thorndike was in charge of the processing and most of the statistical analyses.

The results of the feasibility study were assessed positively. At the 1961 meeting to discuss the results the decision was made to proceed with a 12-country study in mathematics. Mathematics possesses a universal language and a high degree of cross-national overlap in school curricula and was a subject for which the development of standardized tests appeared to be rather straightforward and without problems encountered in developing tests for disciplines such as civics. We could hardly foresee the controversies that were to arise among mathematics educators about the inclusion of content areas and the relative weight that should be assigned to them.

Contrary to our expectations most persons involved in the test construction in mathematics thought that the content was to the disadvantage of students in their own country – even the British whose contributions to the test development had dominated. We were, it should be admitted, imprudent in not drawing upon a wider international range of mathematics educators. Such a step would probably not have made the early mathematics tests much different, but it would certainly have made them less controversial. Another technical problem that surfaced right from the beginning was that of proper sampling. Very few countries had had experience at that time of drawing nationally representative, random samples of school and student populations for educational research.

Setting Up an International Machinery

The organizational "machinery" had to be set up for the IEA research effort, which would span the next decade and cost at least 1 million preinflation U.S. dollars. The resulting organization was called the International Association for the Evaluation of Educational Achievement, which became known under the acronym IEA. The decision-making body on matters of overall policy and operational implications was the IEA Council, on which each institution had one representative. The council had at least one statutory meeting per year. Between council meetings, decisions could be made either by a standing committee that met more frequently or by the chairman of the organisation, a post to which I was elected in 1962. The chairman had at his disposal a full-time coordinator. During the first years, the chairman was also the technical director of the survey work, but later the two functions were split. The IEA was, until 1967 a rather loose association; at that time it incorporated itself. Before that, it could not sign contracts on research grants. The generous grant in 1962 from the United States Office of Education cooperative research program had to be made available to the University of Chicago, where Benjamin Bloom was the principal investigator. He was, of course, primarily responsible to his university and the U.S. Office of Education not IEA. Since the coordinator was placed at the UNESCO Institute in Hamburg where meetings were held certain funds were subcontracted to that institution via its director, who was responsible to his board and the UNESCO secretariat. Thus, for several years there were lines of authority and responsibility that sometimes worked at cross-purposes with each other and led to conflicts. The decision-making machinery that produced research designs and data processing plans and initiated expensive international meetings was not involved in the authorization of expenses and accounting for them.

Thus, the lesson was learned that an international consortium of researchers and/or research institutions conducting research such as ours *must* be incorporated in order to act with autonomy. Some of the participating national research centers were either completely private and autonomous, such as the National Foundation for Educational Research in England and Wales (NFER) or the Graduate School of Education at the University of Chicago, "representing" England and the United States, respectively, on the IEA Council. Other national research centers were institutions within state-controlled universities that by tradition were autonomous in their research projects once they were funded. But government support had to be solicited in terms of funds and endorsement gained from school and the teachers' unions. This could be quite tricky for studies with important implications for national policy in education. In some countries, such as Hungary and Japan, the national research center responsible for the study was either part of, or reported directly to, the Ministry of Education. This had two implications. In the first place, once the government had decided to participate, the necessary funds were made available. Second, the schools were obliged by ministerial order to cooperate, even if clashes with a teachers' union might result. In these countries the executed samples were pretty much identical with the planned samples and could be relied upon.

Funding was a major problem area in setting up the IEA organization. We instituted right from the beginning, a policy of separating national and international expenses. All expenses that were incurred at the national level such as establishing a national coordinating staff, drawing samples, trying out instruments, and conducting preparatory processing, were to be met by funds raised within the country. Clear-cut international costs, such as setting up and maintaining a coordinating staff and a data-processing center, computer time for central data processing and statistical analyses, and international meetings, had to be covered by internationally raised and earmarked funds. Practically all international costs were carried by one single grant. For the Six Subject Survey international expenditures were multifunded by grants from private foundations as well as governments.

There are three different kinds of funding problems that international ventures of the IEA type have to face:

1. Problems of *coordination* to synchronize international and national funding. There is no point in gaining funding in separate countries if international financial support is lacking, and vice versa.

When a project is multifunded, grant givers may require that their contributions cover identifiable parts of the project for a particular period or phase of the project. In the Six Subject Survey a grant from one foundation was given under the condition that it be used exclusively to support the development of instruments used in the evaluation of science education. Since all the subject area studies were conducted simultaneously with the same staff, and all data were processed together by the same data-processing team, it was impossible in practice to comply with this condition.

2. Problems of *timing*. Both national and international grants are usually given under conditions spelled out in a research proposal with a precise timetable. If the coordination of the timing of grants fails the entire project is delayed, and in countries where funds have been appropriated for certain fiscal years researchers run into difficulties.

3. There are finally, *bureaucratic* problems that ensue from the strings attached to funds or regulations that have to be met. Such problems are, of course encountered in national as well as cross-national research, but they are magnified in the latter by international variability in regulations and by differences in behavior. It is in the nature of scientific inquiry that it is impossible to predict not only outcomes but the course of the research process itself. There is a wide margin of uncertainty about when and how the venture one is engaged in is going to end. In planning industrial manufacturing, one plans for the processing of an already known, or clearly envisaged, product. But in planning research one cannot know what the end product is going to look like.

Thus, both the timetable and the budget in a research proposal are at best informed guesswork. The difficulties in making a number of national research institutions move in a lock step fashion and stick to an agreed upon timetable are enormous. Those in grant-giving agencies who are monitoring the research venture attach great importance to the way the project is progressing and how the line items in the budget are followed, if not for any other reason than because they are easy things to refer to in accounting.

Sometimes special requirements can be of considerable nuisance because they run counter to the academic ethos. I remember spending a half-hour talking over the telephone with a government official trying to explain to him that IEA could not possibly reject the participation of a certain country which had shown convincingly that its national research center had the competence to participate. In one case a ministry of education did not release data because the processing was going to be conducted in the United States, and we were told that in that country there were concerns about what the CIA might do with the information! Another ministry urged us to drop the statistical analyses for that particular country because its level of performance was embarrassing.

Competence Building

The first major IEA research venture, the mathematics survey discussed above, was conducted in 12 countries, that is, it involved 12 research institutions, known as national centers. As a rule, the heads of these institutes had been at the Hamburg meetings at the end of the 1950s and in the early 1960s. Thus they had been involved personally in the planning and execution of both the feasibility and the early mathematics study. When we embarked on the Six Subject Survey, the number of participating countries increased from 12 to 21, among them four developing countries. Several of the institutes, or national centers, that joined at this stage had little experience in survey research. Though they employed researchers of high quality, competence in survey studies was almost nil. In two cases, the heads of national centers had doctorates in developmental psychology but had no background at all in testing, measurement, and evaluation. Thus, at this stage attention had to be given to competence building.

Within each national center one, usually full-time, person was named technical officer and put in charge of the day-to-day operations of the project. All the technical officers were brought together on several occasions for combined briefing and training sessions. The directors of the participating institutes needed to consider the technical aspects of the surveys at the council meetings, when decisions were made on the general research strategy. In many cases special assistance had to be provided by the IEA coordinating center. The coordinator had to travel to an Asian country and assist in the actual drawing of samples. The technology used in data collection and data processing, such as using answer cards that could be read by a machine and from which data could be transferred directly to magnetic tape, at that time was new to the majority of research institutes.

During the late 1960s it became increasingly clear that IEA should also bring its competence to bear in building up research capabilities, primarily in the countries that participated in IEA projects. The IEA discharged its duties in competence building by two types of seminars and workshops. In the summer of 1968 the first seminar on research and the educational process was held near Stockholm where English was the working language, followed by similar seminars with German- and French-speaking participants.

In 1971 IEA organised an international 6-week seminar on curriculum development and evaluation in Gränna, Sweden, with 125 participants from some 25 countries in the Third World. This seminar was supported by several organizations such as the Ford Foundation, the Swedish International Development Authority, and the German Ministry for Economic Cooperation. Benjamin Bloom served as the seminar director and Neville Postlethwaite, then the executive director of IEA, as the chief administrator.

The organization is still pursuing the task of competence building. In 1976 a survey of elementary and secondary school leavers in Botswana was conducted with IEA instruments as part of a review of the educational systems of the country, which I was directing in my capacity as chairman of the Botswana National Commission on Education.

The Image of IEA as an "Olympic Contest"

Because the IEA research ventures were launched during the post-Sputnik period, our cross-nationally comparative study was inevitably affected by the climate created by the race for superiority in science and technology. As early as the 1950s many Americans believed that the fight for world supremacy had to be fought in classrooms by increasing the number of students who took science and by raising educational standards. The National Defence Education Act was passed in the fall of 1958 for the purpose of strengthening the infrastructure of American technology. Massive resources were made available in the United States for programs to upgrade mathematics and science curricula and instruction. When the IEA study was launched, what in the minds of some academics was perceived as a major exercise in basic research was perceived by others as an international contest in mathematics. Now, it would at last be possible to find out which country scored highest.

In early 1967, when the two volumes that reported the outcomes of the 12-country mathematics study were released, there were press briefings in London, in connection with a IEA Council meeting, and in Chicago. At the first great efforts were made to play down the "horse race" aspect by referring to the fact that countries had different curricula. We pointed out that differences in average performance between countries could not without great reservations be interpreted as reflecting differences in the efficacy of mathematics education because of the impact of social and economic differences on student competence. Furthermore, the structure and selectivity of the systems played an important role. Although 13-year-olds in England and Germany, who had transferred to academic selective secondary schools, had already been confronted with algebra and geometry, this was generally not the case in Sweden and the United States, the two countries with the lowest average performances in mathematics at that age level. Despite efforts to point out such causes for differences in national scores, the outcry was tremendous in both these countries.

Theoretical Framework and Research Strategy

Initially, we entertained a grandiose theoretical conception of the IEA project. We wanted, first, to develop internationally valid measures of "output" that is, student competence in the key subject areas. Second, we wanted to measure the "input" of teacher competence, teaching materials, teaching time, and method of instruction in the educational process. These inputs had to be related to "outputs" in each country in terms of student achievements and attitudes. Finally we would be in a position to determine the relative importance of various input factors.

With hindsight this appears to be a rather simplistic conceptualization. We should keep in mind that the IEA survey was initially conceived before such massive attempts as the Coleman report, the Plowden Commission, and the Jencks study had been made to disentangle the relative importance of home background and schooling. The more sophisticated methods of multivariate analysis employed in these and other studies had not yet provided a more realistic picture of what was possible within the framework of a cross-sectional survey approach.

The theoretical framework employed in the 12-country feasibility study and the early mathematics survey was a rather primitive one. At that stage we simply wanted to employ quantitative methods in comparative education research which had previously been historically and qualitatively oriented. During the post-Spunik hysteria, judgments about the relative merits and shortcomings of national systems of education had been plentiful but without systematic empirical backing. There were no international standards that could be expressed operationally in test or examination scores. There were no instruments by means of which one could assess cross-nationally the level of student competence in various systems. The group of researchers that coalesced in the early history of IEA, who possessed a solid background in psychometric methods and an interest in evaluation set about developing the instruments required.

At the beginning of its work the IEA Council had a subcommittee to generate hypotheses about how cognitive and noncognitive outcomes of schooling were related to school structure, teaching methods, school resources, and the socioeconomic background of students. The ruminations of the hypothesis committee resulted in a long list, which required the collection of a great amount of data measuring a large number of independent variables.

In the Six Subject Survey we had on the output side measures of cognitive outcomes of instruction as assessed by standardized achievement tests and measures of affective outcomes, such as student attitudes toward schooling in general and the particular disciplines.

Great caution had to be exercised in interpreting student cognitive competence as an outcome of schoolteaching only. Family background is of great importance by the time of school entry. Parental help and concern continued to influence student progress throughout the school career. Given the same quality of teaching, children from illiterate homes could not be expected to reach the same level of competence as those with educated parents. The interpretation of affective measures was more tricky because one could not, with a cross-sectional design, determine the extent to which a certain attitude or level of motivation was an input to or an output of the school experiences of a child. Measures, such as Like School and School Motivation, that could not unequivocally be assigned to either the input or the output side, were labeled "kindred" variables.

As mentioned above, one overriding purpose of the survey exercise was to identify *independent* variables, factors in the social, economic, and – above all – pedagogical domain that accounted for differences between students within schools as well as between schools within countries. We soon realized that hypothesis generation had to be systematized within the framework of theory building. Internationally recognized researchers from various social science disciplines were brought together to elaborate an input-output model and identify variables that they conceived as related to the cognitive affective outcomes of schooling. A separate grant from the U.S. Office of Education enabled IEA to hold two international meetings during which economists, sociologists, psychologists, anthropologists, and comparative educationists – some 20 people – worked with IEA representatives. At these meetings, which took place in Hamburg and Lake Mohonk in New York State in 1966 and 1967, attempts were made to identify key variables and develop hypotheses about their interrelationships. Initial efforts were made to operationalize these variables by suggesting how they should be measured. The report, consisting of commissioned papers and a summing up of the proceedings was edited by Professor Donald Super. Guided by the outcomes of these meetings, we compiled a long list of hypotheses – prohibitively long for realistic field use. Operationalization would have required lengthy tests and questionnaires that would have taken days of work by school principals and teachers to generate all the requisite information. A heroic attempt was made to narrow down the list and to translate the suggested variables into questionnaire items.

The conceptualization of our research strategy in an input-output model was beset with limitations that in retrospect are rather obvious. Since we conceived of our study, there has been a shift in what Kuhn refers to as research paradigms. The straightforward paradigm with representative samples and strict quantitative and standardized methods to test hypotheses uniformly over a number of age levels and countries seemed at the time to be self-evident. We never seriously considered an alternative strategy, for example limiting ourselves to a selection of a few schools and classrooms that could be subjected to intensive, qualitative observations. We certainly expected too much from the broadly collected information that was obtained by questionnaires from the students about their home background and from the teachers about how they taught.

The reporting of the IEA Six Subject Survey has, with ample reason, been accused of a lack of a "focused analytic perspective" (Inkeles). The authors of the reports for the six subject areas – apart from application of the common multivariate technique – used different analytic emphases, which resulted in reporting without a common analytical strategy to make the cross-national and cross-subject comparisons. An advantage of this individualism is characterization of the Six Subject Survey by what Inkeles refers to as a "catholicity of perspectives."

The lack of shared analytical focus can be ascribed to the fact that the IEA research was a *collective* enterprise, which within a strictly agreed upon, descriptive framework for data collection had to accommodate various theoretical conceptions. We were also caught in a tremendous wealth of information that, due to time limitations, was only schematically analyzed; uni- and bivariates were run off and stepwise multiple regression analyses were conducted in all six subject areas. Those who assisted us in planning data processing and statistical analyses were steering us, not we them. The data sets, therefore, were – in the first round – to use Inkeles's term, highly "under-analyzed." I also think that we were not successful in relating characteristics of national systems to student performance. But this does not imply that the researchers who conducted the analyses reported on in the national case study volume did not do what they could with the data available to them.

The above can be illustrated by two examples. In analyzing data from the feasibility study, Thorndike came up with the idea of intercorrelating the 12 participating countries over the more than 100 test items, which covered reading, arithmetic, science, geography, and abstract intelligence. The resulting intercorrelation matrix was factor analyzed, and two different clusters of countries, one Anglophone and one Francophone, emerged with factor loadings in different subject areas. This was an indication of interesting differences in cognitive profiles between the two types of countries. C. P. Snow's "two-culture" hypothesis was tested for a series of countries. The hypothesis, not surprisingly, turned out to be valid only for Snow's own country, England.

All comparativists in educational research have experiences attesting to national differences due to historical, cultural, and economic circumstances which affect formal educational systems and ought to be taken into account in conducting empirical studies of differences between national systems. Such factors were, however, difficult to accommodate within our research paradigm and, therefore largely neglected.

Since IEA wanted to assess what schools did to the children in various national systems of education, the most rational research strategy would have been to *follow* the students at various levels over at least 1 school year and to measure the *gains* achieved during that period among pupils taught by the same teacher. A cross-sectional survey only provides information about students *after* they have been taught, not only by the teacher in charge of a particular subject during a given school year, but by several other teachers during previous school years as well. The lack of information about student status prior to being instructed by their present teacher hardly permits valid conclusions about how much competence in a given year is accounted for by the teaching during that year. The lack of preinstruction scores also makes it difficult, not to say impossible, to decide in what order the independent variables should be entered into the multiple-regression analyses. Above all, the cross-sectional design makes it very difficult to disentangle the influence of school factors from the background factors that the student carries with him to school. Highly sophisticated methods of multivariate statistical analysis cannot substitute for the lack of longitudinal information.

Four developing countries participated in the Six Subject Survey. The instruments employed were not suitable for them because of insufficient room at the "floor" level of the test (i.e., there were too few easy items). A high proportion of students in these countries had difficulties in reading and understanding the instructions of the group administered test, even after six or seven years of elementary schooling. Apparently, different sets of tests need to be developed for the two categories of countries.

Because of my emphasis on shortcomings, I have not dealt with the pioneering virtues of the IEA research. One feature in the methodology employed has been the *replication* of the same kind of measure and analyses over several national systems of education, which allows conclusions to be drawn at a higher level of generalization than is usually the case in educational research. Generalizations in studies of education are usually tied to the special conditions in a particular regional or national system. Different settings and "school climates" influence the relationship between schooling and achievement.

Concluding Observations

Some of the weaknesses of early IEA research simply resulted from the fact that these surveys were the first of their kind; flaws associated with pioneering ventures were inevitable. Other errors stemmed from this research paradigm: the use of an input-output model, extensiveness of scope, and emphasis on quantitative methods and statistical techniques with no reliance at all on qualitative observations and anthropological methods. There are important questions in the comparative study of educational systems that cannot be answered by means of extensive survey techniques and problems that have to be tackled by intensive studies of a few classrooms in the respective countries. Such an approach has been taken in later IEA studies.

FREE

EduQuest™ Booklet and Video

To receive your FREE EduQuest booklet on technology in the classroom and your FREE video of "EduQuest: The Journey Begins," simply fill out and mail this card or call 1 800 453-7178. But hurry, supplies are limited.

Name

Title

School Name

Street Address

City _____ State _____ Zip

Phone ( )_____ School District

Appraising the Quality of Secondary Education: Cross-national Assessments of Achievements[*]

Background

The first attempts to carry out systematic and quantitatively oriented assessments of educational achievements across nations were conducted under the auspices of Sputnik in the late 1950s. Comparative education, although rooted in what German educators referred to as *Auslandskunde* and what the British did in their training of colonial civil servants, emerged around 1960 as an acknowledged field of scholarly specialization. A major research endeavor, the IEA evaluation surveys, was baptized soon after the launching of Sputnik.

By the mid-1950s the quality of American school education came under attack and was defined, by some critics, as a matter of national security. The year after Sputnik was launched the Eisenhower administration submitted legislation to Congress for upgrading certain aspects of American education (mainly science, mathematics, and graduate education) that were regarded as weak spots in the system. This legislation was enacted under the dubious label National Defense Education Act.

Concerns such as those just hinted at seem to appear in a cyclical fashion. It seems not to be coincidental that in 1983-84 half a dozen major reports were published, almost at the same time, one of them by a National Commission. All of them focus on the quality of American education, especially at the secondary level. The concerns are at least as grave – dramatized, for example, by the title of the report by the National Commission, "A Nation at Risk" – as they were in the late 1950s and early 1960s, but the auspices are now different in two major respects:

(1) Japan, not the Soviet Union, is this time regarded as a threat, not in terms of military technology and weaponry but in terms of its competitive trade power on the world market. Japan is even hitting the heartland of microtechnology and other intelligence industries, namely the Silicon Valley. Superior competitive power on the world market is assumed to be a reflection of superiority in the educational and research prerequisites for high technology.

[*] Presentation given at the U.S. National Academy of Education meeting in Stockholm (June 1984).

(2) Steps taken to improve American education by the Eisenhower, Kennedy and – not least – the Johnson administration by means of massive Federal programs were taken in an expanding economy. By mid-1964 a Task Force, chaired by John Gardner and with Ralph Tyler and Clark Kerr among its members, submitted a report to President Johnson recommending far-reaching steps for improving education, including compensatory education for the disadvantaged. On the copy I saw in the White House executive office, while conducting an OECD review on Federal policies in education, Bill Moyers, then Presidential press secretary, had written, "Ought not to be published before election day." The Task Force recommendations would have cost many billions of dollars. Given the policy of the present administration, Federal initiatives are being reduced, partly by an unwillingness to involve "the Feds" and partly by financial restraints in a stagnating economy with a huge budget deficit.

Two Kinds of Impact of Cross-National Assessments

Given the political background just mentioned, it would be tempting to develop further the policy aspects of the efforts that have been made over the last twenty-five years to assess educational systems cross-nationally and, in particular, those by the International Association for the Evaluation of Educational Achievement (IEA). But since I am here primarily concerned with the scholarly aspects of these endeavors and not with their policy implications, I shall concentrate on some central theoretical and methodological aspects of conducting cross-national comparisons. Nevertheless, I cannot fully resist the temptation and shall therefore later in my presentation, return to some of the experiences we gained of the repercussions on the policy debate of the IEA research.

"Comparing the Incomparable"

In the mid-1960s, when we were conducting the first international mathematics survey, when I one day entered the office of Professor George Bereday, my recently deceased colleague at Teachers College, Columbia University, he greeted me by saying: "My friend, you are trying to compare the incomparable." I do not remember what I replied but could have said then, but not today: "My friend, what we are trying to do by means of the empirical methods – tests, questionnaires and the statistical paraphernalia that goes with them – represents some progress. You people in the comparative education establishment either fall back on your gut feelings or on impressions from educational tourism when you make your comparisons and come up with your generalizations about the strengths and failings of various systems of education, national or others." Although I might have thought so, I certainly did not say so, even though those were the heydays of a flourishing social science with a firm belief in what a rational, positivist and quantitative approach could achieve. My hesitation was probably due to the fact that George Bereday, with his solid background in the humanities, was right in one fundamental respect. We could at best compare those things that we were able to measure, in this case certain cognitive outcomes of school teaching. Indeed, we had made it easy for ourselves by starting with mathematics, which was the most universal of all school subjects. Typically, science followed suit a few years later. But what about subjects, such as civics, history and literature, which we began to survey soon afterwards? School education has a much broader spectrum of objectives than the segment of it constituted by the limited cognitive part. Half a century ago, when Ralph Tyler and his co-workers embarked upon what in the history of education is referred to as the Eight Year Study, they set out to include the affective and social outcomes, such as independence, study skills, cooperation and the like. IEA tried to include measures of student attitudes, but without much success, except in the surveys of literature and civic education.

The school has always tried to achieve more than just instill certain cognitive competencies as defined by separate school subjects. The non-cognitive aspects, which for the first time in the history of educational research were assessed in the Eight Year Study, do not easily lend themselves to measurements in strictly quantifiable terms. You can by means of inventories and questionnaires try to measure interest and attitudes toward, for instance, schooling in general or certain school subjects, as we tried to do in the IEA surveys. But how do you in a comprehensive way cover such intangible and elusive fields as those defined as social skills, cooperation, responsibility and independence, all of them important objectives allegedly pursued in our schools?

It is, indeed, highly presumptuous to advance generalizations about the overall quality of a certain system of education, be it local, regional or national, on the basis of test scores only in, for instance, mathematics and science. But this is precisely what is frequently done. The public debate following the publications of the IEA surveys in mathematics and science is a case in point. When the first mathematics survey was published, critics of American education found the low average performance of the high school seniors confirmed their misgivings about the standard achieved in the American high school without taking into account that about 75 per cent of the 17 to 18-year-olds in the United States were compared with 10 to 30 per cent in the West European countries. In Sweden, the low mean score at the 13-year-old level was blamed on the school reform, which in the early 1960s when the data were collected had not affected more than about half of the total population of 13-year-olds. The low score was cited in the 1970 election campaign as an example of what qualitative impairment the reform has led to. Then, in 1973, when the first international science education survey was published and it was found that the 14-year-olds in Sweden had achieved the same level of competence as in other European countries, this put an end to the debate on low standards resulting from the school reform. The findings also contributed to more realistic comparisons between on the one hand retentive or comprehensive and on the other selective systems of education. As I just pointed out, mass education cannot be compared with élite education in terms of mean scores of highly different proportions of the relevant age groups. Furthermore, these studies contributed to throwing light on the price paid in terms of attrition, even of talent, in a selective system. Whatever selection criteria used – test scores, marks, or teacher ratings – they are all correlated with social background indicators. The IEA surveys thereby contributed to providing a better empirical base for the discussion on quality and selectivity in secondary education.

Taking into account all the caveats and qualifications that can be subsumed under the heading "comparing the incomparable," a case can nevertheless be made for attempts to conduct such comparisons. After all, careful measurements with standardized instruments can provide educators with tangible data which are more accessible to rational information treatment than the general impressions and gut feelings derived from brief visits to schools. Empirical evidence could at least supplement such gut feelings and thereby broaden the basis for evaluative judgments. The OECD Policy Reviews can be cited as examples of attempts of this latter character. In his wide-ranging critical review, commissioned by the National Academy of Education, Alex Inkeles gave IEA credit for having embarked upon a field of scholarly inquiry where little previous groundwork had been done. We had tried to quantify in a field abounding with comparative folklore.

A "Positivist" Research Paradigm

It would at this point be tempting to try to review the theoretical and methodological problems we encounter and have to cope with in conducting cross-national assessments and to draw the lessons, not least from the mistakes we made in the IEA studies. This would be to indulge in hindsight wisdom, not to say in futile efforts to proof-read life! What we undertook ought to be seen in its proper setting, namely the state of the art of the social sciences in the early 1960s. Being children of an era with a positivist climate, we attempted a quantitative approach in order to arrive at certain generalizations of the kind that positivist social science research was eagerly trying to achieve. But it was not our main aim to establish an international score board of achievements or to conduct an international olympics.

Our overall scholarly ambition was to study how the outcomes of school instruction in certain school subjects were related to national characteristics as well as to indicators of home background, school resources and methods of instruction. Such relationships were to be studied according to a uniform methodology across countries. In each country parallel analyses were to identify the variables that were "strategic" in determining student achievements. Furthermore, in each country the relative importance of these "input" variables and their interaction were to be assessed. By doing this in a dozen or more countries one would be able to arrive at more powerful generalizations about the determinants of achievement than if the relationships were analyzed in one country only.

Given the scope of the exercise – in the Six Subject Survey we were dealing with tens of thousands of teachers and a quarter of a million of students – the only possible sources of information were questionnaires completed by students, teachers, and school principals, with all the shallowness and inaccuracies that go with such an approach.

Inkeles in his review thinks that the IEA researchers "under-utilized" the information they collected, which might be true given the time pressure under which the project had to be conducted. With the wisdom we have gained with hindsight we were not particularly successful in achieving our overall goal, namely to identify the most "important" input factors, that is to say those variables that were at the top in accounting for between-student and between-school variance. In some subject areas home background came out as overwhelmingly powerful and in others not. (French as a foreign language and Reading comprehension were the extremes.) But we arrived at very little information about what mattered at the classroom level. Thus, the findings expected to yield cross-national generalizations were not particularly illuminating and conclusive.

We used the most sophisticated statistical technique available at that time, step-wise multiple regression analysis. Secondary analyses of our data, seem to show that we should have used a somewhat different approach that would have raised the significance of whatever factors that turned up in our analyses.

Why were we not very successful? I think there are two major reasons:

(1) I have already pointed out the self-imposed limitations set by the research paradigm we opted for. We were in a way caught up in the dilemma between, on the one hand, national representativity, and, on the other, studies in depth of a few classrooms in each country without certainty about representativity. The latter alternative would most likely have given us some general hints in our search for what mattered in accounting for differences between students, schools and countries. A study of a few classrooms per country with ethnographic depth would have yielded more pertinent information about the inner dynamics of the teacher-learning processes.

I think that a comparative exercise of what succeeded or failed in terms of classroom practices would have been much more worthwhile. IEA has subsequently been attempting to do this in the so-called classroom-environment study.

(2) The second limitation was the cross-sectional character of the study. We measured student competence at the end of the school year and related this to single or composite input variables that had to do with home background, school resources and, to some extent, methods of instruction. But

actual student competence is an outcome of influences that have operated from the day the student was born and reflects the teaching efforts of many teachers over several years. Given the reluctance of the individual teachers to be associated with a given class of students, all teachers in the particular school in the particular subject were averaged in order to create a proxy "teacher." No wonder then that the teacher variables which referred to the actual school year yielded little or nothing. In the second mathematics study attempts have been made to make up for this by testing students in some countries both at the beginning and at the end of the school year, which provides increment scores that more meaningfully could be related to teacher and teaching characteristics pertaining to the actual school year.

Future Uses of Cross-National Assessments

What can, given the lessons I have so far tried to draw, be said about the future worhwhileness of cross-national assessments? I shall make one more general and a few more specific points.

In the first place, a reconceptualization is called for. Not least the Six Subject Survey showed that forces operating outside the classroom setting, particularly the home and its support or lack of support, accounted for more of the inter-individual and between-classroom differences than was accounted for by school and instructional factors only. Thus, we would have to devote more efforts to studying the interaction between the schools and the different socio-cultural settings within which schools in various nations are operating. A good example of this is the comparative study of Japanese and American schools conducted by Professor Azuma and his colleagues.

Data for the first international mathematics study were collected in 12 countries in 1964. Data for the second mathematics study in 25 countries were collected in 1980-81. This makes it possible to compare countries also overtime. Again, such comparisons should be conducted with care, since the purpose of the exercise is not to organize international olympics in mathematics. Some items, so-called anchor items, were common to the two sets of standardized mathematics tests, which makes it possible to compare in a limited sense achievement in 1964 with that in 1981. Some countries have, on the whole, improved student competence during the intervening 17 years, whereas in others there is stagnation or even a deterioration. I want to exemplify this with Table 1.

More than mean scores we should begin to look at the *distribution* of scores for each country separately. Countries differ not only in terms of mean scores but even more so in terms of spread between students and between schools. In some countries the between-school variation as a ratio of between-student variability is as low as about 10 per cent or less, whereas in others it is much larger. For instance, Sweden has a rather low mean score but a high level of

TABLE 1. *Number of 14-Year-Olds in Per cent Who Got Eight "Anchor" Items Right 1964 and 1981 in Nine Countries (Preliminary Findings)*

ITEM No	113	015	016	017	086	118	120	148
Year of Testing	64 81	64 81	64 81	64 81	64 81	64 81	64 81	64 81
Belgium	48 57	71 77	43 38	62 74	36 52	45 41	17 46	39 57
England	38 34	51 49	35 39	61 57	33 34	39 35	19 28	31 34
Finland	48 40	12 54	35 36	48 54	30 44	30 33	10 26	32 37
Israel	35 41	43 67	44 49	65 59	28 62	38 34	19 27	54 45
Japan	62 72	39 74	59 62	77 82	37 51	35 46	35 37	59 59
Netherlands	30 38	42 66	36 45	50 68	19 38	20 38	7 32	27 34
Scotland	37 39	52 53	39 37	62 63	30 36	35 35	17 28	35 34
Sweden	25 23	15 35	22 31	45 44	19 26	30 33	19 23	19 22
U.S.A.	29 41	26 29	28 32	66 70	38 49	36 46	23 25	40 40

TABLE 2. *Between-School Variance in Per cent of Between-Student Variance. Science.*

Country	10-year olds	14-year olds
England	19	33
Finland	28	20
Hungary	40	34
Japan	18	20
Netherlands	23	40
Scotland	29	43
Sweden	15	12
U.S.A.	32	28
Federal Republic of Germany	27	30

homogeneity, whereas England, as can be seen from Table 2, has a comparatively high mean score but has a much larger proportion of its students at the lower end of the distribution than Sweden.

Concluding Remarks

It is to me, and I guess to many colleagues, somewhat distressing to note that concerns about the quality of education and the ensuing interest in conducting cross-national assessments of educational systems should be inspired by economic and/or military competition. I have made reference to the 1958 National Defense Education Act and the report entitled *A Nation at Risk*. In early 1984, the Minister of Foreign Affairs of the Federal Republic of Germany, Hans-Dieter Genscher, at a conference I was attending in Berlin proposed the establishment of élite institutions of higher learning, typically with a focus on bio-technology and micro-electronics, without for a moment discussing the general objectives of higher education in our society and the role that, for instance, humanities can play in making that society more humane.

Without relinquishing the more technocratic approach that I have described here I am convinced that cross-national studies would gain immensely from the participation of educational historians and philosophers. They might help those of us who are lost in the technical labyrinths of the social sciences to compare what is really comparable.

VI. Present Trends and Future Perspectives

A Twenty-five Year Perspective on General Theories in Education (1979)[1]
Purposes of Futurologic Studies in Education (1972)[2]
School as an Institution in a Highly Technological Society (1981)[3]

Introduction

This section deals with present trends and – possible – futures in education. The first essay, however, takes a retrospective look at influential theories in education over the period since the early 1950s.

In 1968-70 the author conducted a futurologic study published under the title *Education in the Year 2000* (Stockholm: National Board of Education, 1972) which later became translated into half a dozen languages. The second essay (from 1972) is an attempt to identify for what purposes futurological studies are conducted. The next contribution emanates from a paper that the author was invited to write in 1981 for a futurological project that UNESCO was conducting. The version published here was given as a guest lecture at the National Institute for Educational Research in Tokyo in 1983. The third essay is an attempt to diagnose the problems that seem to beset secondary schools in most industrial countries today. It is closely related to a study on transition from youth to adulthood that the author conducted jointly with his colleague James Coleman. The joint monograph carries the title *Becoming Adult in a Changing Society* (Paris: OECD, 1985).

The views advanced in these essays have in various respects been elaborated upon more fully in *The School in Question* (London, Oxford University Press, 1979) and in *The Future of Formal Schooling* (Stockholm: Almqvist and Wiksell 1980) both by the present author.

Notes

1. *International Review of Education* (Unesco Institute for Education, Hamburg), Vol. 25:2–3, 1979, 325–345.
2. (OECD) *Alternative Educational Futures in the United States and in Europe* (Paris: CERI/OECD, 1972). 31–56.
3. From *Present Trends in Education and their Main Determinants*. Stockholm: Institute of International Education, University of Stockholm, Report No. 49, 1981.

A Twenty-five Year Perspective on General Theories in Education*

The Scope of the Present Review

"Educational theory" is comprehensively conceived in this paper, particularly since we are concerned with "general" educational theory. Thus, we are not dealing here with "theory-building" in a more narrow and strict sense only, the process whereby the educational thinker and/or researcher attempts to construct a model of the reality he wants to investigate. We shall also include paradigms of thinking which determine not only the theoretical constructs used in research but the entire research strategy as well. For instance, some ten to fifteen years ago quantitative methods and experimental design were, whenever they could possibly be employed, regarded as *sine qua non* in empirical studies. The "neo-positivist" approach has, if not left room for, anyhow been complemented by a more holistic and hermeneutic one. Finally, social and political ideologies enter the picture through their repercussions on educational thinking.

"Paradigms" of Educational Research

When in the late 1930s I embarked on graduate studies in psychology and education, one could hardly identify a single dominating and/or established paradigm for the conduct of educational research. Some of us had obtained our disciplinary background in psychology, others in history or philosophy. Lack of background in psychology was at quite a few universities a more serious handicap for aspiring researchers than lack of background in the humanities. Education as a university-based discipline, established to give prospective teachers some theoretical grounding in pedagogy, was in my home country a meeting ground between two distinct disciplines, history of education and psychology, particularly developmental psychology. Those who wanted to qualify for a professorship were, until the early 1950s, required to produce major publications in both these fields. When the professorships were split, this unreasonable requirement was dropped. The chair that I took in Stockholm in 1953 was labeled "education and educational psychology."

The paradigm for educational research that in the late 1940s and the 1950s became dominant, first at Anglo-Saxon and Scandinavian and then at German

* Originally published in the *International Review of Education*, Vol. 25:2–3, 1979, 325–345. Reproduced by permission of the Unesco Institute for Education, Hamburg, FRG.

universities, was born out of both European positivism of the classical brand as reflected in experimental psychology and the "neo-positivism" of the Vienna brand of the 1930s that spread to the United States and was married to the American modern empiricism as applied in survey research. This paradigm was epitomized in handbooks of behavioral research in general and educational research in particular. One had to go through a ritual consisting of various stages, beginning by stating the problem, then advancing a theory from which certain predictions (hypotheses) were derived which then were tested either in conducting a survey or an experiment, the latter being considered the ideal approach in testing hypotheses in the good tradition of the natural sciences. Survey design as well as field studies or merely field observations were considered inappropriate or insufficient if one wanted to establish causal relationships.

Research paradigms are often anchored in, or at least associated with, ideologies which also can be regarded as models of reality. Thus, the scientific conception of big issues, such as equality of educational opportunity, environmental versus genetic influences on scholastic attainments, and ability grouping, differs considerably between conservatives, liberals, and marxists. In the first place, they each tend to define the problems differently. This can be illustrated by referring to the debate on comprehensive versus selective education that has been a major issue in countries where reforms of the structure of the educational system have been launched.

Educational theories, not only those which are part of social philosophies in general or educational philosophies in particular, but also those which inspire empirical investigations, often originate from or tend to be adopted by general social philosophies and political ideologies. This explains why such a seemingly aloof academic issue as that of genetic versus environmental determinants of intellectual performance could suddenly descend from the serene academic sphere and become a highly emotionally loaded, politically explosive issue in the late 1960s. This was at a time when equality of educational opportunity had moved up the priority scale and when in several countries, not least the United States, massive programs of social intervention were launched and when the civil rights of the minorities became an issue on the top of the nation's agenda. Cyril Burt, whose twin studies were advanced by Jensen as the main evidence in favor of a genetic conception of IQ, was one of the contributors to the so-called Black Papers published by a right-wing group in the British conservative party. A hereditarian conception of IQ was advanced in favor of a selective and competitive system of education that, to use Thomas Jefferson's phrase, would enable the "natural aristocracy" to be identified and become properly rewarded.

The central issue in educational policy in Western Europe has for a long time been to what extent educational provisions for all children up to the age of 15-16 could (and/or should) be offered in a school with a common curriculum and a comprehensive structure. Educators have mostly defined the issue as a pedagogical one. But basically it is, of course political, namely – what value should be attached to the establishment of a unitary school where children with varying home backgrounds can obtain a common frame of reference and where more equality of opportunity might be achieved? But when educational research has been called upon to present evidence, the issue has consistently tended to be scaled down to become pedagogical, and essentially academic. It has been asked: Is it possible and/or feasible to keep children in the same program and the same classroom longer than, say, to the age of 10-11? To what extent do the more able "suffer," i.e., to what extent are they hindered from developing their full potential, in a comprehensive pedagogical climate? British, Swedish, and German educational research over the last quarter of the century, at least until 1970, has been obsessed by these issues. The differentiation problem in Sweden, the structural problem with which the German *Bildungsrat* struggled for several years, and the 11+ issue in England provide ample illustrations to what has been said.

Another overriding policy issue that has had a stimulating influence on educational theory building as well as on educational research and theory building over the last couple of decades has been the one of equality of educational opportunity. As I have argued elsewhere (Husén, *Social Background and Educational Attainment*, Paris 1975), the issue is conceived quite differently by conservatives, liberals and new radicals. Usually, the problem in the 1950s was considered as one of making it possible for the "talent reserve," young people from mostly "lower" social strata, to get access to the advanced education that corresponded to their "inherited" ability. The liberals differed from the conservatives by saying that imbalances between social strata in the number of young people who went on to higher education was due mainly to social and economic barriers and not much to differences in "natural" capacity. Study grants and loans would help the able students from lower classes to get access to advanced education. The radicals challenged the concept of "talent reserve" altogether. It reflected a bourgeois belief that inherited capabilities and not social class determine life chances.

Over the last twenty-five years, however, recognition has increased of the importance of the total social matrix for both upbringing at home and, not least, school learning. Sociologists, for instance Talcott Parsons, began to study the school as an institution, the social psychology of the classroom and the impact of the community, and particularly the family background, on the outcomes of schooling. The sociologists, and in some cases the philosophers (for instance the Frankfurt school in Germany) introduced the socialization perspective in trying to account for what happened to young people at home and in school. Whereas the psychologists had taken the narrow perspective in studying the conditions for learning cognitive material, the socialization theories brought school learning within the perspective of a comprehensive pattern of both conditions and outcomes of an affective and social psychological character. One can refer here to the research by James Coleman on what he called the adolescent society and to his report on the transition to adulthood, or to the socialization research at the Max Planck Institute in Berlin.

No doubt, another widening of the perspective to embrace the total learning situation, including the home background, has been brought about by extensive survey research on both sides of the Atlantic since the early 1960s. Coleman conducted his extensive survey on equality of educational opportunity in the United States on behalf of the Office of Education. The Plowden Commission in England studied what accounted for individual differences in school achievements among 11-year-olds. At the time of the publication of these surveys, the International Association for the Evaluation of Educational Achievements (IEA) had completed its evaluative study of achievements in mathematics in 12 countries. This was soon followed by surveys of six additional subject areas in some twenty countries. All these investigations found that family background accounted for a greater portion of the total variance in achievements than did the school factors that had been measured. This gave rise to an intensive theoretical debate and questions were raised about what the schools contributed. Did they "make any difference?"

Consistent, well-organized theories of educational institutions were advanced not only by sociologists and social psychologists, such as Parsons, Getzels, and Trow, but by political scientists as well, for instance James March.

The basic theoretical notions of how educational systems work, have, in some countries since the late 1960s, been affected by a "red wave." In the United States several of the leading Marxist scholars have typically had their training in economics and have moved into education. Samuel Bowles and Herbert Gintis in their book *Schooling in Capitalist America* (1976) have tried to present a comprehensive picture of the role of the formal system of education and how it relates to society at large. Martin Carnoy and Henry Levin have ventured to study educational change according to the Marxist paradigm. Earlier, some young historians, among whom Michael Katz has been the best-known, tried to look at the emerging public education from the point of view of the Marxist conception of formal schooling as an instrument of molding docile and disciplined workers in an hierarchical class society.

The "revisionists'" attempts to revise and rewrite modern educational history have been challenged and subjected to criticism by Diane Ravitch, who was commissioned by the U.S. National Academy of Education to take a critical look at their writings.

On the balance, the "red wave," which represents a paradigm of thinking that for a long time has been regarded as suspect or has even been an anathema in the Western world, has had stimulating effects in two ways. By challenging conventional idealism in educational theory, those who have come under criticism have been forced to sharpen their arguments. But more importantly, the Marxist approach has contributed to a widening of the perspective on the educational process and its determinants, both historical and socio-economic.

Education has been defined as a "continual mode of interactive experience in which lessons of the past are channelled as resources for the future." Thus, the proper territory of educational theory and educational research could be defined as the study of the conditions for the educative process, the process itself, and its outcomes. But can we talk at all about education as a circumscribed, well-defined unitary discipline in the same sense as we talk about physics or history? I would submit that there is *not* such a thing as a clearcut, distinctly defined discipline of education. The same, by the way, applies to political science. Theories, perspectives, and methods developed in other disciplines are in education brought to bear on problems related to learning, both within and outside the institutional setting provided by the school, the family, and the peer group. Thus, we can hardly identify any comprehensive theory of education, at least not one that lends itself to serve as a framework for empirical studies. I am not here referring to the comprehensive theories that constitute entire, more or less consistent philosophies of education.

For the sake of convenience I am here defining education operationally as a discipline, as sets of theories and methods that educational researchers employ in studying education problems. In what follows I shall review changes in basic paradigms and general theories that have occurred since the early 1950s, which in practice means since the mid-1940s, when international contacts and communication networks within the international community of scholars were re-established.

I submit that the most important changes in general theory that have occurred over the last twenty-five years have been these:

1. A movement in a cross-disciplinary direction in conceiving educational processes and structures.
2. A widening of the perspective from the classroom to society at large; a growing realization that education does not occur in a socio-economic vacuum.
3. A swing from the one-sided application of strict quantitative methods of the approved positivist brand towards methodological catholicism.

I shall first comment on these in turn and then deal with theories and research movements that appear to me to have contributed significantly to innovations and ensuing research.

Inter-disciplinary Character of Recent Educational Theories

Due to historical circumstances educational studies and theory-building at the universities were for a long time oriented towards either the history and/or philosophy of education. In America, where there usually were several professors of education at the same university, those representing the "foundations" of education could more easily, on equal footing, bring about disciplinary cross-fertilization, whereas in Europe where there was only one professor per university, the chairholder or the *Ordinarius*, the situation was more difficult in that respect. In places where a one-sided didactic orientation dominated, it was believed – I for one grew up in that tradition – that the psychology of learning and human development together with the study of individual differences would provide the solutions, that is to say, come up with *the* right methods of teaching.

Education's Disciplinary Affiliations

It would be presumptuous to single out certain fields in education, which over the last twenty-five years have been particularly fertile in terms of generating new theoretical perspectives, methodological innovations, and challenging findings. Such an endeavor would easily reflect only the personal interest and priorities of the author. I shall, however, venture to point out certain fields in educational research that in particular seem to have profited from the interdisciplinary approach. Before doing so it would be appropriate to point out certain fields in educational thinking and research that hardly existed as distinct sub-areas before 1950.

In the first place, *comparative education* as a discipline with an articulate theoretical framework was non-existent before 1950. *Auslandspädagogik* had, of course, been taught for a long time, particularly at institutions which served educators in countries with colonies. But it was until recently mostly of a descriptive character of systems of education in other countries or areas and at best a juxtaposition of them. People like Arnold Anderson and Harold Noah and their students have contributed to make comparative education a discipline with its own analytical concepts. Typically, Anderson came from sociology and Noah from economics. Comparative studies of education and of outcomes of educational systems were first launched in the wake of a Sputnik, when there was, not least in the United States, a preoccupation with what the educational system "produced" for science and technology. The establishment of the UNESCO Institute for Education in Hamburg, the International Institute for Educational Planning in Paris, as well as centers for development education, such as the Stanford International Development Center, and the Center for Comparative Education at the University of Chicago, provided an institutional framework for further development of the discipline.

Around 1960 leading economists, such as Theodore Schultz and Dennison, published studies advancing a human capital theory that they also tried to test empirically. European economists, such as John Vaizey and Friedrich Edding, were also "founding fathers" of the new discipline of *economics of education*. When they and others analyzed economic growth, they found that a major part of it could not be accounted for by those classical growth factors of natural resources and labor. The residual, that sometimes was as high as 50 per cent, was ascribed to the quality of the human capital, the skills and competencies of the labor force as well as improvements in production processes introduced by research and development. Thus "investment" in education brought benefits not only to the individual, who increased his life income by acquiring high level education, but to society as well by boosting the GNP. The simplistic way in which the human capital theory was put, as well as the over-emphasis on the quantitative aspects as reflected in educational planning, has over the last few years left room for more sophisticated conception of the economic implications of education.

Another outcome of the movement towards cross-disciplinary thinking and the widening of the perspective in education is the recent interest in what Lawrence Cremin has referred to as *ecology of education*. If education is defined, as it is by Cremin, as "the deliberate, systematic, and sustained effort to transmit, evoke, or acquire knowledge, attitudes, values, skills, and sensibilities, and any learning that results from the effort, direct and indirect, intended or unintended," then one is struck by the one-sided preoccupation among educational theorists and empiricists alike with education in the classroom. Education is a process that occurs in so many different institutional settings, not least in the family. Furthermore, education, especially the aspect that imparts new skills and competencies in a rapidly changing technological society, is a life-long process. Its objectives are manifold. In spite of the emphasis that with certain intervals is put on the "basics," its objective is, apart from instilling cognitive competencies, to mold character.

The fact that, especially in the modern urbanized society, so many different institutions educate and that significant learning occurs not only in the schools, has led to attempts to advance a comprehensive theory of education that covers the whole range of institutional settings. Such an attempt has been made by Hope Jensen Leichter (ed.) *The Family as Educator* (New York: Teachers College, Columbia University, 1975). It has been inspired by scholars from various disciplines, such as Margaret Mead in social anthropology and Urie Bronfenbrenner in psychology.

There are two fields where theoretical progress as well as methodological innovations have been enhanced by cross-disciplinary thinking and theoretical models, namely curriculum and evaluation research. Curriculum studies launched after 1950 have been more guided by principles of human development and individual differences. Prior to this, people in teacher training representing pedagogy on the one hand and subject matter preparation on the other were in entrenched positions against each other. The marriage between didactics and disciplinary thinking that took place in the 1950s in some leading teacher training institutions was a spectacular development.

Survey research was from the outset characterized by a rather narrow positivist orientation without any theoretical perspectives. In this field one could observe how the tail, the statistical techniques employed, tended to wag the dog instead of vice versa. But over the years, when surveys produced results that challenged conventional wisdom and popular belief, this research inspired in the first place a fruitful methodological discussion, such as that which came after the investigations of Coleman and Jencks.

John Dewey long ago, as early as in 1899, in an address delivered to an audience of psychologists, envisioned a "linking science" of education that would provide techniques for practical application in the classroom. It would play the same role in education as does engineering as a link between science and its practical applications. The descriptive science of psychology was expected to provide a prescriptive science of classroom teaching.

Psychology, consisting of principles of human behavior, was early conceived as a discipline from which educational practice could be derived. Edward Lee Thorndike could be cited as one example of how findings from psychological experiments could be applied to the teaching process. His book on the teaching of mathematics was a consistent attempt to build connections between psychology and classroom practice.

B. F. Skinner developed his theory of operant conditioning and reinforcement and how principles developed in animal laboratories could find extended application over a long period before he began to ponder about the educational applications of the theory. The interest in the direct educational applications suddenly emerged, when he visited a fourth-grade class to which his second daughter went in 1953. In an autobiographical sketch he writes:

"On November 11, as a Visiting Father, I was sitting in the back of the room in an arithmetic class. Suddenly the situation seemed perfectly absurd. Here were twenty extremely valuable organisms. Through no fault of her own the teacher was violating almost everything that we knew about the learning process."

This experience in a way was a "peak" learning experience (Bloom) for Skinner that put him on the track of more systematically relating his learning theory to teaching-learning practices in school. The ambition to widen the perspective beyond the laboratory had, however, come earlier. In his Utopian novel *Walden Two*, published in 1948, he tried to describe a social system, community living, before it became fashionable among young people. The book did not catch much attention when it appeared but became later almost a bible among the generation that turned its back against the "sweat-it-out-society." The year after the crucial school visit Skinner published a seminal article, "The Science of Learning and the Art of Teaching," where he translated his experiences from programming animal behavior into programmed instruction.

Programmed teaching was an application of the theory of operant conditioning and consisted of arranging contingencies of reinforcement. He pointed out that a consistent application of what we know about learning calls for a "thorough revision of classroom practices." This paper, along with other essays in the early 1960s, was published in *Educational Technology*, which strongly influenced educators in the decade it appeared. He was interpreted to have advanced a theory, or rather science, of classroom instruction with a teaching method utilizing proper reinforcements and individualized methods and leading to more effective outcomes. His criticism of traditional classroom practice is epitomized in his famous statement that an American child who in good French manages to say, "Please pass me the salt," gets an A, but a French child who says the same thing gets the salt!

The applications of the Skinnerian learning theory, programmed learning and teaching machines, along with the attempt to define the objectives of school teaching in behavioral outcomes as required by educational technology, were highly *en vogue* in the 1960s. They have indeed had a lasting impact on classroom instruction at various levels, not least by bringing individualised instruction from rhetoric to reality. But the reason why the lasting change brought about by the programmed learning movement has been rather modest has primarily been the lack of a "linking science," what Robert Glaser refers to as "a prescriptive theory of instructional design."

A review of general theories in education would be conspicuously incomplete without including Jean Piaget, although his scholarly work was not primarily intended to reform school teaching. Piaget's work is essentially devoted to studies of cognitive and non-cognitive development with particular emphasis on its epistemological implications. He has in fact written only a couple of short essays that focus on educational problems. Therefore, there is no such thing as a Piagetian educational theory. He has not entertained any ambition to advance a comprehensive theory for classroom learning or for the educative process in general. Piaget's theories do not by themselves constitute a rounded off body of principles for classroom instruction. They serve, as Groen points out, as "a good source of ideas" and are thereby serving heuristic purposes. In spite of having written almost nothing on education as such, Piaget has had a tremendous influence on educators once he was "discovered," several decades after his basic, and rather esoteric, writings appeared. He could serve as an excellent illustration of how basic and theory-oriented research can contribute to "broad conceptions and fundamental paradigms" of human behavior and thereby provide "crucial contexts and guides" for educational practice.

Educational Planning and Development Education

At the beginning of the 1960s education rode on a wave of optimism. It was considered to be a major instrument for social change and progress. In Europe educational reforms were launched under the double banner of equalization of educational opportunities and economic growth. The discovery of "the other America" in the United States, an underclass of some 20 per cent poor people, many living in urban ghettos and belonging to racial minorities, led to President Johnson's "War Against Poverty" that was to be fought mainly by providing the public schools system with big resources for what was referred to as "compensatory education." Educational expenditures in the 1960s in most industrialized countries were allowed to grow exponentially in constant prices by more than 10 per cent per year, while the economies grew at most by some 5 per cent annually.

About 1960, as a parallel development, educational planning emerged as a major activity. Planning the educational system at the national level was then something quite new to the Western countries, whereas it already had a history going back to the 1920s in the Soviet Union, where it was part of the overall management of the economy. By the early 1960s there was what Hans Weiler has referred to as a "planning euphoria." There were two reasons for this. In the first place, the human capital theory had just been advanced by some economists and the prospects of applying it in order to boost economic growth seemed very attractive and justified that education was given a relatively larger share of the new resources than other sectors of the economy. Secondly, the colonies in Africa and Asia were about to gain national independence, and the human capital theory applied in their case meant a comprehensive planning for economic take-off, modernization, and general development.

Educational planning can be cited as a good example of the breakthrough in the 1960s of the general interdisciplinary approach in conceptualizing and tackling educational problems. The field during that time was dominated by the economists with emphasis on the quantitative aspects, such as obtaining reliable demographic and enrollment statistics which were to be projected and matched against financial statistics and projections on economic growth. National development plans, as a rule covering five-year periods, became the standard format of planning. The International Institute for Educational Planning was founded in 1963 and, through its research and training activities, began to have a strong impact in the Third World, not least through the UNESCO educational programs.

In an article where he reviews the development of theories and practices in educational planning. Weiler characterizes the development as a "progression from confidence to doubt and from consensus to disagreement."

Educational planning up to now has been characterized by a conception of education much in the same way as industrial production of manufactured goods is conceived. Yet the basic assumptions, upon which educational planning of the early 1960s was founded, the human capital theory, the possibility of making manpower projections over a considerable time, and the conception of shaping the future by planning alone were challenged. Preoccupation with economic growth led to neglect of the qualitative aspects of educational planning.

The role of planning in bringing about educational reform was also up for a reappraisal. The central role of policy became advanced. At the beginning the educational planner was seen as a technical expert who worked outside the political domain. He obtained his terms of reference from the politicians and went ahead and planned according to their directives. The critical theory of educational planning realized that the planner himself unavoidably was part of a political process. Lack of such a realization accounted for the fact that so many plans were never implemented.

The realization of the importance of the entire setting, for instance the "climate" in a particular school or local school system for the teaching-learning process, is another outcome of the widening of the perspective from didactic trivia to the enframing conditions. Enormous expenditure has gone into efforts to investigate the "right" method of teaching or to evaluate the effects of programs with "categorical" purposes, such as the compensatory programs for the educationally and/or socially disadvantaged. A recent illustrative case in point is that of the evaluations of the "Follow Through" planned experiments in compensatory education in the United States reported in a special issue of the *Harvard Educational Review* in 1978. These and other studies document the importance of the "ecology" of the reform process aimed at changing the system and/or bringing about improvement in student competence. The commitment of the principal and teachers, the participation of parents, and the attitude of the community consistently turn out to be more important than the particular methods and/or pedagogical arrangements. The effects of the latter vary from school to school and from district to district depending upon the prevailing pedagogical climate.

A Future Perspective

By 1970, however, due in large part to world wide economic slowdown and budgetary restraints, optimism left room for criticism, not to speak of disenchantment, to the extent that the "de-schooling" philosophy advanced by Ivan Illich, was taken seriously. I have elsewhere (Husén, *The School in Question*, 1979) presented a picture of the change in attitudes towards education and in the public mood as well as within the educational establishment. The wave of disenchantment has also affected the attitudes towards educational research which rode on high hopes in the 1960s and was given resources that researchers only a decade earlier could scarcely dream of. The setback was partly due to lack of talent that could make good use of the rapidly increased resources; as well, it was due to the narrowness of approach, and the lack of comprehensive and fruitful theories.

Still the classroom perspective dominated and massive research efforts were launched, for instance in Research and Development Centers within that narrow frame of reference. One hoped that a thorough study over a broad descriptive front of classroom learning and of the interaction between students and teachers would help to identify strategic variables in teaching behavior. Such an identification would enable the teacher training institutions to instill in teacher candidates the didactics that would lead to more effective school learning. The very competent and comprehensive summing-up of this research by, for instance, Rosenshine and Gage conveys a picture of theoretical barrenness and lack of balance between massive empirical efforts and paucity of results.

However, over the last twenty-five years there have been theoretical approaches that have stimulated research on classroom learning and have contributed to the opening up of new theoretical vistas. One could here refer to John B. Carroll's model of school learning and Benjamin S. Bloom's theory of mastery learning that in some respects is a further development of Carroll's theory. Bloom has challenged conventional theories in educational psychology to the extent of even dismissing the concept of "inherent" individual differences. In an address to the American Educational Research Association in 1971 Bloom even labelled individual differences "a vanishing point."

Under the influence of the mood of disenchantment the contribution of educational research to educational practice has recently come under critical review, not only by governmental commissions but also by educational researchers themselves. A 672-page volume commissioned by the National Institute of Education and produced under the auspices of the U.S. National Academy, could be cited as a case in point. The book, entitled *Impact of Research on Education: Some Case Studies*, 1978, presents nine cases, such as the influence of the Piagetian theory on educational practice, studies of intellectual differences and their implications for practice and the influence of psychoanalysis on elementary education.

In his paper on the contribution of basic research in education to educational practice, "Paradigm and Practice," Getzels takes the following as his point of departure: "The skepticism of educators about the bearing of research – and particularly of basic or theory-oriented research – on the operation of schools is quite extraordinary." He substantiates this by referring to the resistance among educators against appropriations by U.S. Congress for educational research. Furthermore, while some 4.7 per cent of the budget for health and medical services is devoted to research and development, the corresponding portion for education is a tiny 0.4 per cent. He then goes on to give several illustrations of how basic or theory-oriented research can have profound influence in the operations of schools, and how it can provide "crucial contexts and guides for the substance and method of education." But perhaps the most important function that basic research as institutionalized at the universities can perform is to discover and formulate problems that might otherwise have remained "unpursued for being unformulated." In pursuing basic research the problem is to strike a proper balance between "blind empiricism" on the one hand and "theoretical bias" on the other. Too much of the research in recent years with the easy availability of computers and their power of accommodating an unlimited number of quantified "facts" has become data-oriented without this badly needed support of theoretical and explanatory concepts. This in particular applies to studies of classroom teaching and learning. This, again, teaches us an old lesson: nothing is as practical as a good theory.

Purposes of Futurologic Studies in Education*

Introductory Remarks

The young people we now have in our schools will be entering the most productive, and publicly the most influential, period of their lives in twenty to thirty years, i.e. at the beginning of the next century. The objectives of the education that the school gives them, and the content of the instruction they are subject to, must obviously consider that it is not today's society – much less yesterday's – that these youngsters will take charge of, but rather a society which lies only a few paltry (but oh so important) decades ahead of us, when we reflect upon the process of change that has swept across this society at an accelerated rate since 1945. Accordingly, contemporary educational planning must allow for the effects it is likely to have on the society – not to mention the world – that we are going to have twenty to thirty years from now. Not even that will suffice, however. Let me take the following illustration. The Swedish *Riksdag* passed legislation on a new system of teacher training in 1967. These teachers were expected to be active professionally for an average thirty-five to forty-five years to come. They will be teaching young people whose own productive lives will run for about fifty years. This is by way of saying that the teacher-training decisions taken during the 1960s will have repercussions up to the mid twenty-first century.

The foregoing remarks should suffice to justify futurologic studies in education of the type which seek to define the *consequences* of present-day planning and decisions for tomorrow's school. Could it be that the schools of three decades hence will bear little if any resemblance to the time-honored type we know today? In the present century, at any rate, "education" and "school" have increasingly come to be regarded as synonymous concepts. In Sweden, the establishment of a compulsory elementary school was accompanied by the formal abolition of the guild system, within whose institutional framework training for the handicrafts had taken place. The apprenticeship system for training in the trades continued to linger on for some time. But during the course of the past century, education has increasingly come to be carried on in the institutional forms that regular schooling has established with grades, teacher-led class instruction, tests, marks and examinations. From time immemorial, moreover, we have learned to regard education as a

* Originally published in *Alternative Educational Futures in the United States and in Europe*. Paris: CERI/OECD, 1972, 31–56.

matter exclusively associated with the years of our youth. In other words, the basic and applied knowledge and skills needed to make our way in the world are supposed to be acquired early in life. But already at the beginning of this century the free and voluntary adult education programs sponsored by the various people's movements developed considerably, and to a large extent, at least in Scandinavia, these were detached from the institutional school system. The non-formal voluntary system by means of study circles and evening classes long focussed on giving a basic general education, on imparting certain skills in, for example, the native language and the society-and-nature orientation that the great masses did not receive from the elementary public education, which after all was rather meager. In other words, no question of training for careers or of imparting saleable skills was involved. But we have been witnessing, at least in Sweden, the onsurge of adult education which aims at bread-and-butter goals. Both the traditional programs of adult education and, to some extent, the vocationally-oriented system of adult education, have operated outside the traditional school framework. As regards the voluntary adult education programs, one can discern a deliberate effort to move away from the traditional forms and towards the goals they serve.

Recent developments in adult education have opened our eyes to the fact that education takes in a great deal more than mere formal schooling in the traditional sense. The young people attending school today belong to the generation that has been exposed to television from pre-school years and that will be exposed, as transmission time increases, just as much to what comes out of the magical cathode ray tube as to what comes out of a teacher at his classroom desk. A moment's reflection tells us that the school's sphere of influence has also diminished in this respect. In the society that we have been entering for some time, education is in the process of becoming a lifelong concern for the great majority of people, and thus more than a matter to which one dedicates the years of childhood and youth. In that connection the school as an institution – and under forms that are changing drastically – will answer for only certain limited educational functions.

These sketchy indications should suffice to provide a general background to my principal topic, namely the tasks and methods of futurologic studies.

Three Cardinal Purposes for Futurology

What are the cardinal purposes in education that can be imagined for futurology? As far as I can see, three lines of development suggest themselves.

(1) Research can be confined to identifying the future consequences of contemporary planning and policy decisions relating to school organization, construction, curricula, teaching aids and teacher training. The layout given to a new school plant implies certain notions as to how work will be carried on in the projected building for many decades to come. A structure with

bearing walls, and divided up into classrooms of a certain size, presupposes that these rooms will have a specified number of pupils – regarded as normal for so-called class instruction in today's situation – who are going to imbibe wisdom that is mainly imparted by specially trained teachers. Planning of this kind more or less rules out certain alternatives as to the school's work practices, alternatives which assume in common that practices will vary and that pupils will become more active. In any event, such planning has the effect of making these alternatives less likely to materialize.

The example just cited illustrates how important it is to clarify the long-range implications of today's school decisions. It also illustrates a vital thesis: futurologists do not aspire – or should not aspire – to explain what is supposed to happen, but what can happen. In his book *Dialog i det fria* (Dialogue in the Open), the Swedish writer Sven Fagerberg has a section which he calls "The Soothsayers," especially inspired by an issue about the year 2,000 that the American periodical, *Daedalus*, put out in the summer of 1967. This issue was given over to presenting the results of deliberations made by a committee appointed by the American Academy of Arts and Sciences. Fagerberg says: "Forecasts have . . . a great importance; they compel us to analyse the here and now and to try to understand what is happening at this moment. But they can never tell us what is going to happen." In this way investigation into the future can also help us to create that future.

As long as the investigator sticks to analyzing the import and consequences of contemporary planning and policy decisions, he stands on pretty solid ground and does not have to rely too much on what he sees in the crystal ball – or whatever metaphor one wishes to use to characterize the doings of futurologists. But his task immediately becomes more difficult if he takes a step further and extrapolates the statistical trends that are now observable. And he will be tackling a really formidable task if he goes yet one more step to identify those general development patterns and value trends that will dominate society a quarter-century hence. I shall have something more to say about these riskier ventures presently. But first some more viewpoints about the task of making clear the nature of the ultimate commitment that follows from decisions already taken or implemented.

I assume that all parties endorse the rational principle – by paying lip service, if nothing else – that educational planning, as well as social planning in general, in our changeable society ought to aim at maximum flexibility, the object being to keep open as many acceptable future alternatives as possible. That is a demand which ought to be imposed on those responsible for planning physical facilities and building design guiding school construction. Or to put this principle the other way round, contemporary planning should rule out as few alternatives as possible. This means that the futurologist ought to study present-day policy decision-making from two angles.

First, do today's planning and political decisions harmonize with the general objectives of public policy that have been adopted for the long run?

Second, what future alternatives have been excised by today's actions? When the Swedish Authorities decided, a few decades ago, to go in radically for centralizing schools to urban areas and shutting down the majority of the small rural schools, they were motivated by the prospect of certain administrative benefits, and perhaps economic ones as well: since large-scale educational operation would be more advantageous than continuing with the little red schoolhouse, the latter ought to be closed down. However, the transportation of young people to large urban schools, which followed from the closures, combined with the abandonment of farms to generate a vast depopulation of the countryside. In a recent study, Sixten Marklund has shown that small schools offering middle-department courses (i.e. grades 4-6) do not perform worse than the large schools, indicating that the pure educational advantages of doing away with all the many small rural schools at the lower and middle levels have been of dubious value. On top of that, the social and economic impact on sparsely populated areas has been highly negative.

Politicians are easily tempted to look for short-term solutions to current problems, which is perhaps understandable considering that they are reminded of their mortality at fairly short intervals, i.e. at the regularly recurring elections. Hence they readily go astray when confronted with situations where they have to choose between that which imperils themselves in the short run and that which imperils the voters, i.e. the society, in the long run.

The administrators, especially if they work in a strongly bureaucratic setting, risk (for partially different reasons) losing sight not only of the future, but of the basic meaning of the tasks they have in hand at the moment. Current worries, the day-to-day routine, often assume overwhelming proportions, or are perceived to be so overwhelming that no time is left for thinking in terms of the "long pull." Now it happens to be the very essence of bureaucracy not only to build empires but also to become so engrossed in the formal and technical perfection of a present preoccupation that questioning the real meaning of what one is doing seldom, if ever, comes to mind. A brilliant and illuminating document on this point is to be found in *Grisjakten* (The Pig Hunt), a book written by P. C. Jersild. Secretary Siljeberg is so absorbed with the task his boss in the Ministry has assigned to him – to exterminate all pigs in Sweden as efficiently as possible (starting with the experimental district of the island of Gothland) – that he never stops to ask what purpose all this technical perfection is really supposed to serve.

There is something else which impedes the bureaucratic-political establishment from inquiring into the future consequences of its present actions. During the 1960s we have seen how protests – voiced not least by youth – have become increasingly clamorous against the imputed penchant of authorities to plan and decide over the head of the common man. It is contended, not without reason, that an inner circle of technicians and experts, political experts included, steamroller decisions on city planning, roadbuilding, school construction and water impounding which fly in the face of what a "growing grass-roots" opinion perceives to be desirable long-range objectives. One example, often very much the object of controversy, is the extent to which private automobiles should be allowed to circulate freely in downtown areas. A great deal of prestige readily tends to hang on questions of this kind. That which was planned a long time ago, when the conditions were different, builds up such powerful momentum among the bureaucrats that it rolls on with juggernaut force. Experts and persons in authority who have long worked on and sweated over the issues thereby feel they have become privy to a higher insight, and not infrequently they put of a stiff and even supercilious tone towards the protesters. In other words, they "know better."

(2) The futurologist can try to determine certain trends expressed in numerical terms, such as school enrollments, developments of costs and use of teaching aids, and then extrapolate these trends, for example find out in which direction the curves are pointing. This kind of peering into the future, which amounts to drawing upon demographic data to compute the need for school plants and their sizes, has become routine nowadays in both the local and central school planning. Yet it was not more than a few decades ago that no one in Scandinavia even seemed to think it possible to predict with great accuracy the number of children that would be starting school six or seven years after a certain cohort was born.

Even so, attempts to extrapolate trend curves can have their parlous sides. An example is the estimate of the supply and/or demand for special subject teachers that was made by the 1955 Commission of Inquiry into the Swedish Universities. When the Commission published a special report in 1958 it went on record as saying that secondary school teachers would already be in surplus by the early 1960s, and that the surplus would grow as the decade progressed. The analyses were based on the reported number of secondary school-leavers having completed a *gymnasium* program and passed the *student-examen*, together with the number of matriculants and degree-takers at the faculties of arts and sciences up to the mid-1950s. It could be established that the number of leavers from the pre-university school by and large had increased linearly from 1940 to 1955. The assumption was that this would continue till the mid-1960s at which point the curve would level off, since the increase could not very well be expected to go on as in the past. Further, it was assumed that first-year enrollments in the arts and sciences faculties would not mount substantially. Lastly, the experiences gained from the pilot program with the nine-year comprehensive school were drawn upon for that proportion of pupils in grades 7-9 who had made so-called academic options, which was largely identifiable with the percentage of an age group who had elected to study two foreign languages. It did not take more than a few years for the actual course of events to confute all these assumptions. The curve for secondary school-leavers turned out to increase not linearly but exponentially. Not only that but the subsequent course of events has been described as an "educational explosion," and rightly so. By the mid-1960s when the incidence of *studentexamen* was supposed to have levelled off, the acceleration was greater than ever. Far from stagnating, new admissions to the arts and science faculties increased sharply. The number of secondary pupils with so-called academic options grew apace, especially after the basic school reform of 1962, so that the proportion of pupils making such choices rose to more than two-thirds from about one-third during the 1950s. With the introduction of a universal basic school in 1962, followed by reforms of secondary education in 1964 the educational opportunities were expanded far beyond the prospects envisaged in 1958, and all the earlier forecasts were shattered into the bargain. The predicted surplus of Swedish and modern language teachers in the early 1960s never occurred. As for the liberal arts graduates, the much-talked-about surplus turned out to be a hampering shortage, which for a time even exceeded the shortage of mathematics and science teachers in certain parts of the country.

I have not picked out this example in order to sound wise after the event but because I feel a generous helping of imagination is called for when one tries to extrapolate development trends. In this particular case the acceleration tendencies which already existed ought to have given cause to think about the role of education both as investment and consumption, and hence about its attractiveness as well. If such reflections had been allowed to govern, the forecast could have been corrected. It should also have been possible to predict the short-range effects of broadened educational opportunities.

(3) *Social and political values* are legitimate objects of research for the futurologist. For example, he can study how a pluralistic and a monolithic society respectively function in educational terms. However, the futurologist cannot avoid being drawn into the debate about what kind of future society is being sought. In so doing he can indirectly help to create values and gain their wider adoption. The appearance of tomorrow's society does not follow in any clear-cut and mechanical way from the scientific and technological potentials we have today, and probably not from the ones at our command tomorrow, either. The crux is *if* and *how* we intend to use these potentials. That is determined by the social preferences, i.e. by the prevailing values. Medical science can give us formulas on leading a way of life that will keep us in good shape physically and mentally. But none the less we put ourselves in situations, both on and off the job, that induce stress and break us down physically and mentally. We allow the waste products of technology to spoil our environment to the stage where it poses health hazards not only for coming generations, but also for ourselves.

Will the values that fix priorities and preferences look essentially different two or three decades from now? Will science and technology be more greatly harnessed towards creating a better and healthier environment? And what about notions as to what constitutes the "good life," the life worth living? The Protestant work ethic (pace Max Weber), under which everyone was supposed to stick to his last, and which suffused the life ideal of a large part of my generation in the Western world (and in the socialist countries, too, for that matter) may be superseded by another ethic. As long as the "sweat-it-out" ethic dominates, the awarding of marks on the basis of individual performances in competition will continue to dominate in our schools. The curricula can then talk as piously as they wish about group work, cooperation, consideration and social maturity. Hence one of the cardinal tasks for futurology will be to venture predictions about how priorities are going to look in another few decades. What will then be considered essential and inessential? What will one be living for? All of us have personal experiences of how the value accents can shift in a relatively short time. My own generation was not confronted with the problems that relate to the atomic bomb and the developing countries. We rested, if not securely but ingenuously, in the assurance that the Western way of life was superior and our technical civilization unbeatable. There was no talk of technology being able to harm us in any way; it could only make life richer, better, and elevate us to higher and higher standards of living.

I do not propose here to elaborate on how one undertakes to find out about tomorrow's value priorities. If we look at what has happened to change social and political values during the past century, we often detect certain advance signals of what is in store where needs and values are concerned. Such a study will disclose that events constantly thrust up avant-gardists, many of them leading writers, whose ideas and reactions portend the coming shape of dominant values. These signals that point ahead to the future are to be found among writers, artists and intellectuals, but even more so among articulate young people.

These young people will take over the society of tomorrow. By investigating what they hold to be questions of vital importance, we can arrive at a broader understanding not only of what they accord top priority as young people, but also of what they may be expected to consider most essential in their adult years. The Swedish National Board of Education recently published an attitude survey whose main purpose was to provide source data for instruction in religion. A questionnaire administered to 1,300 pupils in grade 9 showed that racial problems, international problems and questions of human dignity headed the list of philosophical and ethical topics which concerned pupils at the age of 16.

The American investigators who concern themselves with educational policy research have made extremely interesting attempts to map out how vital questions are perceived by more articulate and "deviant" youth, respectively. A group of high school students, all of them engaged in putting out "underground" school newspapers, were invited to a conference, where they gave uninhibited expression to their views on the older generation and the existing society, and portrayed the kind of society they would like to have in the future. Another study included the "hippies" of San Francisco. A third tied into an ongoing international study in 25 countries which seeked to elucidate the value orientations, attitudes and political opinions of university undergraduates.

When I read the analysis of the taped proceedings from the conference attended by the young high school editors, I could not escape the reflection that young people now seem to be reacting in the same way more or less universally. After all, these are individuals who experience the world and its problems more directly and tangibly, not least through the medium of television, than earlier generations, and for whom there exist quite different means than in the past for the common sharing of experience.

According to these youngsters, the school is out of touch with the important things that are happening in the world and is also trying to protect the pupils against unpleasant realities. They consider themselves "manipulated," with the school acting as a propaganda machine. One of them said: "The school system has become an efficient factory in which we are the raw material, who under the pressure of the marking system are turned into automatons and conformists for sale to the highest bidders in the business world." Another student said: "What I want more than anything else in the school is interaction between ideas and feelings and not just neutral, grey knowledge. I want us to get accustomed to people trying to convince us about things."

I should like to comment briefly on both these quotations, since I picked them out in order to illustrate a favorite idea of mine. The day cannot be far off when we stop adhering to the illusion that textbooks or teaching aids in general are supposed to present "objective" knowledge. Efforts in that direction make the books so neuter and dull that they cannot possibly stimulate the motivation of pupils. The latter-day debates in Sweden, for instance, about the tacit value assumptions in the textbooks have shown us that we must try another approach. Quite simply, this means that pupils must be put in touch with the debate and clash of opinions in the larger society outside the school: in other words, that the school systematically expose its pupils to these views and train them in their discussion. We shall be living in a society where intentions are becoming more important than opinions.

Futurology, not least that concerned with development trends under alternative 3, confronts this crucial question: What trends shall be selected for extrapolation? Some of these trends will be decisively influenced by the policy that is based on future assessments of priorities. Other trends will probably remain more stable. It therefore becomes essential to design "alternative futures," all according to the congeries of assumptions one makes.

As for the type of society represented by the industrial countries, it is likely that several of these trends will be reinforced in the future. Just how they will develop will depend *inter alia* on the future's value preferences.

We cannot devise sensible future alternatives unless two fundamental conditions are in hand: (1) we regard education as an integrated system, which means we do not confine ourselves to the school-type subsystems in the conventional sense; and (2) we view the educational system in its social, economic and political context. This boils down to attempts to design "comprehensive" future alternatives.

The factors which characterize the educational system as such are here called endogenous whereas those influences which derive from the total social context are called exogenous. Accordingly, efforts to design alternative futures must embrace certain assumptions (more or less correlated with one another) concerning both kinds of factors, on the one hand assumptions about the society at large and on the other about the educational system as such.

School as an Institution in a Highly Technological Society*

IN 1967 some 150 leading educators from all over the world convened in Williamsburg, Virginia in order to discuss the "world crisis in education." The main working paper prepared by Philip Coombs was subsequently published under that title together with the conference conclusions and recommendations. The main problem in the crisis diagnosis was the imbalance between demand and supply in education. Another problem was the lack of relevant curricula. One year later student unrest broke out at universities all over the world. The main issues as perceived by the students were such things as lack of participation and the tendency to corrupt genuine educational values. These other issues were hardly discussed in Williamsburg – although the writing on the wall was already visible.

In entering upon the hazardous attempt to identify present salient trends in education I shall limit myself to such trends which by all tokens will prevail in the near future, that is to say, in the next ten to twenty years. The problem then is on what grounds certain trends are judged as "salient" and are likely to dominate the immediate future.

Another restriction has to do with the distinction between developed and developing countries, or rather, between highly industrialized countries on the threshold of the post-industrial service society and countries which in the foreseeable future are going to be dependent upon an agricultural economy. This distinction should, however, not be pushed too far, because, as I shall argue, both types of countries have problems with their formal system of education which show a great deal of similarity. The differences between them are very much ones of degrees.

I shall limit myself to the formal system of education, that is to say, the system of institutionalized schooling where children and young people are brought together for several years in an institution called a school in order to be given systematic instruction according to a plan called a curriculum. In my book "The School in Question" (London, Oxford University Press, 1979) I have discussed some criteria that can go into a definition of a school. Nine such criteria are discussed: (1) it is an institution with full-time attendance, (2) certain age specifications for school-entry and school leaving are laid down, (3) the model of instruction is the "frontal" one, (4) the

---

* Lecture given in Tokyo (1983) adapted from *Present Trends in Education and Their Main Determinants*. Stockholm: Institute of International Education, Report No. 49, 1981.

curriculum is graded, (5) the size of the basic unit, the local school house or compound of houses, has grown with urbanization and consolidation of school districts, (6) the size of the system has grown since more children belong to it for an extended number of years, (7) the objectives of the school have been widened from the limited one of imparting cognitive skills and competencies to the ones which constitute social education, (8) the growth has called for better coordination which has led to the growth of the administrative machinery and by the introduction of various specialized services, (9) supervision tends progressively to become tighter and operations more uniform under more centralized regulations.

These criteria apply to schools in the northern hemisphere as they are now. But in several countries, well into the twentieth century, primary schooling was not full-time, but part-time, the age of school entry was kept very flexible and the curriculum was not graded. My point here is that the model of formal schooling which has been borrowed from Europe and North America is the more recent one that emerged in the urban areas where it was convenient to let the children go to school full-time and where their presence was not needed at home.

A Common Denominator

A problem which dominated the Williamsburg conference and which continues to loom large and is shared by most countries in the world, both rich and poor, both developed and developing, is the soaring, so-called social demand for formal education, the enormous pressure for more and more formal education. I have referred to this phenomenon as the "revolution of rising expectations." But there is an important difference between industrialized and non-industrialized countries with regard to how this demand has developed over time. The enrollment statistics studied longitudinally are, indeed, revealing.

In Europe enrollment in secondary and tertiary education in terms of relative participation of the relevant age cohorts rose very slowly from the turn of the century up to about 1950. Sweden can serve as an example. About 1900 only about 2 per cent of the relevant age group took the matriculation examination at the end of upper secondary school that qualified for university entrance. That figure had by 1940 risen to about 4 per cent. The increase had been a linear one without any particular growth spurts. The social composition of the enrollment in advanced education reflected a highly ascriptive society. There was some social mobility that resulted in a small proportion of students (as a rule boys), whose parents were either farmers or manual workers, gaining access to the academic secondary school. But the general attitude was that academic advancement was something more appropriate for young people coming from the upper classes. Ralph Dahrendorf in the late 1950s conducted a study of enrollment and social background at German universities. Schematically expressed, he found that about 50 per cent of the university students came from homes of professionals and/or civil servants that represented about 1 per cent of the working population, whereas only 1 per cent of the students came from working class homes that represented about 50 per cent of the work force. A similar, although not that extreme, picture was found in several surveys conducted in the 1940s and early 1950s in Sweden.

The exponential growth of secondary and tertiary enrollment started in Europe in the early 1950s and reached its peak during the "golden years" of the 1960s, when there was much talk about an "enrollment explosion." During the period 1950-1980 the Gross National Product in Europe and North America grew threefold.

Most developing countries have shown another pattern of growth with regard to their formal system of education. In the first place, they have not gone through a long period of slow, linear growth of their secondary and tertiary education. Sub-Saharan Africa provides a good illustration. When the African Ministers of Education met in Addis Ababa in 1960, certain targets were set for the expansion of formal education with top priority given to primary education. At the next two meetings in Nairobi and Lagos, respectively, it was found that the target set for primary schooling had consistently been under-achieved, whereas secondary and tertiary targets had been highly over-achieved. In several instances secondary education, behind which there was a strong political pressure, had in terms of relative participation, by mid-1970s reached the level of industrial Western Europe by 1945. Thus, many Third World countries have in a way jumped over the period of slow and steady growth that was so characteristic of many of the industrial countries in the Northern hemisphere over a period of almost a century. I shall not try here to conduct any analysis in depth of why there has been such a striking difference between North and South. I think there are several determinates behind it. In the first place, education has been "sold," not least by the aid agencies, to the Third World as the main instrument in bringing about development and economic take-off. Secondly, education earlier became a responsibility of the state in the developing countries, where the costs for post-primary schooling to a large extent has been carried by public funds. In Western Europe and in North America education beyond the mandatory level had to a large extent to be paid for by the parents, which, of course, made the enrollment socially biased and put post-primary schooling beyond the reach of the great masses. There is no doubt that the political pressure which, in developing countries, brought about enrollment explosion at the secondary and tertiary levels even before primary schooling had become universal will prevail in the next couple of decades. The financial implications of such a development are far-reaching, since a student in further-going schooling costs the public purse ten times as much or more than a student in primary education.

A review of the trends of the late 1960s and how they developed

In 1968-70 I conducted a futuristic study under the auspices of the Research and Development Division of the Swedish National Board of Education. The ensuing report identified a dozen salient features of the educational system which would help to broaden the perspective and hopefully yield a tentative answer to the question in what direction the school as an institution was heading.

The outcomes of the attempts I made in the late 1960s to identify salient trends, in the first place in the educational systems of highly industrialized countries, will, in what follows, be used to confront what has occurred on the educational scene since then and what appears to be the overriding tendencies today. Such an exercise should, however, not be regarded as an attempt to "validate" the 1970 notions but rather to give a picture of what kind of unforeseen changes have occurred and whether and to what extent these changes are due to paradigmatic changes. I shall in turn comment on the points I made a decade ago, and then in the perspective of what has happened since then point at the main unidentified changes.

The most conspicuous tendency a decade ago was the quantitative trends which at that time were characterized by the phrase "educational explosion": more young people were staying in school more years. But it was also pointed out that the system, particularly in the industrialized countries, had begun to absorb an increasing number of adults. Education tended to become part of the everyday life of most individuals, that is to say, to become "lifelong". By late 1960s very few people, if any, envisaged two phenomena which in the 1970s had strong repercussions on enrollment in the industrialized countries: the economic slowdown, best characterized by the phrase stagflation, and the sudden demographic changes with drastically diminished birthrates.

The Pill took educational planners by surprise. In some industrialized countries the age groups born in the late 1960s and early 1970s have decreased by up to 40-50 per cent. This is going to have dramatic effects on the enrollment and staffing in secondary and tertiary education. A slowdown, or even a reduction, in absolute numbers can easily occur in spite of an undiminished or even increased participation rate. During the "golden 1960s" new faculty was recruited wholesale, not always with due consideration to quality. This means that institutions of higher learning stuck with a rather young faculty, are going to have difficulties of assigning already tenured staff to meaningful tasks. Turnover due to retirement will be low, particularly since there is in some countries a tendency to raise the retirement age. In the United States the Carnegie Council on Higher Education has estimated that the replacement need of faculty in tertiary institutions would by 1985 be zero. In England a large number of teacher training colleges have been either closed or converted into institutions preparing for professions other than teaching.

The enormous expansion of adult education in the 1970s in Europe and North America was hardly envisaged a decade or two ago, although the idea of "lifelong" or "recurrent" education began to be launched, not least by organizations such as UNESCO and OECD. In Sweden by 1980 the number of part-time, adult students in secondary education *exceeded* that of young people through the age of 18, in spite of the fact that secondary education for the young was practically universal. Quite a few of these adults belonged to the generations that had only had six or seven years of primary school and wanted to upgrade their formal education by attending afternoon or evening schools on a part-time basis. In 1977, when the new University Education Act went into effect, about 60 per cent of those who enrolled at the University of Stockholm were twenty-five years or more. Thus, students of "normal" undergraduate age were in minority!

In the early 1960s economists began to argue that education (and research) were major determinants of *economic growth*. In order to maintain its competitive power on the international market it paid off for a country to invest heavily in education. Education increasingly began to be conceived as a career-determining factor. Not only did education help an individual to cope with an increasingly complex society, it also provided him with the skills and competencies that would make him more employable in a rapidly changing society, where career changes were necessitated by changes in the structure of the economy. The German sociologist Schelsky is quoted as having said that educated talent is modern society's substitute for distinction by family name and inherited wealth. In other words: one could trace a clear tendency towards meritocracy. In spite of the broadening of opportunities for further education and the manifold increase of places available in institutions of further-going education, competition, particularly for university entrance, has increased. This has tended to have strong repercussions on the lower levels of the system with what the Germans refer to as *Leistungsdruck* (achievement pressure) already at the beginning of primary education.

The meritocratic tendency has since then tended to become even stronger, because the employment system more and more tends to use the amount of formal education as the first criterion of selection. This means that in order to secure a good place in the line of jobseekers one has to climb as high up on the educational ladder as possible. In order to secure a favorable position there one has to scramble for marks and good examination results. This has strong repercussions on the teaching and learning that goes on in the classroom. Students tend more and more to learn for external rewards. Under such circumstances quite a lot of superficial ritualism is fostered to the detriment of the pursuit of genuine educational values.

In another context (Husén, *Talent, Equality and Meritocracy*, The Hague 1974) I have tried to analyze more closely the meritocratic syndrome and how it besets highly technological and growth-oriented industrial societies. I contend that the meritocracy is the price we have to pay for economic growth and increased material standard of living. Under such auspices, career-orientation and excessive pragmatism tend to take precedence over learning for personal fulfillment and lead to the neglect of the intangible benefits that accrue to the individual who enjoys studying, for instance, history or literature.

The meritocratic tendency that was amounting during the 1960s as part of the "revolution of rising expectations" has since then become stronger and could be envisaged in the coming decades to lead to an even more intense competition in the educational system as a surplus of young people with advanced education enter a world of work which suffers from a slowdown in economic growth.

Research and development has over a few decades developed into a "knowledge industry" which has tended to put out an exponentially growing amount of information emanating from rapidly specialized scientific disciplines. Given the fact that the number of scientific publications over the last three decades has doubled every five to seven years, the phrase "knowledge explosion" is, indeed, justified. In the 1960s the investments in both fundamental and applied research in some countries quadrupled.

This development has led to certain misgivings in the average person who has difficulties in interpreting what the researchers are doing and increasingly has the uncanny feeling of being in the hands of specialists and technocrats. The impact of applied science on the environment and life in the future society has led to a mounting concern, stronger now than at the end of the 1960s. We have seen a growing tendency among young people to shun away from studies in science and technology which are met by suspicion.

Young people through their teens increasingly stay on in school not only as a result of prolonged mandatory schooling but of prolonged, voluntary further-going schooling as well. This has brought problems of secondary education in countries with universal schooling at that level into focus. In some countries secondary education is regarded as a "disaster area." Young people in school today are spoonfed hour after hour, day after day, at an age when their age-mates in earlier times were out in working life learning adult roles. The issue that pedagogues are faced with could be summed up in two words: participation and relevance. One cannot expect young people to acquire more responsibility and social maturity than the school gives them an opportunity to learn.

Since the 1960s the problem of providing adequate secondary education has in many industrial countries, particularly in many big-city school systems, become aggravated. Increased absenteeism is an indicator that the youngsters have begun to "vote with their feet." Disciplinary problems are commonplace. Those who are early losers in school by failing to acquire an appropriate level of basic skills, in particular the ability to read, tend to give up. If they are promoted to the higher grades they leave school grossly unequipped to cope with the complexities of modern society. The emerging "educational underclass" tends in quite a few industrial countries to become an increasing problem.

The added number of years young people spend in school has tended to *widen the scope of duties the school* is expected to perform. School is no longer a place where only certain cognitive competencies are acquired. The duties have been extended to encompass social and custodial ones. It seemed a decade ago as if the school would have to assume an increasing number of the tasks that so far had been performed by the family. The school as an institution was expected to assume the task of personality-development. In the agrarian society the family, being a unity of production and consumption, was the obvious place for upbringing. The last few decades have tended in the industrial countries to deprive the family of its institutional importance and have enhanced the school's temporal influence but have also added new sources of influence, namely the mass media. The latter have considerably widened the horizon of experience of young people, which is not any longer limited to the home or the village but through the television screen takes in the whole world. This makes today's youth much more globally-minded than previous generations. It has repeatedly been pointed out that in some regions of the world young people watch television at least as many hours as they are exposed to classroom teaching.

The changes that have occurred in the *role of the family* as compared to the one of the school are, of course, closely related to basic changes in the economy. In England during the nineteenth century the emergence of institutionalized schooling was related to the effects of industrialization on the family. Until the 1830s, when child labor in mines and factories was commonplace, there was little pressure for any schooling covering the age from 7 through 12. Instead various philanthropic organizations took the initiative in establishing so-called infant schools, which catered to children from 3 or 4 up to 7 years of age. Such institutions took care of the children at least part of the time when their parents worked long hours. But when child labor was legally prohibited the need to find some kind of institutional care for children of 7 through 12 became acute and led some decades later to legislation which provided for universal primary education.

The next major change in the educative role of the family in the industrialized world occurred rather recently. The most striking feature of this change has been the massive *influx of women into the labor market*. In conjunction with this, the birth rate has gone down and day-care facilities have been considerably expanded. The increased divorce rate and number of children born out of wedlock have resulted in a much higher proportion of single-parent families than some ten to twenty years ago. The care-taking functions of the family have been further reduced by the progressive establishment of institutions which take care of the elderly, such as nursing homes. This has further reduced the contacts between generations.

What so far has been said would seem to indicate an overall weakening of the educative role of the family and increased impact of institutional education. A massive research by survey methods tends to show that family background in modern industrial society accounts for a much larger portion of individual differences in school attainments than do the factors that constitute the pedagogical milieu.

In recent years an increased interest is paid to what has been referred to as "ecology of education". Previously the focus was mainly on the individual child, his background and his school attainments. There has now been a shift towards the study of the entire constellation of factors that constitute the educative milieu in which the child grows up. One such constellation is the family which can be studied as an educative entity.

The criticism launched against the school as an institution in several highly industrialized countries in recent years has led to a debate on the proper division of labor between the family and the school. The critics have accused the school of usurping duties that essentially should be performed by the family. There are signs of what could be called a renaissance of family life. Shortening of working hours, legislation on paid vacation, and the increased role of the father in child care at home are some of these signs. Still, however, the proper division of functions between school and family will remain to be a major issue.

Well until the 1950s institutional schooling was limited to a narrow age range which as a rule covered the age of 6-7 through 13-14, i.e., the compulsory school attendance span. It was based upon the principle that by going to school the individual would learn what he as an adult "needs to know." The school was supposed by and large to provide him with the fare of knowledge and skills that would nourish him for the rest of his life. In a rapidly changing and highly technological society any body of specific knowledge rapidly gets out of date. The individual has to keep on learning in order to cope with the changes brought about by the knowledge industry and its applications in technology. This means that certain basic skills, which constitute the competence to absorb new knowledge, have become essential to the learning that has to go on during the entire life. Such skills that are applicable within a wide range of – largely unforeseen – situations become strategic. Among these competences the most important one is, of course, the ability to learn on one's own.

By the end of the 1960s high hopes were held for what the new *educational technology*, not least educational television, could do in providing an increasing number of individuals with the teaching they needed in order to become educated. These hopes were particularly high among educational planners working with educational problems in the Third World. The bottleneck in trying to cope with the enrollment explosion was the supply of adequately trained teaching staff. The unit costs that were going up in affluent countries did not give rise to serious concern, as long as the economy was expanding and education was allowed to absorb more of the growing resources than other sectors of society. However, new devices, such as programmed instruction, mediated through teaching machines, were often perceived as panaceas that would not only save teaching staff but bring down the costs as well. I have repeatedly pointed out that the school is not to be regarded as a pedagogical factory and that teachers therefore cannot be replaced by machines. In the few cases, where replacement by machines was justified, the pedagogical situation must be regarded as abnormal!

We have now seen both the rise – and particularly the fall – of educational technology with all its gadgetry. We have begun to realize that at the core of the educative process going on in school is the interaction between *individuals*, the teacher and the student. The teacher has in close contact with the student, the task to plan, implement and check the learning that goes on. The teacher's role is to provide the student with adequate learning opportunities, something that requires reasonably stable personal and emotional relationships between the two partners in order to build up the necessary confidence and motivation and to convey to the student that the teacher cares about him.

In the 1960s one could notice that the expansion of the educational system also pertained to its *administrative machinery*. The adminstrative units were increased, partly as a result of consolidation of municipalities and/or school districts. Bureaucratization followed in the wake of the big administrative units which led to weakening of the personal contacts between decision-makers and employees. Another development has been the growth of the school plants, particularly at the secondary level. There are certain advantages of economy of size with big school units. Course offerings and program options can be considerably broadened with access to a diversified teaching staff and a large student body as a necessary correlate. Various services can be improved by having access to specialists for various services.

The typical child at the primary level in some countries goes to a school with an enrollment of some 400-500 students as compared to some 30-60 a few decades earlier. The growth of school units at the secondary level has been of the same scale.

There is, however, no evidence that big schools equip their students with more competence than small schools. The price paid for bigness is paid in the field of social education. The bigger the school, the more it suffers from impersonal formality. When the informal face-to-face, social control that can be exercised in the small school breaks down, then all kinds of formal controls, which require an elaborate system of formal rules backed up by an increasing administrative machinery, have to substitute it. Students in the consolidated, centrally located, big schools have to be transported long distances. The social climate easily becomes influenced by lack of stable relationships between the students and the school staff. Absenteeism, vandalism, and mobbing thrive in a social climate where direct social control is replaced by a system of formal regulations which can be violated by the students without having to suffer the embarrassment and shame which is inevitable in the small setting.

The issue of the school size has been taken up because it is indicative of the realization to rethink the ecology of formal schooling that presently can be noticed in many quarters. Given the role of electronic media and given the highly technological, complex, and meritocratic society in which young people in the industrialized world, and to an increasing extent those in the developing world, are growing up, one has begun to realize the necessity to think about the optimal institutional conditions for the education of young people.

Not least the events of 1968 around the world were reason enough to raise the problem of the *"generation gap."* Young people began to question the values that had guided their elders in the growth-oriented society. They questioned the worthwhileness of the so-called protestant work ethic, with all its drudgery. They began to ask whether the price paid in terms of pollution and exploitation of natural resources was worth the increased standard of living. Many of these "forerunners" challenged the very intentions of the adult generation, which they considered to be imbued with hypocrisy.

According to surveys conducted in the United States with regular intervals, the generation gap seems to have been exaggerated under the impressions of the revolt atmosphere in the late 1960s. The variation in values among the young people turned out to be wider than that between themselves and their elders. But in the industrial world the "forerunners" of the 1960s seem to have been joined by followers in putting more emphasis on expressive values of self-realization than instrumental ones of career-orientation.

A Stocktaking

What, then, can in 1986 be said about the "salient trends" or tendencies identified one and a half decades earlier? To what extent can I today subscribe to them?

By and large the tendencies dominating the educational scene in the late 1960s have prevailed, but there are three overriding and fundamental modifications that cut across them all. In spite of "the events" of the late 1960s at many universities, and in spite of the misgivings about the development in education aired by young people, it was still assumed in 1970 that the educational system would continue to grow with an unshaken political support under the auspices of a growing economy. It was further assumed, in spite of the realization of problems that resulted in some talk about "crisis in the classroom," that the almost euphoric mood that attached high hopes about what education could do in reforming society and improving the life chances of the individual would prevail under the decades to come. In short: the futuristic perspective under which the current trends were observed was a growth-oriented, optimistic one.

What has happened that has forced us to change the "paradigm" by means of which education is studied? The auspices under which education now operates in many countries are largely the following:

(1) There has been a slow-down in economic growth to the point of approaching steady state. The educational system in the northern industrial countries was allowed to grow twice as rapidly as the economy at large and almost doubled its share of the GNP during the "golden years" of the 1960s. It now has to suffer cutbacks and has to face what Kenneth Boulding refers to as a "management of decline." The stagnation is hard to take for people who, over many years, have been used to an uninterrupted growth of resources and who have been setting their expectations and conducted their planning within such a frame of mind.

(2) The educational euphoria of the 1960s has turned into criticisms and misgivings about what the formal system of education achieves and, not least, about the ways in which it is operated. The educational establishment in some countries is highly demoralized by such criticism, which even took proposals about "de-schooling" seriously. Until late 1960s the school as an institution was almost a sacred cow, by and large protected from criticism and attack. However, in the 1970s voices that began to talk about "institutional malaise" became louder. The school became vulnerable to attacks from both left and right. It was accused of discriminating against certain groups and of actively trying to preserve inequalities in society. The standards of competence achieved were said to have declined. The mounting absenteeism and vandalism were pointed out.

(3) The enrollment explosion has, due to the decreased birthrates in the late 1960s, resulted in a decrease of enrollment which now begins to affect secondary and tertiary institutions. This means that quite a few industrialized countries will have to face a surplus of trained teachers, something of great significance for the Third World countries, which, for the foreseeable future, are not going to be affected by the same trends.

In an era of economic constraints the rising costs gave rise to concern. The unit costs, that is to say, the costs per student per year in real terms, tended to go up rapidly in most countries, partly due to the fact that teacher salaries tend to increase more rapidly than the cost of living index. But the main reason for the rising unit costs was that the school could hardly be subjected to any rational cost-efficiency assessment in the same way as the manufacturing industry which in most cases had its efficiency measured by market mechanisms.

Promotion of students from one grade to another has in several countries tended to become automatic which often is convenient for the teacher, who can send the student to somebody else by promoting him. The result is that an increasing number of students after nine or more years leave school without being able to read and write. In some metropolitan school systems one begins to get what I referred to above as a new "educational underclass" – students who right from the beginning of their schooling lag behind and successively more and more fall behind.

We have begun to discover that education is not the Great Equalizer that some nineteenth century liberals hoped it would be. It is an instrument by means of which distinctions are instilled and which tends to reproduce, at least partially, existing differences. We have begun to realize that education by making the poor more competent does not automatically remove poverty. On the contrary, as pointed out above, in a competitive and meritocratic society it creates a new underclass of children with underprivileged background. Its alleged contributions to economic growth have been challenged. The high correlation between amount of formal education and economic success both at the individual and aggregate level has been disputed. A problem of "overeducation," with particular reference to a surplus of university graduates, has emerged in some countries.

In many countries education no longer enjoys the solid political backing that it had until the early 1970s. It has tended to slip down on the political priority scale.

It was pointed out above that many of the problems in education constitute a common denominator between industrial and non-industrial countries. But it was also pointed out that the enrollment trend in the Third World has not followed the pattern of the affluent countries in the Northern hemisphere. The misgivings which have been aired are also partly different. The perhaps most pressing problem in Third World systems of education is the one of reconciling quantity and quality. Because of the strong political pressure for expanding enrollment above primary level, there is a temptation to buy quantity at the cost of quality, something which is evident from evaluations of national systems in terms of student competence. Another overriding problem in Third World countries is the one of achieving more relevance in the content of curriculum. This goes partly back to the colonial heritage, when certain types of schools were imported and when curricula and examinations were set by the colonial rulers. But the lack of relevance in relation both to the indigenous culture and economy depends partly also on the high expectations of what education would bring in subsequent benefits in terms of status and income. This has led to a situation where each stage in the educational system tends to be seen as preparatory for the next stage. The lower stages have no clear competence profiles of their own, and are seen only as stepping stones to the top stages. A third overriding problem which many Third World countries have to come to grips with is the high costs caused not only by the quantity of students, given the shape of the population pyramid, but also by the high level of wastage in terms of repetition and dropouts.

Auspicies for the future

Over the next few years, when the formal educational system can be expected to operate under the auspices of austerity caused by a reduced margin for expansion and lower political priority than earlier, a more realistic frame of mind may be called for with regard to expectations about what education can achieve. To parody a well-known statement: you cannot be expected to do everything to all of the people all of the time. A spirit of entitlement vis-à-vis education has prevailed in the rich countries where not least the State has been looked upon as the Great Benefactor who should carry most of the costs. More realism is also called for in looking at education as an equalizer of life chances and in expecting education to be a panacea for problems which essentially are social and economic in nature.

More specifically, a reappraisal might have to take place in, among others, the following respects:

A more equitable balance between primary education on the one hand and secondary-tertiary on the other will have to be established. This applies particularly to the Third World, where education absorbs by far the larger proportion of public funds than in the rich countries.

Greater flexibility in school attendance with regard both to age of entry and number of days per year of attendance. Part-time attendance with teaching of higher quality will have to be considered.

The role of the teacher in the learning process will be subject to more careful considerations. Given the high proportion of staff costs and the shortage of well qualified teachers, economizing with the teacher's time can considerably reduce the unit cost.

To say that education in many countries today is in trouble is to point at the too obvious. The problems that beset education and call for thorough reappraisals in both industrialized and non-industrialized countries are partly elicited by the troubles that beset the world economy and have brought the expansion in many places to a halt and forced educators to rethink what they can do within the framework of already existing resources. But the problems are to a large extent also institutional, and emanating from the way school operates in the society of today.

Some people have raised the crucial issue of whether things are worse now in education than they were, and asked to what extent we are justified in talking about a "crisis." It is, of course, a matter of taste at what point of trouble one finds this appropriate. In the majority of countries formal educa-, tion is a huge state-run machinery that engulfs more and more individuals for more and more years of their life. It is beset with inner conflicts as are other institutions in society. These conflicts would have to be resolved if the school as an institution is not going to fall apart in the sense that education is sought under other auspices than in public institutions.

There are goal conflicts which are most noticeable when political rhetoric is confronted with everyday reality. The official educational policy in most countries is that the school should contribute to increased equality in life chances. The reality revealed by objective participation studies is that considerable gaps remain between rural and urban areas and between social strata. This applies to countries with highly different social and economic orders. The school serves, as pointed out earlier, to impart distinctions and to sort people for their positions in life. To paraphrase Orwell, those who from the outset are "more equal than others" tend to succeed better. The conflicts between the pursuit of genuine educational goals, such as developing an esthetic taste, comes into conflict with pragmatic goals that thrive in a career-oriented competitive atmosphere where credentials are the most important goals. The quest for equality comes into conflict with quality, when the first has to be bought at the cost of the second in, for instance, admitting people to the university. There are conflicts between various interested parties when it comes to the governance of the system and to making decisions about the day-to-day operation of the school. Administrators clash in their interest with parents and students, students with teachers, and administrators with teachers. Such conflicts easily become acute in big school systems with a highly specialized staff and where the direct access on the part of the "clients," the students and their parents, teachers, school administrators, and other officials, are formalized and remote.

Index